Three Dimensions of Vocabulary Growth

Second Edition

Three Dimensions
of
Vocabulary Growth

Second Edition

Lewis M. Paternoster

Ruth Frager-Stone

AMSCO SCHOOL PUBLICATIONS, INC.
315 HUDSON STREET / NEW YORK, N.Y. 10013

Please visit our Web site at:

www.amscopub.com

Lewis M. Paternoster

Professional Background

Taught in the Stratford (Connecticut) School System from 1956 to 1969 as a member of the English Department. Left this post in 1969 to accept a position with the English Department at Housatonic Community/Technical College in Bridgeport, CT. Retired from the college in 1988 as Professor Emeritus.

Publications

THREE DIMENSIONS OF VOCABULARY GROWTH, 1st Edition
A COMMONSENSE APPROACH TO COMPOSITION

Ruth Frager-Stone

Professional Background

Chaired the English Department in the Stratford (Connecticut) School System from 1951 to 1968, which included two senior high schools. Upon leaving this post in 1968, Professor Frager-Stone accepted a position at Housatonic Community/Technical College as English Department Chair. Retired from the college in 1978 with the honorary academic rank Professor Emeritus.

Publications

THREE DIMENSIONS OF VOCABULARY GROWTH, 1st Edition

Part Opening Illustrations: Hadel Studio

When ordering this book, please specifty either:
R 450 P *or*
THREE DIMENSIONS OF VOCABULARY GROWTH, *Second Edition*

ISBN 1-56765-040-6
New York City Item 56765-040-5

PRINTED IN THE UNITED STATES OF AMERICA

6 7 8 9 10   01

To the Student

This is a book of words probably unlike any other vocabulary book that you may have used in the past. A brief overview should prove helpful to you in formulating your own insights into the book and the writers' objectives.

The primary purpose of the book is to teach you words—to develop your word power. Having said this, it is also a work that will help you to expand your knowledge in fields such as government, literature, history, philosophy, medicine, mythology, and even the Bible. This, then, is a secondary objective of your writers, to provide you with opportunities to learn *from* words as opposed to learning *about* words. You will, for example, glean information about eminent philosophers such as René Descartes and John Locke. The Bible also contributes to language with words such as **tenebrous, maudlin, pontiff**, and **venal.** Let's not forget mythology, which has made major contributions to language: **chimera, Sisyphean, Cassandra, stygian, argonaut,** and **narcissism.** In the field of medicine you will learn facts about **laproscopic surgery** and **cryosurgery.** The medical practices **oncology** and **nephrology** will no longer be a mystery to you. Suffice it to say that there is a wealth of information to be learned *from* words. The possibilities are virtually endless.

There is more, much more! You will learn number and amount prefixes: **sesqui, multi, mille,** and **cent.** You will also learn prefixes of a more general nature: **contra, counter, circum, ante, post,** and **anti.** To build a wide vocabulary, prefixes are essential.

Another section of your book introduces you to etymologies or word origins. Many such etymologies work together to form communities of words. Each community of words is based on an etymon, or original form. One such grouping uses the etymon **pan**, meaning **all.** From it a cluster of words is derived: **panacea, panchromatic, pandemic, panorama, pantheism, pandemonium, pantoscopic,** and there are others. Word clusters make learning words easier than trying to master them one at a time.

The names of particular persons, places, and things are called proper nouns. They are another rich source of words in English: **martinet, chauvinism, draconian, tawdry, protean,** and **quixotic.** There are many others. Each of the entries will be followed by an explanation of just how the word found its way into the English language.

In the last of the dimensions you will be made aware of specific facets of language that you may not yet know about: **malaprops, oxymorons, neologisms, portmanteau words,** and **acronyms.** Each plays a significant role in language use, and one can only marvel at just how much richer language is for having them. Also included in this section are some foreign words and phrases of a kind that can be found in the vocabularies of educated persons: **alfresco, objet d'art, caveat emptor, raison d'être, mea culpa,** and **faux pas.** Such entries add richness to the tapestry of language, a kaleidoscopic array of colors and textures.

Following each lesson is a mix of exercises. They are intended to provide you with the practice needed to learn the lesson's words. Also, every few lessons a cumulative review lesson is provided. This is so you can measure your progress from time to time.

In conclusion, this is not a vocabulary book in the usual sense. The typical vocabulary book teaches words, or something *about* words. The aim of this book, on the other hand, is to impart the habit of learning *from* words. Words themselves are more eloquent than anything that can be said about them. Understand that fact and you are well on your way to vocabulary growth.

It is your writers' fond hope that you find their efforts in this book to be enjoyably informative.

LEWIS M. PATERNOSTER
RUTH FRAGER-STONE

Contents

Dimension One

Part One
The Romance of Words

Dimension One

Part Two
Words from Proper Nouns

Lessons

Dimension Two

Part One
Word Families

Dimension Two

Part Two
Prefixes

Dimension Two

Part Three
Number and Amount Prefixes

Dimension Three

Part One
Foreign Words and Phrases

Dimension Three

Part Two
Medical Specialties

Dimension Three

Part Three
Special Terms and Word Forms

Dimension One
Part One

chimera

The Romance of Words

How did people who could not read or write remember facts? One way was to tell stories about them. There can be no doubt that a fact stays in the memory longer if it is associated with other facts or it fits into a larger pattern. The same holds true for words. If you know an interesting story behind a word, you are likely to remember that word. For example, there is in English the word **nepotism**. It means "the practice of doling out favors on the basis of blood relationship, especially favoritism shown to relatives in making important appointments." The word has an extended meaning also in the political arena.

1

For example, those who worked for the candidate who won an election are oftentimes given positions for which they may or may not be qualified. This is also looked upon as nepotism, although there is no blood relationship involved. In any case, the word nepotism comes from the Latin **nepos** and means "nephew or grandson." This additional information should facilitate your learning the meaning of **nepotism**.

Part One of Dimension One presents information about interesting word origins. Part Two of Dimension One presents words that have found their way into our language via proper nouns. The same principle relative to Part One applies here—tie a word's meaning to something larger than the word itself, and it will make remembering it easier. For instance, the word **protean** means "changeable either in appearance or in principle." The word comes from the Greek **Proteus**, who was a sea god who could change his appearance at will. From the mythological Proteus comes the English word **protean**.

Following each lesson are exercises to test your mastery of the words studied. You will find a mix of types: matching; fill-in; true-false; definitions; and correct usage. These exercises are important. They will point out just how well you can recall the words in the lesson.

Now begin your odyssey into the world of words, a world without which there would be no language, or at best it would be reduced to grunt-like sounds and pantomime gestures, a far cry from where humankind has evolved thanks to language, which made communication possible.

Lesson

1

holocaust: *noun*

The word **holocaust** conjures up the most shameful period to be found in the history of humankind. This heinous crime against Jews and others who were designated as undesirables took place in Nazi Germany during the late 1930's and continued until the war's end. The Nazis coined a euphemism to name what it was they were engaged in—"the final solution." Most of those shipped to concentration camps died or were killed; the bodies were burned in huge crematoriums. The word holocaust comes from the Greek **hol** (whole) + **kaustos** (burned). These Greek etymons tell of the tragic consequences attending the specific circumstances. In a more general sense, any conflagration where there is widespread destruction by **fire** can be considered a holocaust.

Context: The **holocaust** raged uncontrollably, claiming the lives of three brave firefighters.

chagrin: *noun*

The word **chagrin** is built on a French word **chagrin**. Note the spellings are identical. The French **chagrin**, however, means **sad**, while its English counterpart means distress of mind caused by humiliation, disappointment, or failure. Any or all of these can bring on sadness. The word also connotes a sense of embarrassment, which again might give rise to one's being sad. To be chagrined is an experience one can do very nicely without.

Context: Much to his **chagrin**, he learned that his test score was the lowest in his class.

3

vacillate: *verb*

When one **vacillates**, there is indecision. There is a phrase in English which is widely used and means about the same thing as vacillate, and that phrase is **to fudge**—to act in an indecisive manner. This is precisely the meaning of vacillate. To vacillate is to waver, to waver in decision or in opinion. It is built on the Latin **vacillare**, which means **to sway to and fro**. How aptly the spirit and meaning of the word are captured.

> *Context:*   After careful consideration of alternatives, don't **vacillate**; act!

catharsis: *noun*

A **catharsis** is a purging, a cleansing, a spiritual purification that brings with it release from tension or emotional stress. For many Catholics the act of confession to a priest is cathartic. In this regard, it is a spiritual purification which may well bring about the release mentioned above. Many times convicted killers who are about to be executed for their crime(s) admit their guilt and in this way purge themselves of a heavy burden. To a greater or lesser extent, most people have at one time or another in their lives engaged in **catharsis**.

> *Context:*   Many psychologists believe that **catharsis** is the only remedy to cure those who are guiltridden over some shameful episode in their lives.

ennui: *noun*

The word **ennui** (on-WEE) comes from an Old French word that is very similar to its current counterpart—**enui**, which means **displeasure**. Today the meaning of ennui is listlessness, dissatisfaction, or a feeling of discontent that usually results from boredom. It should go without saying that were one dissatisfied, discontented, or bored, **displeasure** would play a role, an important one, in this state of mind. The connection between the Old French **enui** meaning **displeasure** and its current meaning is striking.

> *Context:*   The long, hot summer, which seemed endless, filled me with a pervasive sense of **ennui**.

caveat: *noun*

A **caveat** is a warning or caution. It is derived from the Latin **cavere**, "to take care." In other words, a caveat is a caution or a warning "to take care, to be heedful of consequences." A Latin phrase used widely in English is **caveat emptor**, and it means "Let the buyer beware." Good advice! One buys at his or her own peril. The word also has a meaning attached to jurisprudence, but it is much too narrow for our purposes. Let this serve as a **caveat**; there is this other meaning of the word.

> *Context:* On many prescription and nonprescription drugs, **caveats** are printed on their labels concerning the use of such drugs.

caprice: *noun*

The Latin etymon **caput** means "head" and is the derivation of the word **caprice**. **Caput** meaning "head" can be found in many other English words: **captain, capitate, per capita, cape**, etc. It is a commonly used root word. Returning to the word **caprice**, it should be made clear that it has to do with the head only in an oblique way. To put it another way, the head is only implied in its meaning—"a sudden and unpredictable change or turn of mind." The mind and the head in lay terms are used almost interchangeably. Capriciousness is characterized by impulsive behavior such as changing one's mind. The circle is complete—**caput** meaning "head" to **caprice**, "a turning of the mind."

> *Context:* His decision to leave his job appeared to have been arrived at **capriciously**.

palliate: *verb*

The word **palliate** is derived from the Latin **palliare**, which means "to cloak or to conceal." Today it has two meanings, both of which are more than loosely connected. First, the word **palliate** means "to cover by excuses and/or apologies." The other definition is "to lessen the violence of, to abate." One seems to engage in the first behavior to achieve the second as an end. One palliates—cloaks or conceals the truth—in order to mitigate the consequences of an act while the other offers lame excuses and apologies hoping to attain the same results. In any case, neither of these is a very open or honest response.

> *Context:* The young boy's father attempted to **palliate** his son's tantrum by offering to buy him an ice cream cone.

assuage: *verb*

To **assuage** a friend's grief is "to ease his or her pain." The word is built on the Latin **suavis**, which means "sweet." Perhaps now a better appreciation of the word **suave** can be had. **Suave** means, and this is a very informal meaning, "sweet talk"—or more formally, "smoothly agreeable or polite." Back to assuage. It means "to mollify, to pacify, to lessen the intensity of pain." In a word, its intent is to make a situation sweeter—less bitter. It is much akin to the word **palliate**. If there is a difference, it is in motivation. One assuages with selfless motivation; one palliates, in at least some instances, for selfish motivation.

> *Context:* My disappointment at not winning the science award would not be **assuaged** by kind words and well-meaning praise.

axiom: *noun*

An **axiom** is a maxim widely accepted on its intrinsic merits: its own worth. It is a proposition regarded as a self-evident truth. Axiom finds its way into English via the Greek **axioun**, meaning "think worthy." The linguistic connection between the Greek and English is inescapable. An idea must be considered worthy if it is to be accepted as a self-evident truth. Just as obvious, an axiom must be deemed worthy if it is to be widely accepted on its own merits. A quantum leap is not needed to get from the Greek **axioun** to the English **axiom**.

> *Context:* The **axiom** "Spare the rod and spoil the child" no longer holds sway with child psychologists.

EXERCISES

A. Match each word in Column A with its definition in Column B.

Column A

1. palliate
2. axiom
3. holocaust
4. ennui
5. vacillate
6. caprice
7. assuage

Column B

a. humiliation; embarrassment
b. listlessness; boredom
c. impulsive behavior
d. self-evident truth
e. to cloak; to conceal the truth; to offer lame excuses
f. widespread destruction by fire
g. to mitigate; to lessen pain, physical or emotional

8. chagrin
9. catharsis
10. caveat

h. be irresolute; be indecisive
i. a warning or caution
j. a cleansing and purging of emotional or spiritual stress

B. Select the word from the list provided below that is closest in meaning to the boldface word or words in the sentence.

capriciousness   catharsis   axiom
ennui   caveat   vacillation
holocaust   palliate
chagrin   assuage

1. "Let no man enter here" was a **warning sign** posted at the entrance to the sacred temple.

2. My grandmother had a saying of **self-evident truth** for every possible phase of my behavior, especially if she wished to show disapproval.

3. Because of the bride's **unpredictable changes of mind**, no one invited to be in the wedding party knew what to expect.

4. Much to my **embarrassment**, I spilled the bowl of hot soup all over the tablecloth.

5. Because they were so late for dinner, the young couple tried to **make excuses for** their thoughtless behavior by blaming the heavy traffic.

6. A lightning strike in the forest accounted for the **fiery conflagration** that destroyed hundreds of acres of prime land.

7. Because of his **indecision** about doing his Latin homework or watching the Yankee game on TV, Louis never accomplished either objective.

8. The wealthy young man's **boredom** was equalled only by his sullen attitude.

9. The harmony of the choir singing "How Great Thou Art" proved to be a kind of **purgation** of my deep despondency.

10. His defeat by an unseeded newcomer left the top-ranked tennis star despondent, and any attempt **to mollify** him failed.

C. Listed below are word pairs. Write **S** if they are synonyms; **A** if they are antonyms; **N** if they are neither.

1. caprice—whim

2. chagrin—embarrassment

3. assuage—destroy

4. palliate—reveal

5. holocaust—widespread destruction

6. ennui—annoyance

7. axiom—wisecrack

8. vacillation—decisiveness

9. catharsis—purification

10. caveat—warning

D. Choose two words from the following: vacillate, ennui, caprice, axiom. Write the words in sentences of your own.

Lesson

2

foible: *noun*

The word **foible** comes from an Old French word **feble**, and it meant **weak**. With the passage of time, **feble** changed to its contemporary counterpart **foible**. It means today essentially what it meant in the Old French except that the weakness alluded to is more implied than forthright. A foible is a fault, a minor flaw in character which, of course, implies a kind of human weakness. It should also be noted that the Old French **feble** gave rise to the English word **feeble**, in which case the weakness can apply to physical or intellectual capacities.

> *Context:* One of humanity's **foibles** is its readiness to discredit that with which it disagrees.

fortnight: *noun*

Fortnight is a word seldom used by English-speaking Americans, although the word abounds in English literature. It is built on the Middle English **fourtene night** which in turn derives from the Old English **fewwertyne nigt**. A fortnight is a period of time lasting fourteen nights, or two weeks as English-speaking Americans would put it. Any reader of English literature should know the meaning of fortnight.

> *Context:* Hillary went on holiday to the Caribbean islands for a **fortnight** of fun, sun, and relaxation.

ecdysiast: *noun*

In science, **ecdysis** means "shedding the outer coat or integument," as in the case of snakes, which shed their skins, or in crustaceans, which do the same with their outer shells. In a more restricted sense, H. L. Mencken, a popular writer of humorous fiction, coined the word **ecdysiast**, borrowing from the Greek **ecdysis**. There was, however, a major difference in terms of just what was shed. In Mencken's version, clothes were being shed—more specifically, a costume. An ecdysiast did a striptease, partially disrobing before an audience of men for the most part. This was known as burlesque at the time Mencken coined the word, and it was very popular for obvious reasons. He could not have been more apt in choosing the word to describe what it is a stripper does.

> *Context:*   The most famous **ecdysiast** of the 1940s was Gypsy Rose Lee, who entertained countless audiences of men with her special talent.

grotesque: *adjective*

The word **grotesque** has its roots buried in an Old Italian word—**grottesco**, and it means "of a cave." An Italian phrase makes clearer the connection between the two—the modern word grotesque and the Old Italian, grottesco. The phrase is **pittura grottesca**, and it means "a cave painting." It is a form of art (decorative, for the most part) oftentimes found painted on walls of caves characterized by fantastic human forms often interwoven with foliage or similar figures that distort the natural into absurdity, ugliness, or caricature. The word is used today to mean bizarre, absurdly incongruous, departing from the natural, the typical. The linguistic progression from the Old Italian **grottesco** to the Italian **pittura grottesca** to the English **grotesque** is now complete.

> *Context:*   The fallen soldier lay on the battlefield in such intense pain that his face had become **grotesquely** distorted.

fickle: *adjective*

The word **fickle** means "capricious; casually changeable; not constant in loyalty or affection." A person who is fickle does not know whom she or he likes. Today it's Peter and Jane; tomorrow, John and Joan. It is built on the Middle English **fikel**, which is remarkably close to the word's current spelling. The meanings are a different story. The Middle English etymon means **deceit**, and deceit is a behavior that is engaged in with a conscious intent. Not so with fickle persons. They may not be constant in their attachments, but there is no motivation to deceive. A fickle person is flighty—a bit "flaky." It's just how some people are. The one component lacking in their character is maturity. One expects children to behave in a fashion that is consistent with fickleness.

> *Context:* **Fickle** persons are generally shunned because of their inconstancy, especially regarding personal attachments.

fulminate: *verb*

The Middle Latin word **fulminare** means "to flash with lightning or to strike with lightning." It is the origin of the English word **fulminate**. To fulminate is to send forth censures or invectives. In figurative language it is to hurl denunciations as though they were bolts of lightning. It might be well to note here that fulminic acid also comes from the same origin. It is known for its highly explosive nature. The word fulminate implies an explosion, but the eruption is more emotional than it is real.

> *Context:* Hitler's **fulminations** were both frequent and frightening, especially when he was brought news about how badly the war was going.

dotage: *noun*

The word **dotage** has its origin in Middle Low German—**dotten**, which means "to be foolish." Its English counterpart, dotage, denotes a state of feeblemindedness, especially in old age. It is a sad but true fact of life that some elderly people in their dotage do things or say things that give the appearance of **foolishness**. The word has another meaning, too. Dotage is **foolish affection** as, for example, a married couple who cater to each other's whims too scrupulously, which borders on the foolish.

> *Context:* In his **dotage**, it was sad to witness in the old man the deterioration of what was once a vibrant mind.

expurgate: *verb*

Expurgate is "to remove that which is morally harmful, offensive, or erroneous." This removal relates especially to expunging objectionable parts from works prior to publication. In a word, to some it means editing, to others, censorship. It is built on the Latin prefix **ex**, "out" + **purgare**, "to purge; to cleanse." To purge is to free from impurities as if by **cleansing**, just as an editor might delete an objectionable part of a manuscript. There are those editors who engage in expurgation in the guise of sound editorial judgment.

Context: Many persons view **expurgation** as an abridgement of an author's First Amendment rights.

specious: *adjective*

The Late Latin etymon **speciosus** means "good looks, beauty," and it gave rise to the English word **specious**. It means "deceptively attractive or having the ring of truth but is actually false." For example, an argument that sounds plausible and true at first blush will upon closer scrutiny prove to be lacking merit if it is specious. Bear in mind that the good looks alluded to in the Latin etymon are in fact not what they suggest. Quite to the contrary, since the good looks are deceptive; hence, a specious argument, for instance, has little qualitative substance to merit its serious consideration.

Context: His reason for declining the invitation was patently **specious**, but it was accepted graciously.

ostracize: *verb*

Ostrakon is a Greek word meaning "shell" or "potsherd." From this we get the English word **ostracize**, meaning "to ban" or "to exclude from a group by popular consent." In ancient Athens a citizen could be banished by popular vote of other citizens. The voting was done by dropping pottery fragments, or potsherds, into an urn. Each potsherd bore the name of a person the voter wished to have banished. The person whose name appeared on the greatest number of potsherds was sent away from the city, or ostracized.

Context: Because he was accused of stealing money from its treasury, Ralph was **ostracized** by all members of the Friendly Athletes' Club.

EXERCISES

A. Using the words listed below, write the word that best completes each sentence. The first letter of each word is given to you. The same word may be used in more than one sentence and as different parts of speech.

foibles   dotage
ecdysiast   ostracized

fulminations   specious   expurgated
fortnight   grotesque(ly)   fickle

1. The g_____ mask worn by the clown caused a sensation among the children.

2. One of the f_____ of mankind's d_____ is that an elderly person may engage in public f_____ that make that person appear to be pathetically foolish.

3. Because of her slovenly appearance, the e_____ was fired from her job in the burlesque show after only a f_____.

4. In China, all news releases are e_____ by government officials, a form of censorship.

5. When the body was finally recovered from the water, it was g_____ misshapen.

6. What s_____ promises are being made by advertisers, especially those on television.

7. After the scandal involving members of her family, all of Marcia's old friends o_____ her.

8. Sometimes supposed friends give f_____ responses to requests for help from old chums.

B. Match the definition in Column B with the word it defines in Column A.

Column A

1. specious
2. dotage
3. fortnight
4. fickle
5. ecdysiast
6. grotesque
7. fulminate
8. expurgate
9. foible
10. ostracize

Column B

a. incongruous 6
b. to explode 7
c. one who sheds outer layers 5
d. state of foolishness, especially in the elderly 2
e. a minor character flaw 9
f. inconstant; changeable 4
g. reject; banish 10
h. having a deceptive appearance of truth 1
i. two weeks of time 3
j. to purge; to cleanse 8

C. From the words below choose the definition that conveys the idea of the word. Write the letter of the definition.

1. fulminate
   (a) to fantasize (b) to rage (c) to whisper (d) to swell up

2. specious
   (a) ugly (b) ridiculous (c) acceptable (d) false

3. dotage
   (a) adolescence (b) puberty (c) foolishness (d) concentration

4. grotesque
   (a) cavernous (b) bizarre (c) huge (d) ordinary

5. ecdysiast
   (a) a snake (b) an exhibitionist (c) a lizard (d) a stripper

6. foible
   (a) an aluminum wrapper (b) a minor character flaw
   (c) a fable (d) a weak excuse

7. fortnight
   (a) ten days (b) four nights (c) two weeks (d) forthright

8. ostracize
   (a) acknowledge (b) apologize (c) shun (d) accept

9. fickle
   (a) fanciful (b) undependable (c) constant (d) trickle

10. expurgate
    (a) explain (b) extend (c) expunge (d) expect

D. Choose two words from the following: fortnight, grotesque, specious, ostracize. Write your two words in your own sentences.

Lesson

3

turgid: *adjective*

The Latin **turgere** means "to be swollen" and is the origin of the word **turgid**. **Turgid** may be used in either a literal or a figurative sense. A limb, for instance, that has accumulated fluid may become swollen and therefore turgid. Water on the knee is a case in point. On the other hand, a river that has overflowed its banks can be described as swollen or turgid. This is a literal use of the word in both instances since there is an actual swelling. In addition to this usage, there is a figurative context. Turgid prose, for example, is swollen in that it is bombastic, pompous, inflated, all of which imply a swelling of sorts. The word is used quite freely in both contexts.

Context: The teacher's written comments indicated that the student's prose was **turgid** and in dire need of editing.

calumniate: *verb*

The word **calumniate** is derived from the Latin **calumnia**, "to deceive." To calumniate is to utter false charges maliciously to damage another's reputation. It is important to note that calumny if it is to succeed requires deception. The calumniator must in some way deceive his readers or listeners. They must believe that the charges he imputes are indeed true.

Context: His political adversary became desperate in the final hours and resorted to **calumny**, which in the end failed.

chimera: *noun*

Greek contributed to the English word **chimera** (ka-MERE-a). It really has a fanciful origin. In Greek mythology there is a word **chimaira**, an imaginary animal having a lion's head vomiting flame, a goat's body, and a serpent's tail. What could be more fanciful, more illusory, than such a creature? Today the word **chimera** means "an illusion of the mind—an unrealizable dream." This certainly is consistent with the Greek **chimaira**—an illusory creature. As a matter of fact, it is strikingly vivid.

> *Context:*   Many people who have become disenchanted with war believe that lasting peace is the **chimera** of fools.

nirvana: *noun*

The word **nirvana** has several meanings of special religious significance, but for our purposes a more general treatment would be more appropriate and useful. Nirvana comes from the Sanskrit **nirvana** and means "a blowing out, extinguishing." The **blowing out** can be thought of as extinguishing a candle. When nirvana is reached, there is an extinguishing of care, pain, and all external reality. The dictionary defines nirvana as extinguishing of desire and individual consciousness. This can occur only after the individual and cosmic consciousness merge. The latter extinguishes the former, and in so doing the external world no longer exists. There is a more general meaning attached to the word: an ideal condition of rest, harmony, stability, or joy. This meaning has nothing to do with religion.

> *Context:*   Many seek their **nirvana**, but only few ever find it.

avuncular: *adjective*

Avuncular has a fascinating origin. There are those who will complain that it is a word so seldom used that it is not worth the time and effort to learn. Wrong! It appears in literature often enough to make adding it to one's vocabulary a worthwhile effort. Avuncular comes from the Latin **avuncul(us)** and means "a mother's brother" or in other words one's uncle. The current meaning of avuncular is "characteristic of an uncle." By extension, the word can relate to any person who behaves in a kindly uncle-like fashion. Some teachers, especially teachers of elementary students, strike avuncular poses in both manner and speech.

> *Context:*   The policeman's **avuncular** appearance put the young boy at ease.

alpha and omega: *noun*

Alpha and omega are the first and last letters of the Greek alphabet. Incidentally, the first and second letters of the same alphabet are **alpha and beta**. Sound familiar? The compound in current usage means the beginning and the end. For instance, the Supreme Court's ruling on desegregation is the alpha and omega where Constitutional law is concerned. In the Bible one finds, "I am the Alpha and the Omega, the beginning and the ending, saith the Lord" (Revelation 1:8).

> *Context:*   An **alpha and omega** attaches itself to all living creatures without exception—a beginning and an end.

nebulous: *adjective*

Nebulous means "hazy, vague, indistinct." It is derived from the Latin **nebulosus**, "full of mist." This makes for a nice connection between the Latin and English counterparts. A heavy mist is in essence fog, and that which is foggy is indistinct, vague. A comment can be nebulous if it is unclear, and so too can an idea. The key word is clarity or a lack thereof. When words are studied etymologically, they are, for the most part, remarkably consistent in their current usage and their distant past.

> *Context:*   The debate coach belabored the point again and again that **nebulous** ideas do not win competitions.

bane: *noun*

While Latin and Greek dominate the foreign languages that have influenced English, there are others. For example, Old High German is the origin of the English word **bane**, which means a person or thing that ruins or spoils. It is something or someone noxious, poisonous. The word element **bano** from Old High German means "death." That which is poisonous or noxious can lead to death. Note that bane does not always mean harm in a physical sense. It can also mean a person or thing that ruins or spoils. In this context, Dennis the Menace is Mr. Wilson's bane.

> *Context:*   The **bane** of many harmless animals is the indiscriminate use of pesticides.

imprecation: *noun*

Imprecation is a Latin borrowing, and it comes from **imprecari,** meaning "to pray." Praying in this context is unusual. Generally prayers are offered for the sake of good, not evil. An example of an imprecation might make this clearer: "May God strike you dead!" The praying is evil in its intent. The dictionary defines the word as "to invoke evil upon; to curse." A better feel for the word might be had were one to think of a blessing as an antonym for the word imprecation.

> *Context:* The convicted killer's **imprecation** directed at the jury reverberated throughout the courtroom.

frenetic: *adjective*

Frenetic has an especially unusual origin. It comes from the Greek **phrenitiko,** and it means "brain disease." As the word is used currently there is no reference to the brain either stated or implied. The word means "frenzied, frantic." Having said this, one might suppose that frenzied, frantic behavior is a hallmark symptom of those who do suffer some form of brain disease. The connection between brain disease and frenzied behavior is all too obvious. In terms of its use today, frenetic behavior generally does not apply to brain disease, although it might characterize the behavior of someone suffering from a brain disorder.

> *Context:* The **frenetic** call to 911 reported a murder.

EXERCISES

A. Match each word in column A with its definition in column B.

Column A

1. chimera
2. avuncular
3. bane
4. calumniate
5. frenetic
6. imprecation
7. turgid

Column B

a. to make false charges
b. a fanciful illusion
c. swollen; inflated
d. hazy; indistinct
e. something noxious or poisonous
f. frantic; frenzied
g. curse; evil invocation

8. nirvana   h. the beginning and end; all-in-all *10* *9*
9. alpha and omega   i. an ideal condition of rest, harmony; stability *3*
10. nebulous   j. having characteristics of a benevolent uncle *8*

B. Write the letter in each group that uses the boldface word correctly.

1. a. Randolph spent his entire allowance on food for the **chimera**.
   b. Ulysses piloted his vessel skillfully between the dangerous monsters, **Scylla and Chimera**.
   c. Nancy's belief that her marriage was ideally perfect proved to be a **chimera**.

2. a. The **calumniatory** articles in the newspaper convinced voters that the senator should not be returned to office.
   b. Mixing the water with the **calumny** powder resulted in a doubtful remedy for indigestion.
   c. Her supporters depended upon **calumny** to elicit a favorable verdict for the woman accused of committing a felony.

3. a. The ritual of magic **imprecations** resulted in a blessed healing for the crippled man.
   b. Depending upon **imprecations**, the teacher conducted a lesson on the difference in meaning between "infer" and "imply."
   c. Hurling **imprecations** at the crowd, the motorist tried to escape its wrath.

4. a. "I can never be **frenetic** enough to qualify as a lady in my mother's eyes," said the placid teenage girl.
   b. The boy's **frenetic** behavior caused his doctor to give him a sedative.
   c. **Frenetics** can best be taught only by an accomplished linguist.

5. a. Adam received a grade of D+ on his theme paper because his **turgid** prose made his ideas impossible to comprehend.
   b. Her brother's room was so **turgid** that Mary refused to attempt cleaning it.
   c. People said Henry was **turgid** because he was so painfully thin.

6. a. The mongrel dog was a mean, **avuncular** pet.
   b. To say that a woman is **avuncular** is a contradiction in terms.
   c. Only an **avuncular** man can dislike children intensely.

7. a. **Alpha and Omega** were lovers until Frankie shot them down.
   b. **Alpha and Omega** was the only fraternity that Frankie wanted to join.
   c. Nostradamus is thought by some believers to be the **alpha and omega** of prophecy.

8. a. The professor was popular because his **nebulous** lectures were of such clarity.
   b. Explanations of the origin of the universe remain **nebulous**.
   c. The idea was so **nebulous** that even the slowest person in the audience understood it instantly.

9. a. "You are the **bane** of my existence," said the mother to her obstreperous child.
   b. The censors tried to **bane** from the school library any book they thought contained specious philosophy.
   c. The pharmacist recommended a controversial **bane** as a life-saving drug.

10. a. **Nirvana** is a promise to all liars that they will go to heaven when they die.
    b. Andy's life was so frenetic that he often said that he lived a **nirvana**-like life.
    c. Floating lazily on the warm water in the pool, Jane felt that she had discovered **nirvana**.

C. Write the word from the list given below that best completes the meaning of each sentence.

chimera	turgid
calumnious	bane
avuncular	alpha and omega
nirvana	nebulous
frenetic	imprecations

1. Unable to have any children of his own, Aaron always displayed an _____ attitude toward his sister's family.

2. Because I was half-asleep, all the proctor's directions about taking the exam were _____ in my mind.

3. The husband arrested for abusing his wife shouted _____ at the police.

4. "My goodness," said Elaine to her friend, "why get so _____ over losing an earring?"

5. "Students who chew gum—especially bubble gum—in class are the _____ of my profession," said the junior high school teacher.

6. People waiting in line at the supermarket cashier's station amused themselves by reading the _____ gossip in the scandal sheets.

7. The magician claimed to be the _____ of prestidigitation.

8. The capricious floods of spring turned the brook into a _____ river.

9. After the cold, snowy winter, spring seemed like _____ .

10. It is a _____ to expect to get an A on the exam if you don't study.

D. Choose two words from the following: nirvana, nebulous, bane, frenetic. Write your words in sentences of your own.

Lesson

4

cenotaph: *noun*

A **cenotaph** is a tomb or monument erected in honor of a person whose body is buried elsewhere. It is derived from two Greek etymons: **kenos**, "empty" + **taphos**, "tomb." There are many such monuments in the world today. One of the more famous is the Washington Monument found in Washington, D.C. The parallel between the meanings of the Greek etymons and that of their English counterpart is striking. Incidentally, where are **epitaphs** found? Of course, on tombstones.

> *Context:* In Egypt there are no **cenotaphs** because pharaohs and kings were buried in the tombs erected in their honor.

unctuous: *adjective*

The Latin **unctum** means "ointment." An ointment is characterized as a viscous fluid or a salve. A viscous fluid tends to be as slippery as engine oil so that engine parts will not wear unduly. The word **unctuous** as defined in a dictionary is "oily, greasy, excessively smooth." By extension an unctuous person is a slippery devil. In a religious context, unction is the **oil** used to anoint the sick and dying. The epitome of an unctuous person is the fawning nephew who butters up his rich uncle in the hope of inheriting a fortune.

> *Context:* The **unctuous** student heaped praise on his teacher hoping to earn an A grade.

vicissitude: *noun*

Vicissitude means one of the sudden or unexpected turns often encountered in one's life. It could take the form of an activity, or it may be related to one's environment or state of health. Take for example a young boy who because his father was transferred in his job to another city must learn to adjust to making new friends, adapting to an unfamiliar environment, and the countless other inconveniences that attend such a move. This can be thought of as one of life's vicissitudes. Perhaps the best way to express the idea is to use a popular cliché— "life's ups and downs." Most if not all people have experienced these **shifts** in their lives. The word is built on the Latin **vicis**, which means **change** (shift?), and the connection between it and the word's current meaning is inescapable.

Context: Robert Burns, the Scottish poet, no doubt had life's **vicissitudes** in mind when he penned the oft-quoted line concerning the best laid plans of mice and men.

titillate: *verb*

Titillate comes from the Latin word element **titillare** and means "to tickle." The tickling alludes to the senses, such as Pavarotti's exquisite tenor voice can titillate the ear just as a Gauguin can titillate the eye, or a world-class chef's creativity can titillate the palate. The word means to excite pleasurably, agreeably—to tickle?

Context: One's sense of humor can be **titillated** by a well-told story having an excellently crafted punch line.

moribund: *adjective*

Moribundis is the Latin etymon from which the word **moribund** has been derived. The Latin **moribundus** means "to die." There is no reference implied or otherwise that indicates when the dying will happen. On the other hand, the English version is more precise. It means the point of death, about to die. This is the essential difference between the English and Latin versions. The former suggests that death is in the offing; the latter makes no such reference. Note also that moribund extends to many things other than the human body: governments, societies, technologies, etc.

Context: Communism languished in a **moribund** state decades before its demise.

badinage: *noun*

Latin and Greek have made thousands of contributions to the English language, but this is not one of them. The word **badinage** has its origin in the French **badin**, which means "jester, joker." The English version badinage means "light playful banter or a playful kind of teasing." Who would be more apt to engage in lighthearted, humorous banter than a jester, a joker? Keep in mind that badinage characterizes a good-natured kind of teasing, not in any way mean-spirited.

Context: The host's **badinage** led to a lively repartee that bordered on the hilarious.

sesquipedalian: *noun or adjective*

This is a word that you will undoubtedly never have occasion to use, but its origin is such that to omit it from a work of this kind would be unpardonable. The word **sesquipedalian** comes from the Latin **sesqui** meaning "one and one-half" and the other element **ped** means "foot." Taken together, they mean one and one-half feet, and a sesquipedalian is a word that is unusually long. To suggest that the word is actually one and one-half feet long is hyperbole, but the idea should be clear. The word can also refer to a person who is given to using long words—a William F. Buckley. Incidentally, a **sesquicentennial** celebration marks the occasion of reaching 150 years—one and one-half centuries.

Context: The word **sesquipedalian** itself is a classic example of a sesquipedalian.

extirpate: *verb*

This is another of those words that carry with it a powerful notion and should be used with care. The Latin etymon **ex + tirpat** means "plucked up by the stem." To extirpate is to exterminate; to wipe out; to pull up by the root leaving no trace. One can easily discern that extirpate is an impact word that has a rather limited application. A synonym for extirpate is **expunge:** to strike or blot out; to wipe out or destroy.

Context: No one really believes that the drug trade will be **extirpated** so long as there is a ready-to-buy market available to drug dealers.

apotheosis: *noun*

Apotheosis is yet another English word owing its origin to the Greek language. It is built on two word elements: **apo**, "related to" + **theos**, "god." The denotative meaning of apotheosis is "exalted, perfect example, deification, or glorified." For example, Mother Teresa is the apotheosis of the Christian life. She has an unadulterated love and compassion for all humankind. It is a word that should be reserved for very special occasions and precious few people.

Context: The brave soldier's selfless act was the **apotheosis** of heroism on the field of battle.

swastika: *noun*

The word **swastika** has become a symbol of Nazi tyranny and the unspeakable crimes against humanity. Its origin presents one of humankind's most tragic ironies. The word originates from the Sanskrit **svastika** and means "good-luck charm." Thankfully, the swastika was not the Nazi good-luck charm.

Context: It is sad to note **swastikas** waving in parades held by neo-Nazis in many places across the world.

EXERCISES

A. Write the letter of each correct answer.

1. In the following sentence who is **unctuous**?
   Jerome's sales pitch was so smooth that Bill found him repulsive.
   (a) Jerome   (b) Bill

2. Which item gives the best definition of **badinage**?
   (a) a bandage   (b) light-hearted banter   (c) an argument
   (d) a good-luck charm

3. Which of the following can be termed a **sesquipedalian**?
   (a) an ant   (b) a horseshoe crab   (c) a full grown boa constrictor
   (d) an overly long word

4. The crowd was **titillated** by the somber news that the president had been assassinated.
   (a) true   (b) false

5. The pope was exalted as the **apotheosis** of Roman Catholicism.
   (a) true   (b) false

6. Lester was an unusually active athlete, so full of life that the commentators described him as **moribund**.
   (a) true   (b) false

7. The words **extirpate** and **expunge** are close enough in meaning to be considered synonyms.
   (a) true   (b) false

8. Which of the following is associated with the word **swastika**?
   (a) Christianity   (b) Taoism   (c) Nazism   (d) Islam

9. Is the following sentence true or false in context?
   Because Henry knew that the **vicissitudes** of life made the future stable and predictable, he decided to remain in his job.
   (a) true   (b) false

10. A place where a monument is erected in honor of a person whose body is buried elsewhere is called a(n)_____.
    (a) cenotaph   (b) monolith   (c) obelisk

   B. Match the word in Column A to its correct definition in Column B.

Column A

1. vicissitude
2. unctuous
3. apotheosis
4. badinage
5. extirpate
6. titillate
7. swastika
8. sesquipedalian
9. moribund
10. cenotaph

Column B

a. unusually long 8
b. the Washington Monument, for example 10
c. oily; smooth 2
d. sudden change in one's routine 1
e. to excite pleasurably 6
f. deity; glorification 3
g. playful teasing 4
h. to wipe out completely 5
i. obsolescent; about to die 9
j. symbol of tyranny 7

REVIEW OF LESSONS 1 - 4

A. Read the following paragraphs; answer the questions by writing the correct names.

In Charles Dickens' novel DAVID COPPERFIELD, David first thinks of his stepfather as a kind of uncle figure. Later, however, he discovered his stepfather's belief that he was the end-all and be-all of perfect fatherhood. Unfortunately, he could not tolerate any lighthearted teasing between David and his mother.

David was suddenly faced with an unforeseen change in his life—the death of his mother and his going to live with his great Aunt Betsy who would not allow any untidy behavior in her home.

David met many new friends, among them Mr. Micawber, a man who spoke in rather bombastic terms.

David met and married Dora, but to his chagrin he found that Dora could not cook or keep house. Her early death made the marriage very short-lived.

Also into David's life came an unctuous little clerk, Uriah Heep, who made false accusations against David's employer.

Eventually the pain David suffered because of the death of Dora was lessened by the love of his second wife, Agnes.

1. Who spoke in turgid language?

2. Who caused David chagrin?

3. What one word could express the idea of a change in David's life?

4. Did David find his stepfather to be the alpha and omega of fatherhood?

5. Who assuaged David's sorrow over the death of Dora?

6. Who hated slovenly habits?

7. Who engaged in badinage?

8. Who was once thought of as avuncular?

9. Who made calumnious statements?

10. Why was David's marriage ephemeral?

B. Match the word with its definition.

Column A

1. catharsis
2. titillate
3. extirpate
4. foible
5. vacillate
6. axiom
7. apotheosis
8. turgid
9. ennui
10. chagrin

Column B

a. minor weakness; character flaw
b. swollen; distended
c. self-evident truth
d. waver
e. deification
f. boredom
g. to wipe out completely
h. a cleansing; a purging
i. to tickle
j. embarrassment

Lesson

5

apocalypse: *noun*

The word **apocalypse** has a biblical background. The last book of the New Testament—Revelation—is the source. When referring to this use of the word, it is capitalized—Apocalypse. There is, however, another use of the word when it appears in lower case—**apocalypse**. In either usage the word means "a prophetic revelation, disclosure, or discovery." The origin of the word is the Greek **apokalyptein**, which means "to uncover." This meaning is quite apt inasmuch as a revelation is a kind of uncovering, revealing. Generally, the uncovering relates to a striking disclosure. Perhaps the most striking revelation is found in the New Testament. A reference is made to the four major plagues of humankind: War, Famine, Pestilence, and Death. They are more commonly known as the Four Horsemen of the Apocalypse.

Context: The **apocalyptic** horsemen have made their presence felt throughout the history of humankind—a fearfully brutish presence.

inimical: *adjective*

From the Latin root **inimicus** meaning "enemy" the word **inimical** is derived. The dictionary defines it as "unfriendly, hostile, harmful in effect." Quite literally, that which is harmful, hostile, or adverse to one's best interests can be considered **an enemy**—inimical. The word can be used in a wide range of contexts. For example, where one's health is concerned, a poor diet or smoking or lack of exercise can all be inimical. All forms of disease are inimical. One's bearing or tone of voice can be inimical if it is patently unfriendly or hostile. It is a word that has versatility in its use and belongs in the vocabulary of an educated person.

> *Context:*   There are those instances where too much exercise can be **inimical** to one's well-being.

vagary: *noun*

A **vagary** is an unpredictable action or notion. This sounds much like the meaning of the word **caprice**, a word already studied. It should, because **vagary and caprice are synonyms**. The former comes from the Latin **vagari**, "to wander." Wandering implies an aimless activity—purposeless, unpredictable, capricious—all of which are consistent with the Latin **vagari**. Perhaps the phrase "flights of fancy" can help to recall the word's meaning.

> *Context:*   While life's **vagaries** may not be productive, they can add spice to a humdrum existence.

austere: *adjective*

The dictionary definition of **austere** is "rigidly abstemious, unalterably sparing, solemn." It comes from the Greek **austeros**, which means **harsh or severe**. The word has both multiple meanings and wide application. For instance, it can be used to indicate how austere spending can bring about fiscal stability to governments. On the other hand, **austere** means "stern, forbidding in manner or in appearance." Many school teachers unfortunately take on an austere countenance—stern, forbidding. In addition to these meanings, **austere** also refers to that which is "simple, unadorned, grave, somber."

> *Context:*   There is but one solution to deficit budgets—**austerity**.

parochial: *adjective*

Parochial is a word that comes to English having a religious connection. The word comes from the Latin **parochia** and means "parish." The church parish is the smallest unit into which the Catholic religion is broken. It represents Catholicism at the provincial level. **Parochial** means "confined or restricted as if within the border of a parish." One's thinking on any topic might be parochial if it is provincial, narrow, restricted in scope. This is consistent with the Latin meaning "parish"—Catholicism at a provincial level. While there is no stigma attached to the word **parish**, there is pejorative meaning attached to parochial. One's thoughts and actions should be more catholic in scope—universal?

> *Context:* Many younger teens feel that their parents' views on dating are far too **parochial**.

demagogue: *noun*

The use of the word **demagogue** imposes three requirements on the user. First, demagogues are people, a very necessary imposition. Next, demagogues are leaders. Finally, demagogues are able to use popular prejudices and false claims and promises to further their own goal, which is to retain power. The speeches of demagogues which pander to prejudices and espouse false claims are referred to as demagogery. The word is built on the Greek **demos**, "people" + **agogos**, "leading." Hitler is the quintessential demagogue. Incidentally, a **pedagogue** is "a leader of children," from **paidos**, "child" + agogos. Teachers, if they are too formal or pedantic, are often referred to as pedagogues. For that matter any person who acts in a teacher-like manner consistent with pedantry can be thought of as pedagogic.

> *Context:* **Demagoguery** is rife in the political arena, especially during political campaigns.

truckle: *verb*

The word **truckle** comes from the compound **truckle bed**, which is a low bed moving on casters and usually pushed under another bed when not in use. It comes from late Middle English **trocle**, meaning **roller**. The truckle bed (or trundle bed, another name for it) moved around on casters, another name for rollers. Now the word truckle when used as a verb means "to submit, to yield obsequiously, or to act in a subservient manner." It takes no extraordinary powers of deduction to make a connection between the verb **truckle** and the noun **truckle bed**. The truckle bed is pushed on rollers **under** another bed when not in use. The meanings "subservient" and "obsequious" indicate behavior that implies subordination, which in turn denotes belonging to a lower class, an **under** class.

> *Context:* The niece's **truckling** attention was an obvious sham that did not go undetected by her rich uncle.

torpor: *noun*

Torpor is characterized by activity that is lacking in energy, or sluggish in functioning. It comes from the Latin **torpere** and means "to be numb." Webster defines numb as to be deprived of the power to feel or to move normally. The adjective form is **torpid**. Synonyms for **torpid** are "slow, dull, apathetic, lethargic." These pretty much capture the essence of **numb** as it relates to the Latin **torpere**.

> *Context:*   The youngster's **torpid** behavior was of concern to his parents since the lad's energy level was generally quite high.

licentious: *adjective*

The words **licentious** and **license** have the same linguistic backdrop. They are both derived from the Latin **licentia**, meaning "freedom." The word **license** connotes that a licensed individual has the **freedom** to engage in whatever it is that the license permits. Licentious relates to another kind of freedom. Here freedom refers to freedom relative to moral discipline, sexual restraint, or behaving in a manner inconsistent with rules and standards imposed by a society. The licentious person believes that he is free of civilized restraints. The noun **libertine** is one who is characterized as licentious. It comes from the Latin **libertus** and means "a freed man," free of civilizing restraints.

> *Context:*   The frightened woman became terrified after the ominous-looking stranger made a **licentious** remark.

charisma: *noun*

The Greek word element **charis** means "favor," and from it is derived the word **charisma**. There are those few individuals who have influence or authority over large numbers of people. They possess charisma. Perhaps some logical explanation can reconcile the Greek **charis** meaning "favor" and the word's current meaning. In a very real sense, the charismatic person is **favored** by the crowd, and it is this **favor** which allows the crowd to be influenced. Both Winston Churchill and Franklin Delano Roosevelt had charisma. So too did John F. Kennedy, and the Kennedy name has charisma which persists to this very day. A person's motivation has little to do with charisma. The influence can be either for good or for bad.

> *Context:*   Many political pundits believe that Ronald Reagan was one of America's most **charismatic** presidents.

EXERCISES

A. Select the word or phrase that best completes the meaning of the sentence.

1. An **austere** regimen is (a) a complicated lifestyle   (b) a military regiment   (c) a simple, self-denying lifestyle   (d) a dissolute lifestyle.

2. Smoking cigarettes is **inimical** to (a) one's peace of mind   (b) one's health   (c) one's job   (d) one's marriage.

3. Hitler was a **demagogue** because (a) he told good bedtime stories   (b) he was semi-literate   (c) he acted like a teacher   (d) he appealed to Germans' prejudices.

4. Our **torpid** behavior resulted from (a) a ferocious tornado   (b) humid, sultry weather   (c) a swim in the cold ocean water   (d) an exciting ski trip.

5. The actor was termed **charismatic** because (a) he waved to the crowd   (b) he exuded undeniable charm   (c) he was a demagogue   (d) he ran for political office.

6. An **apocalypse** is (a) a horse race   (b) a local primary election   (c) a forecasting of disaster   (d) an apothecary's diagnosis of illness.

7. Because Alton was often said to be **licentious**, the neighbors thought (a) he had a driver's license   (b) he had been given liberty from jail   (c) he flattered women with charming compliments   (d) he was an unprincipled scoundrel.

8. To **truckle** is (a) to behave in a subservient manner   (b) to truck baggage   (c) to dance to a musical genre popular in the 1950s.

9. The word **vagary** refers to (a) a wandering vagrant   (b) unpredictable fortunes in life   (c) various planned activities   (d) viable planned budgets.

10. Eustacia was thought to have a **parochial** mind because (a) she was liberal in her political thinking   (b) she was Roman Catholic   (c) she had Puritan ancestors   (d) she had an extremely narrow point of view on morality.

B. Match the definition in Column B with the word it best defines in Column A.

Column A   Column B

1. austere   a. hostile; harmful 7
2. licentious   b. stern; unadorned 1
3. apocalypse   c. a leader who makes false promises to gain power 5
4. vagary   d. to submit; to be subservient 9
5. demagogue   e. discovery; prophetic revelation 3
6. torpor   f. personal charm that allows one to hold sway
7. inimical   over people 10
8. parochial   g. unpredictable idea 4
9. truckle   h. provincial; narrow 8
10. charisma   i. numbness; apathy 6
                  j. unrestrained 2

C. If the boldface words in the following sentences complete the sentence meaningfully, write True; if not, write False.

1. Of the Four Horsemen of the **Apocalypse** the most feared is probably Death.

2. Shakespeare's jesters often composed songs about life's **vagaries**.

3. Jeremy was accused of being licentious because he had such a **parochial** point of view about dating women.

4. "Papa Doc" ruled as a **demagogue** in Haiti for many years because he was subservient to his opponents.

5. The new superintendent of schools believed that students' attitudes were **inimical** to his improving the quality of education they received.

6. When the reader first meets Mr. Rochester in Brontë's novel *Jane Eyre*, he is so **austere** that he is a most unsympathetic character.

7. The star of the baseball team made certain he had an unusually heavy lunch so that he would be **torpid** enough to make several home runs.

8. In spite of the politician's unpopular beliefs, he was so **charismatic** that he won the primary easily.

D. Choose two of the following words: austere, parochial, torpor, charisma. Use the words in your own sentences.

Lesson

6

vestige: *noun*

The word **vestige** has its origin in the Latin **vestigium**, meaning "footprint or trace." At one time **footprint** was the current usage, but users let it fall out of grace and it is now listed by dictionaries as archaic. In time the word took on a broader meaning—"a trace or visible sign left by something vanished or lost," a footprint in a way. Fossils are one vestige that most people know about. They are vestiges of former archeological times. Another vestige in humans is the appendix, which at one time eons ago had a purpose which no longer exists. The appendix is currently a **vestigial appendage**. In terms of its second meaning, "trace," think of one's not showing a vestige of remorse, a vestige of honesty, a vestige of forgiveness.

> *Context:* The gold pocket watch was the last **vestige** of his father's legacy to him.

peremptory: *adjective*

From the Latin **perimere**, which means "to take away fully," the word **peremptory** is formed. Its meaning is "absolute, final, haughty, dictatorial." Juxtapose these definitions and the Latin **perimere**, and the connection is obvious. For example, a peremptory command leaves no room for discussion; it is not negotiable. It is final. What in fact has been taken away in the Latin is one's right to challenge a peremptory command. Sitting judges in a courtroom often speak peremptorily since theirs is the final word in matters of procedure and law.

Context: The teacher's **peremptory** manner left little doubt that he would be a strict disciplinarian.

audacious: *adjective*

The word **audacious** is derived from the Latin **audere**, meaning **to dare**. Its definition is "bold, adventurous, intrepid." The words bold, adventurous, and intrepid imply "daring behavior." Also note that audacious imputes a reckless kind of behavior, which is, of course, another way of characterizing the word **daring** from the Latin **audere**.

Context: It was an **audacious** effort to attempt climbing the mountain during the brutally cold winter.

monolithic: *adjective*

Monolithic is derived from two Greek words which appear in the etymology of many English words—**monos**, "single," and **lithos**, "stone." Many **obelisks** of ancient Egypt were **monolithic** in both form and structure; that is, they were composed of a single, solid stone. The Washington Monument is monolithic in form only, for it has a hollow structure, not an undifferentiated whole as is the true monolith. The term has been extended to describe anything that is one massive whole, exhibiting solid conformity and one harmonious pattern throughout. The Catholic Church is monolithic. The Communist Party was at one time a monolith.

Context: The **monoliths** found on Easter Island still confound those who study them.

obelisk: *noun*

An **obelisk** is a four-sided monolithic (one stone) pillar, tapering as it rises and terminating in a pyramid; it is also a mark of reference (an inverted spit or dagger †) found in textbooks. The word **obelisk** is built on the Greek **obelos**, "a spit; a pointed pillar." The Washington Monument again has the form of an **obelisk** but is not composed of a single stone. Examples of true obelisks are the obelisk in the Place de la Concorde in Paris and Cleopatra's Needle in New York.

Context: The movie about an extraterrestrial culture took the viewer to a city filled with strange structures and **obelisks** rising majestically into the sky.

akimbo: *adjective, adverb*

The expression **arms akimbo** is used quite frequently to describe a position in which a person's hands are placed on the hips with the elbows extended outward. The expression comes from the Middle English word **kenebowe**, which means "jug handle." The picture of someone standing arms akimbo—looking like a two-handled jug—is strikingly vivid.

> *Context:*   The policeman stood arms **akimbo** berating the motorist who had just violated three basic rules of driving.

cursory: *adjective*

The word **cursory** means "superficially done; done hastily without taking note of details." It's almost as though one were in a hurry to get done whatever it is that is being done. It should be apparent that cursory behavior features quickness at the expense of thoroughness. The word is built on the Latin **cursor** and means "running," which is consistent with the word's current definition. To do something in a cursory manner is to do it in haste, almost like running through it. The word also connotes inattention, a primary characteristic of the word cursory.

> *Context:*   Before the crime lab technicians arrived, the detective gave the room a **cursory** examination.

eponym: *noun*

The English word **eponym** has its origin in the Greek word element **eponumos**, which means "named after." Its current meaning is the derivation of a name of a city, country, era, institution, or other place or thing from the name of a person. A classic example is the city Rome, Italy, which takes its name from Romulus. Eponyms are not all that uncommon: Washington, D.C., ohm, volt, Cadillac—all come to English from someone's name. The Greek **eponumos** again means "named after," and it is a close approximation to the word's current definition.

> *Context:*   The names of many famous people have been taken and used as **eponyms** for places or things.

penchant: *noun*

From the French **pencher** the English word **penchant** is derived. **Pencher** means "to incline, to lean." The meaning of **penchant** is not too unlike that of its French counterpart—"a strong taste or liking for something, a preference." This gets us back to the French **pencher**, meaning "to incline, to lean." A strong taste or liking for something is certainly an inclination toward something, a preference. Actually the

French borrowed from the Latin **pendere**, meaning "to weigh." In a sense, when one has a penchant for something, his preference outweighs his possible dislike of the thing.

> *Context:*   His **penchant** for playing golf was such that it caused a serious home problem.

asinine: *adjective*

The Latin word element **asinus** means "jackass," and it is the origin of its English counterpart **asinine**. A jackass has the reputation for being a remarkably stupid animal. **Asinine** means "silly, stupid, unintelligent"—a jackass. A silly remark, foolish behavior, or frivolous thinking, if silly or doltish, is asinine. The word can be used in many different contexts, but the bottom line returns to a jackass from the Latin **asinus**.

> *Context:*   It was a student's **asinine** remark that provoked the teacher's asperity.

EXERCISES

A. Match each word in Column A with its definition in Column B.

Column A

1. audacious
2. obelisk
3. cursory
4. monolithic
5. penchant
6. vestige
7. asinine
8. peremptory
9. eponym
10. akimbo

Column B

a. absolute; authoritative 8
b. trace; remnant 6
c. silly; stupid 7
d. reckless; intrepid 1
e. massive; solid 4
f. hands on hips, elbows bent 10
g. the person for whom something is named 9
h. hasty; superficial 3
i. a preference; strong taste for 5
j. 4-sided tapered pillar; a mark of reference 2

B. In the following sentences choose the word or phrase that best completes the meaning of the sentences.

1. Standing _____, the farmer's wife shouted lustily at the cow in the middle of the road blocking traffic.
   (a) royally   (b) daintily   (c) arms akimbo   (d) hands folded

2. Mount Rushmore National Memorial located in the Black Hills of South Dakota is a likeness of Washington, Jefferson, Lincoln, and T. Roosevelt carved into a mountain of rock, a(n) _____.
   (a) monolith   (b) eponym   (c) epigraphy

3. Naming Ella Grasso Boulevard after the late governor of Connecticut is called _____.
   (a) a synonym   (b) an eponym   (c) a metonym   (d) an antonym

4. When they resorted to cannibalism, the survivors of the plane crash admitted that the last _____ of civilized behavior were disappearing.
   (a) veracities   (b) verbosities   (c) vestiges   (d) polemics

5. The boys in the family all had a _____ for watching professional football competition on TV.
   (a) flatulence   (b) penchant   (c) catharsis   (d) vestige

6. Because the camp counselor made such final and absolute decisions, the campers all agreed she was a/an _____ person.
   (a) peremptory   (b) indecisive   (c) passive   (d) meek

7. My cousin had the _____ to question the credentials of the newly appointed basketball coach.
   (a) cowardice   (b) timidity   (c) charisma   (d) audacity

8. The tour guide took us to the Place de la Concorde in Paris, explaining that a true _____ is composed of a single four-sided stone tapering to a pyramid as it rises.
   (a) gravestone   (b) war memorial   (c) obelisk   (d) plaque

9. Jack's answer to the teacher's question was so _____ that the entire class collapsed into laughter.
   (a) ambiguous   (b) clever   (c) asinine   (d) intellectual

10. A _____ examination showed no sign of broken bones after Lenny fell off his skateboard.
    (a) thorough   (b) cursory   (c) lengthy   (d) fearsome

   C. Listed next are word pairs. Write **S** if they are synonyms; **A** if they are antonyms; **N** if they are neither.

1. akimbo—akin

2. audacious—fainthearted

3. monolithic—massive

4. peremptory—submissive

5. penchant—proclivity

6. eponym—epitome

7. vestige—trace

8. obelisk—gravestone

9. asinine—foolish

10. cursory—thorough

D. Choose two of the following words: audacious, cursory, vestige, penchant. Use your words in your own sentences.

Lesson
7

penury: *noun*

Penury means "poverty, absence of resources, destitution." It is built on the Latin **penuria**, which means "want." Certainly anyone who is living in poverty or who is destitute **wants**—more money, a better diet, more affordable housing, etc. The wants of the impoverished are endless. Bear in mind that penurious individuals are not simply poor; they are penniless, living wretched lives. It is yet another power word that should be used on carefully considered occasions.

> *Context:* Most homeless people live **penurious** lives, forgoing the barest essentials of life.

explicate: *verb*

To **explicate** is "to provide detailed explanation." The word is built on the Latin prefix **ex**, "out" + **plicare**, "to fold." Figuratively, to explicate is "to get the wrinkles out, to unfold" as it were. There are occasions when explication is vital to a full understanding. Common sense should guide one in the matter of determining when explication is required and when it is not.

> *Context:* Since the professor's students seemed not to grasp the concept, he provided a more thorough **explication**.

obfuscate: *verb*

To **obfuscate** is "to make obscure, to confuse, to darken." It is built on the Latin prefix **ob**, "in the way" + **fuscus**, "dark brown." To render an idea obscure or confused can readily be accomplished were

41

one to cover (figuratively) it over with a **dark brown** something which gets in the way of understanding. Obfuscation generally implies a deliberate attempt to confuse, to darken. In this sense, it is something that one should avoid doing.

> *Context:*   **Obfuscation** is a ploy engaged in by some politicians in order to mask their real intentions.

excoriate: *verb*

To **excoriate** is "to censure in a scathing manner." It is much more severe than is a reprimand or a scolding. From Latin comes the word's origin: **ex**, "away" + **corium**, "skin; hide." In a figurative sense, to excoriate is "to tear away the flesh (skin)." The late Richard Nixon, for example, was excoriated by the press and by many others for his involvement in the Watergate scandal. It is a powerful word that evokes strong feelings, and it should be used with care.

> *Context:*   The captain of the college debate team **excoriated** his opponent, which in the end cost him the win.

impugn: *verb*

To have one's honesty or integrity **impugned** is to have it opposed or attacked as false. It is being called into question. **Impugn** finds its way into English from the Latin **impugnare**, which means "to fight against." The words **pugilist** and **repugnant** are derived from this same source. A pugilist is a prizefighter. Repugnant means arousing disgust or repulsion. Would not one fight against (if only figuratively) that which arouses disgust? The Latin **repugnare** and **impugnare** mean the same thing—"to fight against." Finally, there is a word **pugnacious**—"eager to fight." Those with chips on their shoulders just spoiling for a fight are pugnacious, from **pugnare** meaning "to fight." Many other subtle links exist in language, and only after they are known does language bare itself as a veritable treasure trove, the use of which is accorded to humankind alone.

> *Context:*   Many people **impugned** the loyalty of those who fled to Canada to avoid having to serve during the Vietnam conflict.

cozen: *verb*

In the Italian the word **cozzone** means "a horse trader." It has two meanings in English: "to deceive by petty trickery or fraud; to persuade someone to do something by cajoling or wheedling." Webster defines horse trader as one whose dealings are characterized by shrewd and vigorous bargaining (sometimes with deception and fraudulent intent). One who has been **cozened** has been "had." Put another way, the victim has been tricked or "conned" by a wily horse trader. The primary intent of many telemarketing operations is to cozen those on the other end of the phone.

Context: Many elderly people have been **cozened** by smooth-talking "salesmen" who sometimes swindle them out of their life's savings.

emulate: *verb*

Emulate finds its origin in the Latin **aemulus**, "rivaling." The word's current meaning is "to strive to equal or to excel, to imitate." If anything, the rivaling alluded to in the Latin root is not mean-spirited as are some other rivalries. It is more in the nature of a son imitating his father, or a young football player emulating Joe Montana. In any case, the person being emulated should take comfort in the knowledge that someone thinks highly enough of him to want to be like him one day.

Context: Too often youngsters tend to **emulate** negative role models—famous personalities who are taking drugs, or who beat their wives, etc.

obtuse: *adjective*

The word **obtuse** suggests "lacking sharpness (of the mind)." The Latin **obtusus** is its derivation, and it means "blunt, dull." The dullness of the English version of obtuse has two meanings: dullness of the mind, and in mathematics it is an angle exceeding 90° but less than 180°. In other words, the angle lacks sharpness, or acuteness. Both of these meanings are used quite extensively

Context: The customer charged the salesperson for being **obtuse** because she could not understand what the problem was.

adamant: *adjective*

Adamant means "unyielding, inflexible, especially in the face of opposition." Its linguistic heritage can be traced back to the Greek

adamas, "hardest metal." Bear in mind that the hardness alluded to is transformed in the English version. An adamant position, for instance, refers to one that is unyielding, inflexible, unshakable, procrustean. It is not like a physical hardness, a hardness of touch. It is rather a hardness of the mind—unbending. Incidentally, the word diamond is built on this Greek root word **adamas**. Perhaps one can now better understand the connection between the Greek **adamas** and **diamond**. The words even look somewhat alike.

> *Context:* His position against cigarette smoking was **adamant**; nothing would change is mind.

virulent: *adjective*

The word **virulent** has two meanings. One definition is "extremely toxic," or in this same vein it is used to characterize a toxin, or a microorganism that is deadly, such as AIDS. This is the meaning closest to the Latin **virulentus**, designating "poison." That which is virulent can kill just as easily as can a poison. But there is another meaning of the word virulent—"bitterly hostile or antagonistic; hateful; maliciously spiteful." None of these can be fatal; none of them is a poison in a literal sense. One can, for instance, compose a virulent letter, or make virulent criticism. Neither of these can cause physical harm as can a virulent bacterium. It is important to be mindful of these distinctions. Incidentally, perhaps now one can appreciate more fully the word **virus**, which is built on this same Latin root. Some viruses are deadly; others are not.

> *Context:* The bubonic plague was a **virulent** disease that caused the deaths of seventy million people during the 14th century.

EXERCISES

A. Match the word in Column B with the word it defines in Column A.

Column A

Column B

d 1. obfuscate

a. attack; fight against

b 2. cozen

b. toxic; hateful

J 3. excoriate c. destitution; dire need
A 4. impugn d. to explain fully
D 5. explicate e. dull; blunt
E 6. obtuse f. try to equal; imitate
G 7. adamant g. inflexible; unyielding
B 8. virulent h. to confuse; to obscure
~ 9. penury i. to cajole; to deceive
F 10. emulate j. to censure harshly; to flay

B. Choose the word or phrase in each group that best conveys the meaning of the boldface word in each sentence.

1. The jury agreed that the broker's young assistant was trying to **obfuscate** his participation in insider trading.
(a) explain (b) cover-up (c) excuse (d) clarify

2. My brother says I am so **obtuse** that I never get the point of his jokes.
(a) bright (b) stupid (c) quick-witted (d) sharp

3. Florida police warn winter homeowners not to let door-to-door salesmen **cozen** them into signing contracts for home improvements.
(a) frighten (b) trick (c) force (d) threaten

4. A **virulent** epidemic swept through the county, causing schools to close for several days at a time.
(a) varied (b) nontoxic (c) masculine (d) deadly

5. When the neighbors termed Jonah **penurious**, they meant that
(a) he always carried small change (b) he had a virulent disease (c) he was in dire need of food and clothing (d) he was constantly in and out of jail.

6. **Excoriated** by the media because he was convicted for murdering his neighbor, the man was released ten years later when another prisoner admitted to the crime.
(a) excused (b) denounced scathingly (c) harassed (d) praised

7. Joe's father was **adamant** about his resolution forbidding Joe to drive the car without permission.
(a) indecisive (b) inflexible (c) capricious (d) avuncular

8. "How dare you **impugn** my motives for leaving you?" demanded the battered wife of her spouse.
(a) palliate (b) obfuscate (c) attack as false (d) praise

9. **Explicating** endlessly, the politician managed to stall the vote on the issue of cutting taxes.
(a) assuaging (b) explaining (c) extirpating (d) impugning

10. Aspiring to be a country singer, Henry decided to **emulate** Garth Brooks.
(a) imitate (b) praise (c) improve on (d) ignore

    C. Complete each sentence by writing the appropriate word from the following list.

penurious   excoriated
explication   impugn
obfuscate   cozened
emulate   virulent
obtuse   adamant

1. It was easy to recognize that my aunt was a school teacher because she always went into a long-winded _____ when asked a simple question.

2. Anyone who could not understand the rudiments of first year algebra was considered _____ by the math teacher.

3. Because Elsa's one goal in life was to be a ballet dancer, she tried to _____ Margot Fontaine.

4. The confusing, long-winded explication of Plato's "Parable of the Cave" by the student orator served only to further _____ the central idea of the Parable.

5. We discovered that a family new to our church was so _____ that the children had no warm winter clothing.

6. The scandal sheets that _____ the reputations of celebrities are repugnant to me.

7. An extremely _____ strain of Asiatic flu caused the board of education to close the schools for a week.

8. Anita's parents were _____ about their decision forbidding her to stay out later than eleven P.M. even on Friday night.

9. My neighbor, an elderly widow, was _____ into investing her life savings in a gold brick business venture.

10. When it was learned that the mayoral candidate was arrested for public drunkenness, his character was _____ by the press, and he was forced to withdraw from the race.

D. Choose two of the following words: emulate, obtuse, adamant, virulent. Use your words in sentences of your own.

Lesson

8

exurb: *noun*

Most people are familiar with the words **urban** and **suburban**. There is, however, a third word less commonly known that indicates areas where people live in relation to a metropolitan city, and that word is **exurb**. These areas are found outside a city and beyond what are usually classified as suburbs. For the most part, those who are well-to-do live in exurbs. The word is built on the Latin prefix **ex**, meaning "outside," and **urbs**, meaning "city."

> *Context:* Stately homes with expensive foreign autos parked in tandem are often found in an **exurb**.

exult: *verb*

The word **exult** is derived from the Latin etymon **ex**, meaning "up," and **saltare**, "to leap." The literal translation of the Latin is "to leap up." While this is an accurate translation, it does not quite capture the full flavor of the word **exult**. The leaping up is brought about by joy, jubilation, and this is what is missing in the Latin definition. Note that there is another word in English that is a look-alike to **exult**, and that is **exalt**. The latter word means "to glorify, to extol" and is not to be confused with **exult**.

> *Context:* The football fans who **exult** over the team's efforts contribute mightily to their winning games.

euphemism: *noun*

A **euphemism** is a substitute word or expression that is used to avoid a word or expression that might offend some individuals or suggest to them that which is unpleasant. For instance, the expression **passed away** is a **euphemism** for the word **died**. In Germany an **erostess** is a **euphemism** for the word **prostitute**. The ultimate use of euphemisms was one coined in Nazi Germany—the **final solution**—for the extermination of over nine million people. A more recent euphemism for decimating a population is **ethnic cleansing**, another attempt to mask the reality of what took place. The word is derived from the Greek elements **eu**, "good, well" + **pheme**, "speech." The **good speech** is intended to convey the idea of inoffensiveness regarding the use of language.

> *Context:* Some car dealers have used the **euphemism** "previously owned auto" in place of "used car."

flatulent: *adj.*

The word **flatulent** has two meanings, one literal and the other figurative. The first of these is a condition where there is excessive gas in the digestive tract. The second meaning of **flatulent** is "to be pompous, pretentious, without real substance or worth." The word is built on the Latin **flatus** and means "blowing wind." Think of someone you know who is a braggart, who overvalues his or her personal abilities, a blowhard. It does not require a quantum leap to get from this current meaning to the Latin **flatus**, meaning "blowing wind."

> *Context:* The speaker's **flatulent** comments made painfully clear to his audience that he was an egotistical bore.

facade: *noun*

The Italian word for face is **faccia**, and it is the origin of its English counterpart, **facade**. The English version has two very different meanings. The first of these is the face of a building, especially the principal face. The second of these meanings is an artificial or deceptive front; a face that gives a false, superficial, or artificial appearance. The word is used frequently in both contexts. There is a widely known phrase that captures the essence of the word—**putting on a false front or face**. This is what the word means in the latter context.

> *Context:* The boy's parents put on a brave front to bolster their son's spirits, but it was too obvious that it was merely a **facade**.

euphoria: *noun*

The Greek etymon **euphoros** means "healthy" and is the origin of its English counterpart, euphoria. It means a feeling of great happiness or well-being. Note that this feeling is oftentimes unexplainable. In fact, in psychology the word euphoria relates to a feeling of well-being, an exaggerated one having no basis in truth or reality. While this may be the case in psychology, it is not always so in terms of the word's more general usage. There are instances where one can point to an event having been the cause of euphoria. For example, a young girl who is given an engagement ring may be in a state of euphoria for days. Back to the Greek **euphoros**, meaning "healthy." A state of euphoria brings with it boundless joy. Might not this mental state also promote better health in a broader sense? In short, euphoric states of mind can and oftentimes do induce better health, especially one's mental health.

Context: I awakened on my wedding day in a state of unparalleled **euphoria**.

expatiate: *verb*

As is the case of many other words found in the English language, **expatiate** owes its origin to the Latin. The prefix **ex**, "out" + **spatium**, "space," combine to make the word **expatiate**. It means "to wander, to move about freely or at will." While this definition is acceptable, it is much too broad to be of much use. In a much narrower sense, expatiate means to speak or to write at great length and in great detail without restraint. The word suggests a kind of discourse, verbal or written, that seems to go on endlessly. In a sense, such communication goes outside the space that would normally be allotted such activity. "To expatiate" is used in a derogatory sense, and should be avoided if at all possible.

Context: The speaker **expatiated** on his journey to Africa, omitting not a solitary detail, much to the distress of his audience.

heinous: *adj.*

A heinous (HAY-ness) deed is shockingly evil, outrageously bad. It has its origin in the Middle French **haineus**, from **haine**, meaning **hate**. That which is heinous is so wicked that the act is a hateful one. The word should be used sparingly to characterize those misdeeds that are the very hallmarks of evil. For example, Hitler's crimes against the Jews

9. Pleading with the jury to **exculpate** Jerome, the lawyer was trying (a) to free him from prison   (b) to bring Jerome to trial (c) to clear Jerome of blame   (d) to calumniate Jerome.

10. If Elizabeth was **euphoric** when she won the short story contest, she was (a) anesthetized   (b) moribund   (c) elated (d) peremptory.

   C. Write S if the words below are synonyms; write A if they are antonyms; write N if neither.

1. euphoric—elated

2. exultant—downcast

3. flatulent—flat

4. facade—false front

5. expatiate—be patriotic

6. heinous—admirable

7. exurb—exalted

8. euphemism—inoffensive expression

9. exigency—emergency

10. exculpate—execute

   D. Choose two of the following words: euphemism, exurbs, facade, euphoria. Use your two words in your own sentences.

REVIEW OF LESSONS 1 - 8

   A. Write the word in parentheses that best completes the meaning of the sentence.

1. A politically correct (vagary, euphemism, caprice) for the term "chairman" is "chairperson."

2. Imagine my (chagrin, frenzy, titillation) when I realized I had introduced my new sister-in-law to her own cousin.

3. I found the stranger's (moribund, avuncular, nebulous) attitude toward my young nephew to be very annoying.

4. Members of the opposition party said that the rival candidate's campaign speech was filled with (monolithic, specious, penchant) reasoning.

5. Believing that Joan of Arc was the (demagogue, chimera, apotheosis) of Christian sainthood, her followers worshipped her as their savior from oppression.

6. Students tried to avoid Dr. Quint's class because she always (extirpated, expatiated, exculpated) in infinitesimal detail about every word in every sentence of every lesson.

7. Climbing up the rock face at Yosemite was the most (audacious, austere, adamant) project we had ever attempted in our mountain-climbing adventures.

8. "If you girls must (impugn, assuage, emulate) a famous woman, let it be Mother Teresa rather than Jezebel," advised the guidance counselor.

9. Lying in the muddy trench as the bombs spread horror over the battlefield, the soldiers felt that the last (imprecations, vestiges, foibles) of civilization were disappearing.

10. The (virulent, torpid, grotesque) gargoyles found on buildings such as Notre Dame in Paris are intended to keep evil spirits from entering the cathedral.

B. Write the letter C if the boldface word is consistent with sentence meaning, or write I if it is not.

1. If a person is filled with a sense of **ennui**, he or she is fraught with excitement and pleasure.

2. An **ecdysiast** is a reptile or a crustacean that sheds its outer skin or shell.

3. To **fulminate** is to hurl denunciations, invectives, or censures.

4. The Washington Monument is an example of a **cenotaph**.

5. **Turgid** prose is what English teachers appreciate most in student writing.

6. A **parochial** view is one that is all-embracing.

7. That which is **licentious** has to do with freedom, specifically freedom of speech.

8. To **fulminate** and to **calumniate** are fairly close in meaning.

9. A **chimera** is a goat having a lion's tail and vomiting flame.

10. To be **chagrined** is to be distressed of mind caused by humiliating failure.

   C. Match the following words with their meanings.

Column A

1. holocaust
2. assuage
3. titillate
4. alpha and omega
5. badinage
6. emulate
7. avuncular
8. vagary
9. axiom
10. euphoria
11. foible
12. obfuscate
13. peremptory
14. heinous
15. fortnight

Column B

a. a self-evident truth
b. haughty; dictatorial
c. a minor flaw in character
d. a conflagration; widespread destruction caused by fire
e. an unpredictable action
f. a period of two weeks
g. feeling of great happiness or well-being
h. to mollify; to pacify
i. to make obscure
j. shockingly evil
k. light, playful banter
l. strive to equal
m. to excite pleasurably
n. the beginning and the end
o. characteristic of a kindly uncle

Lesson

9

anachronism: *noun*

The prefix **ana**, "backward" + **chronos**, "time," are the etymons on which the word **anachronism** is built. An anachronism is a person or thing which is chronologically out of place. For instance, Shakespeare was guilty of falling into this time warp when Brutus, while ruminating in his garden on the eve of Caesar's assassination, hears a clock strike the hour. There were no mechanical clocks in use at this time. They had not yet been invented. Be mindful that not only persons or things can be anachronistic. One's thinking on a given subject can be anachronistic. Many psychologists, for instance, believe the bromide about sparing the rod and spoiling the child is anachronistic thinking. It is out of sync and has no place in the framework of child rearing.

> *Context:* Many young folks today feel that anyone over the age of forty is an **anachronism**.

poltergeist: *noun*

The Old High German etymons **poltern**, "to knock" + **geist**, "ghost," combine to form the word **poltergeist**. Literally the word according to the root elements is a ghost that knocks, a noisy ghost, if one prefers. The current definition is compatible with this definition: a noisy, mischievous ghost held responsible for unexplained rappings (knockings?) and other mysterious sounds. Poltergeists are not generally considered to be malevolent spirits. Rather they tend to engage in playful kinds of pranks more bothersome than hurtful. Perhaps the most famous poltergeist is "Casper the Ghost" who can be found in the animated cartoon world.

Context: There are those who deny the existence of **poltergeists** and further contend that they are the product of over-active imaginations.

histrionic: *adj.*

Histrionic finds its way into English via the Latin etymon **histrio**, "actor." There is a nice tie-in to the word's current meaning—"theatrical, deliberately affected; artificial in behavior or in speech; excessively dramatic or emotional." In brief, histrionics is an act performed for the benefit of an audience, which is essentially what actors do. Note that histrionics is not acceptable social form and should be avoided. Leave acting to actors.

Context: Parents who engage in **histrionics** in defense of their child at school only make matters worse.

bellwether: *noun*

There are two meanings that apply to the word **bellwether**. The word is derived from the Old Saxon **wither**, "a castrated male sheep." Middle English added **bell** to the Old Saxon, and together meant a male sheep with a bell tied round its neck so that the flock could more easily follow it. In a sense, a very loose sense, the bellwether sheep was leader of the flock. A more general use of the word is one that takes the lead or initiative—a leader. This leadership can assume any form: military, political, scientific, etc.

Context: The sales of new homes is a **bellwether** economic indicator that forecasts stability in the market place.

banal: *adj.*

The Middle French **ban** means "of compulsory feudal service or serfdom" and is the origin of the English word **banal**. It means "wanting originality, common." During the Middle Ages, serfs were referred to by the landed gentry as **commoners**. By extension a banal existence or turn of phrase is **common** in the sense that each is hackneyed, trite, **commonplace**. Today its full meaning is "devoid of freshness, originality."

> *Context:* **Banal** expressions should be avoided in both written and spoken language.

exude: *verb*
The word **exude** has both a figurative and a literal meaning attached to it. Literally it means to ooze out; to cause to spread in all directions as would burning rubber exude a bubbling, resinous substance. The exudation is literal in this instance. On the other hand, there is a figurative use of ooze. The oozing is implied, as in one's exuding charm, grace, loathing, love—all of which **seem** to ooze from the skin's pores. It is a figurative use of language. The word is built on the Latin prefix **ex**, "out of" + **sudare**, "sweat." Does not sweat ooze out from the skin's pores? The parallel between the Latin and the English versions is striking.

> *Context:* At the birthday party, the children **exuded** a special kind of joy that was manifestly obvious.

catholic: *adj.*

Catholic: *noun*
There are two different uses of the word catholic depending on whether or not it appears in lower or upper case. **Catholic** (upper case) is a religion and needs no explication here. Then there is the word **catholic** (lower case), which means "broad in sympathies, tastes, or interests." On to the word's derivation. It comes from the Greek **katholikos**, which means "general, universal." Note how nicely the **universal** fits Catholic (upper case). Certainly there is a universality associated with Catholicism in that it is practiced worldwide. In terms of catholic (lower case) there is just as nice a parallel. For example, one's taste relative to food or reading may, if sufficiently inclusive, be catholic. Or a preference for objet d'art may be catholic just as any other broad interest or taste. Such tastes or interests must be wide ranging and inclusive if they are to be catholic.

> *Context:* Education must be a **catholic** enterprise if students are to benefit from it.

pontiff: *noun*

The word **pontiff** finds its roots buried deep in Latin as do so many other words that have become part of the English language. It is built on the Latin **pontifex** and means "bridge maker." More often than not, it is used to designate the pope, spiritual leader of the Catholic Church. In a sense, he is the **maker of bridges**, especially those between the temporal and spiritual worlds. Beyond this specific reference, the word takes on a more general meaning, one that is more belittling in its usage. Also, it changes grammatically from noun to verb—pontificate. It means "to speak in a pompous or dogmatic manner." While the pope may not be pompous, he is dogmatic in matters of religion. His is the final word in this regard.

Context: The **pontiff** bestowed his blessing on the crowd that had gathered in St. Peter's Square.
Teachers who **pontificate** rather than teach seldom win the esteem of their students.

brogue: *noun*

The word **brogue** is derived from the Irish word **barrog**, meaning "a grip or hold." Actually the grip or hold referred to is on the tongue. Once the Irish language grips the tongue, it seems never to quite relinquish its hold. More than other speech habits, the brogue of the Irish persists in manifesting itself even when the speaker communicates in some other dialect or tongue.

Context: An Irish brogue fits the tongue like an old shoe.

idiosyncracy: *noun*

The word **idiosyncracy** comes from the Greek **idios**, "own" + **sunkrasis**, "mixture; temperament." An idiosyncracy is a physiological or temperamental characteristic peculiar to an individual; it is his or her own mixture, if you will. An example of a physiological idiosyncracy is Carol Burnett's tugging on her ear at the end of each of her television shows. The behavior is peculiar to Carol Burnett alone. A temperamental idiosyncracy might be buying expensive clothing that really is unneeded whenever one is emotionally distressed. Groups can also exhibit idiosyncrasies. A football team, for example, whose members touch the team mascot's head before every game engage in this kind of "odd" behavior.

Context: A baseball pitcher who will not step on the foul line on his way to or from the dugout is being **idiosyncratic**.

EXERCISES

A. Match each definition in Column B with the word it defines in Column A.

Column A

1. poltergeist *G*
2. brogue *B*
3. idiosyncracy *F*
4. exude *J*
5. catholic *I*
6. histrionic *H*
7. pontiff *C*
8. anachronism *A*
9. banal *E*
10. bellwether *D*

Column B

a. chronologically out of place
b. grip, hold
c. spiritual leader
d. an indicator of trends; a leader
e. lacking originality; stale
f. peculiar trait; eccentricity
g. a noisy, impish ghost
h. theatrical, artificial
i. universal
j. ooze; display abundantly

B. Using the clues below, write the words defined. The letters corresponding to the shaded squares will show if you have a particular liking for this type of puzzle.

1. a playful wraith

2. display abundantly

3. a spiritual leader

4. an eccentricity

5. melodramatic

6. ordinary

7. something chronologically out of place

8. indicator of trends

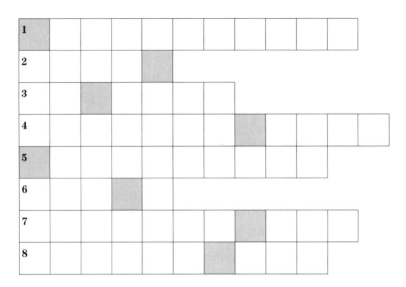

C. Read the passage below, then answer the questions that follow.

All of us students who were in Mr. Jorgenson's English class last period of the day certainly were not fascinated with English, at least not the way it was taught by him. There were, however, other things going on in the classroom besides an analysis of SILAS MARNER.

Last Friday, for instance, Amy who generally oozes charm ad nauseum put on her own private show. When she saw the grade her theme received—a flat-out F—she cried and then pretended to faint, entertaining the class no end with her dramatic overacting. To add to the drama Irma, her friend, accompanied her to the girls' room ostensibly to mollify her despair. Mr. Jorgenson hadn't an inkling that he was being "put on." While they were gone, Mr. Jorgenson continued with his critique of several other papers. Anita's was filled with figures of speech that were both tired and unoriginal. John had misspelled the word for "noisy ghost." Jorgenson continued by voicing his concern over careless spelling errors, misused commas, and a host of other mistakes. These he said would eventually lead to failure in composition. He continued returning papers as he spoke. When Raymond's paper was returned, he displayed his usual odd behavior—taking off his glasses and wiping them, then crossing his hands in a prayerful position. Finally, he crossed his fingers before he looked at his grade.

Last, I should mention that my mom had Mr. Jorgenson for English 12 more than 25 years ago, and she informed me that his teaching methods hadn't changed one iota. He was, she said, a dinosaur in the field of education.

At that point, the bell rang and the class ended. In fairness, it wasn't a dull day, not at all.

Answer these questions.

1. Who misspelled the word **poltergeist**?

2. What histrionic display entertained the class?

3. Which student had an unusual idiosyncrasy?

4. Who was criticized for banality in composition?

5. Who usually exuded charm?

6. What did Mr. Jorgenson consider to be a bellwether of eventual failure in composition?

7. What word characterizes Mr. Jorgenson's outmoded teaching approach to composition?

D. Choose two of the following words: anachronism, histrionic, exude, idiosyncrasy. Use your words in sentences of your own.

Lesson

10

aegis: *noun*

Aegis means "protection, sponsorship." In Greek mythology aegis referred to the shield or breastplate of Zeus and Athena. Needless to say, a breastplate or shield is meant to protect, and it should come as no surprise that one of the word's meanings is "protection." There is another meaning attached to the word, and that is sponsorship, which implies an assumed responsibility for the sponsor—an obligation to provide protection of one kind or another: financial, political, military, the arts, whatever.

> *Context:* Under the **aegis** of the United Nations, it was decided by member nations to send in a contingent of armed soldiers.

coruscate: *verb*

The English **coruscate** has its origin in the Latin **coruscat**, which means "to flash." The American Heritage Dictionary defines the word as "to give forth flashes of light." Two synonyms for the word flash are **sparkle** and **glitter** and these words precisely define the meaning of coruscate. Blue-white diamonds have a tendency to **coruscate** when exposed to bright light. They tend to sparkle or flash brilliantly.

> *Context:* The exquisite crystal chandelier **coruscated** brightly when the overhead lights were turned on.

quintessence: *noun*

The word **quintessence** dates back to the ancient Greek view of the universe. Empedocles held that the universe consisted of four elements—earth, air, fire, and water. Aristotle added to these basic elements a fifth (Latin **quinta**) essence, which he called **ether**. It was this fifth essence that was the purest and most concentrated, for it made up all of the heavenly bodies. Hence the quintessence of a thing is its purest and most concentrated form. How does Shakespeare apply the word when he has the disillusioned Hamlet say, "What a piece of work is a man . . . And yet, to me, what is this quintessence of dust?"

> *Context:* Technology and technocrats are **quintessential** elements of the 1990s, which have spawned the age of modems, bytes, bits, and the now ubiquitous internet.

nepotism: *noun*

Nepotism is the practice of doling out favors on the basis of blood relationship, especially favoritism shown to relatives in making important appointments. Many people believe that nepotism is the reality of politics—take care of your own first. The meaning of nepotism is a rational derivation from the Latin **nepos**, meaning "nephew or grandson."

> *Context:* **Nepotism** is especially rampant in the corporate world where sons, nieces, nephews, and cousins are shown preferential treatment.

rue: *noun; verb*

The noun **rue**, meaning **regret**, is not often seen in modern English prose. On the other hand the noun **rue** designating an aromatic Eurasian plant is in current use. That there is a relationship between the nouns and our more common verb **rue**, meaning "to regret" or "to repent," seems plausible. The oils of rue were used medicinally, possibly the reason that the plant was once also called **herb of grace**. In the famous mad scene in Hamlet, Ophelia uses a double meaning when she distributes flowers and herbs to characters in the play. To Queen Gertrude she says: ". . . There's rue for you, and here's some for me. We may call it herb of grace o' Sundays. O' you must wear your rue with a difference." Ophelia may have meant that rue for Gertrude symbolized a need to repent, while for Ophelia it symbolized sorrow or regret.

Context: The abused wife's sentiments were expressed very vividly when she shouted that she **rued** the day she met her spouse.

ephemeral: *adjective*
Derived from the Greek **ephemeros**, "daily," the English word **ephemeral** means "short-lived." We do not confine our definition of the word to its literal sense of lasting one day only, but we do indicate by the word the idea of something lasting a very short time. The word **ephemera** designates the genus of mayflies, insects that live in the adult stage for only a few hours. They are called mayflies because they swarm in May, or dayflies because their lifespan is so short.

Context: Many former celebrities complain that fame is **ephemeral**—short-lived.

sub rosa: *adverb*
New Latin provides the backdrop for the English compound **sub rosa**. One might be able to guess at the meanings of two Latin word elements: **sub**, "under," + **rosa**, "rose." The Latin and the English have the same spellings. Many years ago there was an ancient custom of hanging a rose over a council table to indicate symbolically that all present at this meeting were sworn to secrecy. Today **sub rosa** means "privately, confidentially, in secret," which is fairly close to the word's original meaning. What is lost is the symbolic reference to the rose.

Context: Much of what passes for foreign policy issues is discussed **sub rosa**.

recondite: *adjective*
From the Latin **recondere**, which means "to conceal," the word **recondite** is forged. The **concealment** referred to in the Latin is for the most part unintended. Rather it is the nature of what it is one is reading or listening to. Einstein's theories relating to space and time are recondite by virtue of their very complex nature. To the neophyte such weighty subjects are incomprehensible. **Recondite** today means "not easily understood, abstruse, obscure." It is in this context that the Latin **recondere**, meaning "to conceal," is used. There is nothing sinister attached to the concealment found in the Latin **recondere**.

Context: The professor delivered a lecture on the **recondite** philosophy of René Descartes.

pogrom: *noun*

This word is derived from Yiddish, the language of Eastern European Jews. An often-persecuted minority in Russia, the Jews there borrowed the Russian word for devastation—**pogrom**—and gave it the meaning it now has in English: "an organized massacre of defenseless people." Notorious pogroms have been perpetrated by the czarist government against the Jews in Russia and by Hitler against the Jews in Germany and throughout Europe.

> *Context:*   **Pogroms** and an absolute control by government officials seem to coexist.

poignant: *adjective*

Derived from the Old French **poindre**, meaning "to sting," the English word **poignant** means "painfully moving or piercingly effective." We often use the word to describe a touching novel or movie or some news story that affects us emotionally. In a figurative sense, it is your heart which is stung by the poignant incident.

> *Context:*   To see a mother and her child reunited after not seeing each other for so many years was a **poignant** event to witness.

EXERCISES

A. Match the definition in Column B with the word it defines in Column A.

Column A

1. quintessence D
2. rue F
3. ephemeral H
4. aegis B
5. sub rosa I
6. poignant A
7. coruscate C
8. nepotism J

Column B

a. heartrending; touching
b. protection; sponsorship
c. sparkle
d. purest; most concentrated form
e. abstruse; obscure
f. regret; repent
g. organized massacre of defenseless people
h. short-lived

9. recondite ⊨   i. secretly
10. pogrom ᴳ⁻   j. favoring one's relatives or friends in making important appointments

B. In which of the following sentences are the boldface words used correctly? Designate by writing C if correct; N if not correct.

1. **Coruscating** sequins on the soprano's dress diverted our attention from her aria.

2. "You will **rue** the day you ever threatened me," exclaimed the occupant of room 13 to his landlord.

3. **Pogroms** were established by the government in order to assist people in finding good homes.

4. The incursion of U.N. troops into the warring nation took place under the **aegis** of the U.N. Security Council.

5. A fraternity house at Yale has no windows; the doors open only to those who know a special password, indicating that the fraternity's business is conducted **sub rosa**.

6. Cold and unfeeling described the serial killer's **poignant** plea for mercy.

7. The passage assigned for reading concerned the various theories about the formation of the universe and were so **recondite** that I was able to understand them quickly and easily.

8. My grandfather always seemed to me to be the **quintessential** gentleman.

9. John's uncle, who was the manager of the whole restaurant chain, denied there was any **nepotism** involved when he hired John as an accountant.

10. The etched crystal stemware was so fragile that the antique dealer warned us, "This crystal is as **ephemeral** as the Rock of Gibraltar."

C. Choose the item that best conveys the meaning of the boldface word in each sentence.

1. A person who **rues** an action is (a) happy about it   (b) boasts of it   (c) regrets it   (d) forgets it.

2. Council meetings held **sub rosa** are (a) open to the public   (b) confined to family members   (c) secret   (d) given roses.

3. The most **poignant** article I ever read concerned (a) the crowning of the king   (b) the baby's rescue from a kidnapper   (c) the unctuous behavior of a store clerk   (d) the audacity of a thief.

4. The **quintessential** rock musicians are represented by (a) Duke Ellington   (b) the Vienna Boy's Choir   (c) the Rolling Stones   (d) the New York Philharmonic.

5. **Coruscating** past the light from the street lamp, the raindrops (a) were torpid   (b) disappeared   (c) sparkled   (d) were assuaged.

6. Something that would be considered **ephemeral** is (a) the flash of a lightning bug   (b) an elephant's lifespan   (c) Niagara Falls   (d) the Pacific Ocean.

7. Instituted usually by the ruling powers, a **pogrom** is (a) a welfare program   (b) a massacre of defenseless people   (c) a program to rehabilitate defenseless people   (d) a celebration of religious beliefs.

8. When a person who is head of personnel in a large corporation is accused of **nepotism**, it is because he has (a) hired a 15 year old   (b) hired his wife   (c) hired an applicant without experience   (d) hired a retired person.

9. Asked to contribute to a cause that is not under the **aegis** of a nationally reliable charity, one should (a) send off a contribution in the return mail   (b) investigate the charity   (c) contribute without question   (d) become frenetic.

10. If a lecturer's expatiation of his theme is **recondite**, his audience would find it (a) crystal clear   (b) disorganized   (c) obscure   (d) inflammatory.

   D. Choose two of the following words: aegis, quintessence, nepotism, ephemeral. Use your words in two sentences of your own.

Lesson

11

carouse: *verb*

Carouse is a word generally associated with unseemly behavior, especially when such conduct results from excessive drinking—spirits, that is. The word comes from the Italian **carosello**, which means "a kind of tournament." Unfortunately the tournament alluded to is more in the nature of a drinking contest than a reference to knights jousting for sport and honor. Carousing is "to drink excessively, and then to indulge in drunken merrymaking." The connection between the Italian and English versions is tenuous at best, but it is one possible explanation.

> *Context:*   He paid the price for a night of **carousing** the morning after when he awakened with a screaming hangover.

pastiche: *noun*

The word **pastiche** is a borrowing from the Italian word **pasticcio**, which is "a dramatic or literary work," especially a musical piece. A **pasticcio** is the product of borrowed fragments or motifs from various sources, a kind of melange. The current definition suggests a less kind meaning—"a hodgepodge." **Pasticcio** has its roots in the Latin **pasta**, which means "paste." This would suggest a rather obvious connection among the Latin, Italian, and English. It may well be that a **pastiche** or **pasticcio** is a pasting together of fragments from other sources. A pastiche oftentimes takes the form of a satire.

> *Context:*   The evening included a **pastiche** of songs from the 1890s.

acrimony: *noun*

Acrimony means **sharpness** or **harshness**, especially when they relate to one's nature, speech, or disposition. It finds its way into English from the Latin etymon **acerb(us)**, which means "sharp, sour, or bitter." This is precisely what acrimony is—sharpness, sourness, or bitterness. If you have ever been in the company of someone who is acrimonious, you may recall a sharp phrase, a bitterness that cloaks the very words spoken. There is another word in English that has the same lineage—**acerbic**. It means pretty much what acrimony means, and the words can be used interchangeably. Acrimony and acerbic are not synonyms since the former is a noun and the latter, an adjective.

> *Context:* The **acrimony** in his reply was obvious, and it only served to heighten the heated debate.

bifurcate: *verb*

Bifurcate is made up of two Latin elements, the prefix **bi**, "two" + **furcus**, "fork." One would logically assume that when combined the two Latin roots would mean "two forks," but that is not the case. What is suggested is "one fork having two prongs or tines." The current meaning of bifurcate is "divided into two branches or parts." In most cases the division is not to be taken literally. The United States before, during, and even after the Civil War was a nation plagued by a bifurcation—those who opposed slavery and those who advocated it.

> *Context:* The Vietnam war caused a **bifurcation** of thinking in many Americans: was it a just or an unjust war?

spurious: *adjective*

The word **spurious** means "not genuine, not authentic, not true." Its origin is found in the Late Latin word element **spurius**, meaning "illegitimate." Certainly that which is "not true or not genuine" can be thought of as illegitimate and therefore spurious. Note the similarities between the Latin spelling **spurius** and the English **spurious**.

> *Context:* The Senator claimed that the charge of sexual harassment against him was **spurious** and not worthy of a reply.

asperity: *noun*

Asperity is another English word much in the mold of the words already studied: **acrimonious** and **acerbic**, both adjectives. It finds its roots in the Latin **asper**, which means "rough." The current definition of asperity is "ill-temper, irritability, sharpness of tone, temper, or manner." In its most common application the **roughness** from the Latin **asper** relates to temperament. Keep in mind that the words **acrimony** and **acerbity** have about the same meaning as the word **asperity**, and note that they are all nouns.

Context: His abrupt response evidenced an **asperity** that made clear his opposition to the proposal.

sycophant: *noun*
This word is built on two Greek elements: **sykos**, "fig" + **phainein**, "to show." Some persons attempting to curry favor with those in high places became informers, advancing themselves by offering to denounce criminals to the authorities. A criminal was pointed out by a sign known as the "gesture of the fig." Consequently, one who made this gesture became an accuser. The word sycophant denotes a person who is willing to demean himself by being a "yes-man" or an "apple polisher" for selfish, personal reasons.

Context: It isn't fair, but sometimes **sycophants** advance themselves at their jobs over others who are eminently more qualified.

clairvoyant: *noun*
Clairvoyant is derived from the French **clair**, which means "clear," and **voyant** which means "seeing." Literally it means to have a clear mental image of things that others cannot see, or to know of events that have not yet happened. There is on record official documentation to support this phenomenon. Clairvoyants have led police to remote places where kidnap victims were held, and they had no more information at hand than did the police. There have been too many other incidents involving clairvoyance—too many to dismiss or reject out of hand. Scientists are puzzled. They have no empirical proof that clairvoyance exists and are reluctant to accept it into the scientific community with a stamp of approval. It has remained an unsolved mystery for many centuries.

Context: Many years ago **clairvoyants** were declared witches and burned alive to purge the devil from their bodies.

carnal: *adjective*
Carn is a Latin root word that means "flesh." **Carnal**, which is built on this etymon, means "marked by sexuality, given to crude

pleasures of the flesh." **Carn**, the Latin root, is the origin of not only the word carnal, but others as well: **incarnate, carnivorous, carrion**, and **carnival**. The last word—carnival—has an interesting origin. Preceding the Lenten religious holiday, Catholics in places across the world come together to make merry and to bid a fond farewell to flesh. Lent is that period of time (forty days) when Catholics are forbidden to eat meat (flesh?). The Latin **carn**, "flesh" + **vale**, "farewell," make up the word which means literally "farewell flesh." Check the meanings of the following words. What exactly do they have to do with flesh: **incarnate, carnivorous**, and **carrion**. What about the word **carnage**?

> *Context:* Many notable historians attribute the decline and fall of the Roman Empire to **carnal** decadence, a pernicious forerunner of cultural decay.

anthology: *noun*

Anthos, "flower" + **legein**, "to gather" form the English word **anthology**—a gathering of the flowers of literature, the passages of literary excellence, into one place. Today any collection of literary works is called an anthology, whether it represents an age, a type, the best of one nationality, or some other unifying theme. We also speak of anthologies of music or of works of art when they are collected together in a book. Obviously the definition of the word has departed somewhat from its original, etymological significance.

> *Context:* Literature **anthologies** are almost always part of course studies, especially at the college level.

EXERCISES

A. Choose the word in each group that does not belong with the others.

1. chaste, pure, virginal, carnal

2. sedate, carousing, calm, reserved

3. whole, united, pastiche, uniform

4. matter-of-fact, clairvoyant, unimaginative, stolid

5. benign, good-humored, kind-hearted, acrimonious

6. rectangular, bifurcated, squared, triangular

7. spurious, genuine, true, legitimate

8. pleasantness, asperity, affability, cordiality

9. loyal, trustworthy, sycophantic, dependable

10. anthology, novella, epic poem, short story

B. Match the definition in Column B with the word it defines in Column A.

Column A

1. clairvoyant F
2. carouse C
3. carnal J
4. anthology H
5. pastiche A
6. bifurcate D
7. asperity E
8. spurious I
9. acrimonious B
10. sycophant G

Column B

a. hodgepodge; melange
b. bitter; sour
c. to make merry; imbibe
d. divide into two parts
e. harshness; roughness
f. able to see things that are not visible; having second sight
g. apple polisher; flatterer
h. collection of literary, musical, or artistic works
i. counterfeit; specious
j. sensual; fleshly

C. Select the sentence in which the boldface word is used correctly. Write the letter of your choice.

1. a. The portrait of Dorian Gray revealed that in spite of his virtuous appearance he had actually been a **carnal** man.
   b. Because she was so chaste everyone said Loretta was **carnal**.
   c. Chastity is often associated with a **carnal** appetite.

2. a. Only a **pastiche** chef can create a mouth-watering pie.
   b. Because the story had a unified plot with beginning, middle, and end, the critics called it a **pastiche**.
   c. The collage was a **pastiche** of hundreds of bits of colored papers.

3. a. The children wanted to ride on the **carouse** at the amusement park.
   b. The nurse could not **carouse** her patient from sleep.
   c. After winning the ball game, the team **caroused** in spite of the coach's admonition to go straight home.

4. a. The **clairvoyant** led the police to the spot where the body was buried.
   b. Esther was so matter-of-fact and unimaginative that the neighbors said she was **clairvoyant**.
   c. Humpty-Dumpty was so **clairvoyant** that he fell off the wall.

5. a. If you put some **acrimony** on that wheel it probably won't squeal so much.
   b. The woman demanded excessive **acrimony** as one of the stipulations of the divorce settlement.
   c. The **acrimony** evident in the political debate disgusted the audience.

6. a. When they reached the **bifurcation** in the trail, the hikers had to make a decision about which direction to choose.
   b. An octopus is a marvel of **bifurcation**.
   c. The jury was split into three groups by their **bifurcated** opinions.

7. a. The author wrote his **anthology** under an assumed name.
   b. I found the poem I was looking for in an old **anthology** in the bookcase.
   c. My friend assured me that an **anthology** contained a single novel only.

8. a. "I refuse to bow down and flatter the boss," claimed the **sycophant**.
   b. Because my neighbor had grown a flourishing fig tree, we called him a **sycophant**.
   c. Willing to be a **sycophant**, the corporate manager's aide was a "yes-man" from the day he was hired.

9. a. Sam endeared himself to all his friends because of his **asperity**.
   b. His constant toothache may have been the cause of Sam's **asperity**.
   c. Because of his **asperity** in running the race, Sam won by a wide margin.

10. a. Usually the **spurious** gems cost more than those documented as genuine.

   b. Having checked the offered money against the list of serial numbers that she had been given, the cashier refused to accept the customer's **spurious** $100 bill.

   c. The king's son claimed his place on the throne because of his **spurious** title.

   D. Choose two of the following words: pastiche, acrimony, spurious, sycophant. Use your two words in your own sentences.

Lesson

12

harass: *verb*

The Old French **harer** provides the origin of the English word **harass** (huh-RASS). **Harer** meant "to set a dog upon." To be set upon by a dog is to be badgered—to be nipped and barked at persistently, unrelentingly. The current meaning of harass is "to torment without letup." Keep in mind that the torment must be both chronic and mean-spirited. One final note—a dog is not required to harass. It is done with regularity by people of all kinds—some uncaring students harass teachers, too many husbands harass their wives, and in all fairness some wives do the same to husbands.

> *Context:* The detective was charged with **harassing** the public defender's client.

mordant: *adjective*

Mordant comes to English by way of Middle French. It is derived from **mordre**, which means "to bite." The biting alluded to is not to be taken literally. Rather it is in the nature of being **caustic, sharp**, or **biting**. A remark, piece of writing, speech, or observation may be mordant if it is consistent with one of these meanings. There is another use of the word **mordant** as a noun; however, it is so restricted in meaning that it is hardly worthwhile presenting. Briefly, mordant (noun) is a corrosive or acid used in etching.

> *Context:* The newspaper editorial presented a **mordant** point of view relative to the mayor's plan to veto the council's budget proposal.

debilitate: *verb*

The word **debilitate** is defined as **to enfeeble, to weaken**. It is built on the Latin etymon **debilis**, meaning "to impair the strength of," which is pretty close to the word's current meaning. Its usage is wide-ranging and can fit nicely into many contexts: cancer and tuberculosis are debilitating diseases; old age tends to debilitate the mind; gloomy economic forecasts can have a debilitating effect on the stock market. Just about anything can be debilitating if it enfeebles, weakens.

> *Context:* Participating in a marathon has a **debilitating** effect on a runner's stamina.

manifest: *verb; noun; adjective; adverb*

Manifest is another of those words that have an extraordinary versatility. It can be used as four different parts of speech. The word is built on the Latin **manus**, "hand" + **festus**, "gripped." The current definition of manifest is "easily understood or readily perceived by the senses, especially by sight." To put it another way, when some understanding seems suddenly to become manifest, it is as though one is guided to the understanding by someone's taking that person's hand and pointing out the truth. Perhaps the following may be of some help: **manifest** (noun) is a list of cargo carried by some kind of conveyance—truck, rail, ship, etc. It is this manifest that makes clear just what it is that is being shipped. It is a detailed list of the cargo. As a verb: "The truth eventually **manifested** itself." As adjective: "It was a **manifest** error on his part." As adverb: "It was **manifestly** the wrong choice to have been made."

> *Context:* The red blotches on the child's chest and abdomen made it **manifestly** clear to the doctor that measles was the culprit.

decadent: *adjective*

Decadent means "a period of decline or decay, especially of moral decay." It is **manifestly** apparent that the word **decay** is built into the word **decadent**. The Late Latin **decadere**, which means "to fall or to sink," is the origin of its English counterpart. Both these words—fall and sink—are implicit in the word **decay**. **Decadent** can be applied in almost any context: cultures become decadent; morality, politics, the legal profession—all can become decadent. The word has wide application which makes it a very useful one to add to your vocabulary.

Context: Many scholars of history believe the widespread moral **decadence** that pervaded the Roman Empire was in part responsible for its fall.

vicarious: *adjective*

From the Latin **vicis**, meaning "alteration, change, or stead," the word **vicarious** is derived. Vicarious expresses a substitution, either real or imaginary. If you should ask another person to be a vicarious participant for you at a meeting, for example, you are asking this person to take your place. You can enjoy the thrill of shooting an elephant vicariously by substituting yourself in your imagination for the big-game hunter. Arnold Bennett was once severely taken to task by a reader who assumed that the novelist had gone out to witness a hanging so that he could describe it in his novel THE OLD WIVES' TALE. Bennett replied that he had never actually seen a real hanging; he had only read accounts by people who had. In this case Bennett was reporting a vicarious experience and the reader was experiencing horror third-hand—but still vicariously.

Context: One can experience **vicariously** a vacation to tropical islands by reading travel brochures.

trepidation: *noun*

The etymon **trepidare** comes from the Latin and it means "to be in a state of confusion." The current definition of **trepidation**, the English word built on this word element, is "a state of alarm or dread, apprehension, fear." All of these frames of mind can and often do bring on confusion, and this is the link between the Latin and the English versions. To do something with trepidation is to do it with fear, anxiety. In a word, one is scared!

Context: The mailman approached the pit bull with **trepidation** because he had never seen it before, and he didn't know what to expect.

melee: *noun*

A **melee** (MAY-lay) is "a confused struggle, turmoil, a jumble." It is derived from an Old French word **mesler**, which means "to mix." The mixing alluded to is the kind one would expect to find in a state of confusion, turmoil, or a jumble. Each of these words implies a kind of **mixing**, especially the word **jumble**, which is one definition of melee.

Context: After the hard-fought football game, fans engaged in a
melee during which the goal posts were torn down.

implacable: *adjective*

The word **implacable** comes from the Latin prefix **im**, "not" **pla-
care**, " to calm." Together the Latin elements mean **not to be calmed**,
and this is pretty much what the word means today: incapable of
appeasement or mitigation, not to be palliated. An implacable foe is
one who will not be mollified or will not be calmed. There is another
English word built on this same root—**placate**. It has the opposite
meaning of **implacable**. To be placated is to be appeased, palliated, or
mitigated.

Context: The environmental group was an **implacable** foe of any
legislation that would endanger national forests.

nexus: *noun*

The Latin **nectere** is the derivation of the English word **nexus**.
The Latin roots mean "to bind, to fasten." The word in a more contemporaneous setting denotes "a means of connecting, or a tie, a link." In
a real sense, to connect, to tie, or to link suggests at the least **a
binding or fastening** of sorts. If, for instance, one is writing or
speaking about two disparate ideas, a nexus may be required in order
to connect (tie, link) these ideas in an understandable way. In many
instances in this book, a nexus has been established between the Latin
and the English, and it is this connection that makes understanding
the work easier.

Context: One **nexus** between man and his god is religion.

EXERCISES

A. Match the definition in Column B with the word it defines in
Column A.

Column A   Column B

1. trepidation ⌐   a. decayed; corrupt
2. implacable ⊢   b. a jumble; brawl

3. harass *G*   c. to weaken; wear out
4. manifest *I*   d. a link; connection
5. nexus *D*   e. caustic; incisive
6. mordant *E*   f. experiencing through imagination
7. decadent *A*   g. to torment continually; besiege
8. melee *B*   h. inexorable; unrelenting
9. vicarious *F*   i. visible; easily understood
10. debilitate *C*   j. anxiety; apprehension

B. Write the letter of the word or phrase that best conveys the meaning of the sentence.

1. Joseph was _____ in his demand that his brother, Benjamin, be sent to Egypt as a hostage for the wheat sent to his family.
   (a) unctuous (b) implacable (c) relenting (d) debilitating

2. The _____ between human beings and their origin is still a debatable premise today.
   (a) distance (b) anachronism (c) nexus (d) caveat

3. Jake's _____ humor repelled many of the listeners to his morning radio broadcast.
   (a) charming (b) mordant (c) delightful (d) austere

4. "Why are you always involved in some kind of bloody _____ ?" demanded the school nurse as she bandaged Arthur's injured hand.
   (a) award program (b) musical (c) library search (d) melee

5. Many Americans feel that most TV programs are _____ and should be abolished.
   (a) cable (b) decadent (c) moral (d) humorous

6. The people rallied in the public square to _____ their displeasure with the edict of the governor.
   (a) conceal (b) disparage (c) manifest (d) atone for

7. The dermatologist said the outbreak of rash on my face and arms was probably caused by _____ over the approaching final exams in chemistry.
   (a) intrepid feelings (b) audaciousness (c) trepidation
   (d) caprice

8. I have visited many far-away places, met both famous and ficti-
tious people, and lived in past ages all _____ through reading.
(a) firsthand   (b) vicariously   (c) sub rosa   (d) turgidly

9. Lack of exercise can be extremely _____ especially to muscles
which lose tone and strength.
(a) healthy   (b) debilitating   (c) invigorating   (d) pleasurable

10. Mr. Jones complained bitterly about _____ phone calls from so-
licitors asking for money.
(a) innocuous   (b) inimical   (c) harassing   (d) mordant

C. In the passage below, choose the word in parentheses that best
indicates correct usage in the context of the sentence. Write the
words in a numbered list.

Exploring the old house that had been our great-grandmother's,
we entered with (1. trepidation-euphoria) because it was in such run-
down condition. There was a kind of (2. exhilarating-mordant) odor
caused, no doubt, by the rotting floor boards and musty fireplaces.

The (3. austerity-decadence) apparent in the house (4. manifested-
concealed) itself in the (5. invigorating-debilitating) atmosphere surrounding us.

The kitchen looked as if some (6. feast-melee) had once taken place
there, as if some (7. implacable-plausible) force had caused senseless
chaos. Perhaps someone had been (8. ridiculed-harassed) beyond human endurance and had literally gone to pieces.

As we continued to explore, we began to sense a (9. nexus-gulf)
between the present and the past to the point where we were actually
experiencing a (10. vicarious-capricious) relationship with our ancestral forebears.

D. Choose two of the following words: debilitate, decadent, vicarious, trepidation. Use your words in your own sentences.

REVIEW OF LESSONS 1 - 12

A. Write the letter of the item that gives the best meaning to the
sentence.

1. If an editor **expurgates** a passage from the text of a Shakespearean play, he is
(a) adding a footnote   (b) putting the passage in italics   (c) omitting it entirely   (d) praising it.

2. My brother decided to spend New Year's Eve **carousing**.
(a) reading   (b) merrymaking   (c) going to bed early   (d) watching TV

3. The politician asserted that global peace was a **chimera**.
(a) an illusion of the mind   (b) a vagary   (c) a heinous idea
(d) a virulent epidemic

4. The cave paintings that were found by the spelunkers were anatomically **grotesque**.
(a) moribund   (b) avuncular   (c) bizarre   (d) perfect

5. "If I chose to **emulate** anyone it would be Bill Cosby," stated the aspiring young comedian.
(a) obfuscate   (b) imitate   (c) exculpate   (d) palliate

6. Because his sales pitch was too **unctuous**, I shut the door on the home-improvement representative.
(a) charismatic   (b) ephemeral   (c) straightforward   (d) excessively smooth

7. One of Almira's **foibles** was to ruin her appearance with excessive green eye make-up.
(a) shortcomings   (b) strengths   (c) banes   (d) vestiges

8. My great-grandson who is only seven years old made me laugh by saying he was **penurious**.
(a) poignant   (b) inimical   (c) monolithic   (d) destitute

9. Under the **aegis** of the Salvation Army, food and water were rushed to the survivors of a devastating hurricane.
(a) torpor   (b) sponsorship   (c) facade   (d) ennui

10. The **euphoria** of winning thousands of dollars in the state lottery wore off somewhat when Alex realized how much his tax bill would be.
(a) nexus   (b) histrionics   (c) joyfulness   (d) catharsis

B. A word from Lessons 1-12 is listed below. Following it are four words or phrases. Two of them define the word and two do not. Identify the two that do not define the boldface word. Write the letters of both items.

1. **exult**
   (a) exalt   (b) be joyful   (c) to celebrate   (d) to be sad

2. **exurbs**
   (a) far outside a city   (b) a metropolitan area   (c) beyond the suburbs   (d) an inner city blighted area

3. **poltergeist**
   (a) a malevolent spirit   (b) a ghost   (c) a playful spirit
   (d) a German soldier

4. **bellwether**
   (a) a town crier   (b) a leader   (c) a male sheep with a bell tied around its neck   (d) one who predicts the weather

5. **coruscate**
   (a) to shine brilliantly   (b) a diamond   (c) to give forth flashes of light   (d) to perform brilliantly, as a virtuoso piano player

6. **ephemeral**
   (a) a short person   (b) a short period of time   (c) brief
   (d) a mayfly

7. **pastiche**
   (a) an ice cream flavor   (b) a hodgepodge   (c) a product of borrowed fragments   (d) an extended musical piece

8. **spurious**
   (a) genuine   (b) ersatz   (c) authentic   (d) not true

9. **acrimony**
   (a) acerbity   (b) harshness of speech   (c) acidity   (d) a pleasantry

10. **catholic**
    (a) a religion   (b) universal   (c) parochial   (d) broad in one's views

C. Match the words from Column A with their definitions from Column B.

Column A

1. banal
2. exude
3. aegis
4. assuage
5. quintessence
6. fickle
7. debilitate
8. histrionic
9. rue
10. sesquipedalian
11. bifurcate
12. melee
13. mordant
14. apocalypse
15. harass

Column B

a. caustic; sharp; biting
b. a thing in its most concentrated form
c. divide into two parts
d. common; trite
e. to ooze out
f. protection
g. regret
h. deliberately affected; theatrical
i. confusion; turmoil
j. to enfeeble; to weaken
k. a prophetic revelation
l. to torment without let up
m. an unusually long word
n. to mollify; to pacify
o. capricious; not constant

Lesson

13

contumacy: *noun*

The Latin **con**, "thoroughly" + **tumēre**, " to swell," when combined are the origin of the English word **contumacy**. It means stubborn resistance to authority. Picture in the mind's eye a child of three or four who rebels against authority by holding his or her breath which, of course, causes the cheeks to puff out. It is this kind of swelling that contumacy implies, more figurative than literal. On the other hand, **tumēre** is the source of the word **tumor**, which indeed does entail a physical swelling, especially in malignant tumors.

    Context: The stubborn child became even more **contumacious** after his mother insisted he finish his peas.

convivial: *adjective*

Literally, thousands of English words have their origin in Latin, and the word **convivial** is one of them. The Latin **con**, "together" + **vivere**, "to live," make up the English counterpart—convivial. To be convivial is to be good company, friendly, or agreeable. One might legitimately assume that a friendly, agreeable person would fit nicely with a group of like-minded people. Most people enjoy being in the company of convivial friends or acquaintances and can live together in harmony as the Latin suggests. In a word, they are fun to be with!

    Context: His **convivial** nature made him a much sought-after guest at social occasions.

indomitable: *adjective*

The Latin **in**, "out" + **domitare**, "to tame," are the source of the English word **indomitable**. It means what the Latin **domitare** suggests—"not to be dominated, not to be tamed." Today the word means unconquerable, incapable of being subdued. If one looks back at the Latin, the same idea can be found—"not to be tamed (conquered, subdued?)." Generally, the word relates to one's spirit. Don Quixote had an indomitable spirit as reflected in the musical version of the novel by Cervantes. Remember the song and lyrics: "To dream the impossible dream . . ."? This requires an indomitable spirit.

Context: The team's **indomitable** will to win led them to victory.

millennium: *noun*

A **millennium** is "a period of one thousand years." From the Latin **mille** meaning **one thousand**, English derives the word millennium. You must know other words beginning with mille: milligram, millipede, million (one thousand thousand), and millisecond. Many commonly used words use this number/amount prefix. Back to millennium. There is another meaning of the word. It is tied to the Bible, and it is that period of time (one thousand years) during which Christ will reign on earth and bring peace and prosperity to all. In a more generic context, millennium is a period of rectitude and happiness, especially in the indefinite future.

Context: Humankind has yet to reach a **millennium** marked by unbridled happiness, universal peace, and heartfelt good will.

emasculate: *verb*

The word **emasculate** means "to deprive of virile procreation power"—the power to beget offspring. More generally it means to deprive of masculine vigor, spirit. An even more generic meaning is "to weaken." Emasculate comes from the Latin **e**, "out" + **masculus**, "male"—figuratively to take out that part of the male that makes procreation possible. The current meaning is not quite so literal. For example, a piece of writing can be edited so extensively that the work is "weakened, deprived of vigor." It has been emasculated. In this context gender has nothing whatever to do with the word. A close linguistic relative of emasculate is the word **eviscerate**—to deprive of vital force or essential parts. This is fairly close to one of the meanings of emasculate. The Latin **eviscerare**, "torn apart; deprived of entrails," is the word's origin. To disembowel (remove the entrails) of a fowl is to **eviscerate**. The House of Representatives oftentimes **eviscerates** a bill pending before it by making countless changes and adding a bunch of riders to it.

> *Context:*   A meager vocabulary more than any other thing tends to **emasculate** one's ability to write.

digress: *verb*

To **digress** is "to turn aside," especially from the main subject of attention. It comes to English via the Latin prefix **dis**, "away" + **gradi**, "to step." **Gradi** is a commonly used etymon that changes in English to **gress**: pro**gress**, "step forward"; e**gress**, "step out"; in**gress**, "step in"; con**gress**, "step together." Digressions are not always bad nor are they always good. They can be instructive, amusing, or reflective. They can also be deadly boring, distracting from the main subject matter.

> *Context:*   Many college professors **digress** although they are not aware of it, and their digressions are oftentimes more interesting than the text of a lecture.

kaleidoscope: *noun*

The Greek etymons **kal(os)**, meaning "beautiful" + **eido(s)**, meaning "shape" + **skopein**, "to view," make up the word **kaleidoscope**. A kaleidoscope is an optical instrument containing bits of colorful glass, beads, etc., held loosely at one end by a rotating tube which when turned shows a continually changing symmetrical form by reflection through the use of mirrors. The meanings of the Greek word elements when combined manifestly suggest the essential meaning of the word—"to view beautiful shapes." In a more general context, **kaleidoscope** means "constantly changing sets of colors." The fall foliage presented itself with ever-changing bounty of colors—a veritable kaleidoscope. This meaning has nothing to do with the tubed version.

> *Context:*   The art instructor wanted a **kaleidoscopic** painting— one whose hues changed with the light reflected on it.

jargon: *noun*

The word **jargon** is derived from the Old French **gargon**, meaning "chattering"—uttering inarticulate speechlike sounds (jabbering?). This is not too different from the word's current meaning, which is unintelligible and meaningless talk. There is, however, another definition, one that is applied most often: the vocabulary peculiar to a particular trade, profession, or group. Take, for example, the computer which has spawned a host of neologisms (**neo**, "new" + **logos**, "word") in order to fill a linguistic vacuum: **byte, internet, modem, mouse, main frame, digital** and **analog** computers. There are many other such words that make up the jargon known as "computerese." There is medical jargon, sports jargon, educational jargon, and on and on.

> *Context:*   Many women find the **jargon** associated with football befuddling, which makes understanding the game almost impossible.

humor: *noun*

In the Middle Ages, before the discovery of the human circulatory system, it was generally believed that the body contained four humors or fluids—blood, phlegm, yellow bile, and black bile. These fluids were thought to be responsible for one's disposition, or one's humor. As one may have already guessed, **humor** originally meant "fluid or moisture." For example, a dull, sluggish person was thought to have too much phlegm, which made him sluggish. From this the word **phlegmatic** finds its way into English, designating either "apathy or calmness." The word for black bile comes from the Greek **melas**, "black" + **chole**, "bile." Too much black bile in one's system resulted in **melancholy**. On the other hand, a person who felt cheerful was thought to have a good or ample supply of blood—hence our word **sanguine** (from **sanguis**, meaning "blood"). Today the word means "in high, cheerful, healthy spirits." Yellow bile, or choler, was a source of irritability. A person who was in a bad humor was said to be **choleric**. The theory that there are four humors, or fluids, affecting our disposition may have been a mistaken one, but perhaps it is not too far removed from the more scientific explanation of glandular secretions which is prevalent today. These words come from a mixing of both Latin and Greek word elements.

> *Context:*   According to people who lived centuries ago, one's **humor** (disposition) was determined by the dominance of one or another fluid or moisture in the body.

aberrant: *adjective*

The word **aberrant** has two meanings, both of them common to current usage. The first is a departure from a normal or typical course.

Space flights have been cancelled due to an aberrant functioning mechanical part. These aberrations are referred to as anomalies, deviations from what would be considered normal. The other meaning of aberrant is to characterize an abnormal alteration in one's mental state. If you had a friend who rarely if ever lost his self-control, and this person was heard shouting at someone in an out of control fashion, then this behavior could be characterized as aberrant—it is an abnormal alteration in your friend's mental state. The noun form is **aberration**.

> *Context:*   The defendant's **aberrant** outburst caused the judge to clear the courtroom of television cameras.

EXERCISES

A. Match the definition in Column B with the word it defines in Column A.

Column A

1. indomitable
2. emasculate
3. jargon
4. aberrant
5. digress
6. humor
7. millennium
8. contumacy
9. convivial
10. kaleidoscope

Column B

a. mood; frame of mind
b. a variegated colorful pattern or scene
c. a period of great happiness or holiness
d. to turn aside; deviate from
e. affable; gregarious
f. gibberish; argot; idiom
g. stubborn resistance to authority
h. invincible; unconquerable
i. to weaken; devitalize
j. irregular; abnormal

B. Write C if the sentences below use the boldface word correctly; if not, write N.

1. "But I **digress**," apologized the speaker after inserting a personal story into his analysis of John Donne's poem, "Death Be Not Proud."

2. My friend's new boyfriend was so **convivial** that he went off and sat silently in a corner all through the party.

3. The Olympic athlete's **indomitable** spirit has been a factor in his gradual improvement from the paralysis that resulted from his high-dive accident.

4. I saw a **kaleidoscope** of colored stars when I fell and hit my head on the icy porch steps.

5. He was so favorably impressed with the prisoner's **contumacious** attitude during the hearing that the judge dismissed all the charges against him.

6. Leroy expected to be worth a **millennium** when he won the sweepstakes.

7. Creating their own **jargon**, the girls had a secret language that no one else could understand.

8. The only **aberration** that made us realize Grandpa was getting senile was his tendency to confuse his great-grandchildren with his own children when they were small.

9. Frances decided she should sign up for a body-building class in order to **emasculate** her torpid muscles.

10. If I am in an irritable **humor** I can blame it on my glandular secretions.

C. Unscramble the jumbled words and match each to its correct definition.

Column A	Column B
1. noccutamy	a. invulnerable; valiant
2. rumho	b. friendly; sociable
3. gesrids	c. gibberish; argot
4. dimitbleano	d. abnormality; deviation
5. caulamstee	e. rebellion against authority
6. livonviac	f. frame of mind
7. grjoan	g. to weaken; to make impotent
8. beraration	h. stray
9. cosdiekalope	i. a time (or period) of great happiness
10. linummieln	j. variegated, colorful pattern

D. Choose two of the following words: digress, humor, jargon, kaleidoscope. Use your two words in your own sentences.

Lesson

14

animosity: *noun*

The dictionary defines **animosity** as "an active display of ill will or hatred." It is generally followed by the word between or against: animosity **between** nations or animosity **against** authority. The Latin etymon **animus** is the source of its English counterpart, and one of its meanings is **wrath**, which parallels the denotation of animosity. Also, bear in mind that **animus**, the Latin etymon, is also an English word meaning "ill will; hostile feeling; antagonism." These words should be used with care inasmuch as they convey an intense idea—hatred.

Context: The **animosity** between the two neighbors manifested itself as they shouted at each other at fever pitch.

antemeridian: *noun*

Who has not used the designation A.M. to mean before midday? **Antemeridian** is a cumbersome word to say or to write. Along came some enterprising person and took the letter **a** from the prefix **ante** and the letter **m** from the word element **meridian** and came up with A.M. The word is built on the Greek **ante**, "before" + **medius**, "middle" + **dies**, "day"—"before the middle of the day." Perhaps the designation P.M. is obvious now—**post**, "after."

Context: The word **antemeridian** is seldom used today since it has been replaced by the more efficient abbreviation A.M. (P.M. in the case of **postmeridian**).

91

ecumenical: *adjective*

Oecumenic(us) is the Late Latin word element that is the origin of the English word **ecumenical**. The Latin etymon means "belonging to the whole inhabited world." That covers a lot of ground, but the word is meant to be all-encompassing. It means "universal" or in a more spiritual context—"pertaining to the Christian church world-wide." When, for example, the papacy convenes an ecumenical conference, prelates from all over the world attend. The word is used in a secular context more often than not.

> *Context:*   The United Nations is an organization that has an **ecumenical** agenda.

travail: *noun*

Late Latin once again comes to the fore and makes yet another contribution to English. While the Latin **trepali(um)** may not look much like the English word **travail**, its meaning does fit nicely with the Latin to provide a logical connection between the two. **Trepali(um)** in Latin means, of all things, "a torture chamber." What can one expect to experience in a torture chamber but pain, anguish, suffering? This is precisely the word's meaning today—"pain or suffering resulting from mental or physical anguish."

> *Context:*   The **travail** the two parents experienced after losing their only son was obvious to all.

pernicious: *adjective*

The Latin prefix **per**, "intensifies," and **nex**, "violent death," are the source of the English word **pernicious**. It means "tending to cause death or serious injury; deadly; causing great harm; destructive; ruinous." All of these suggest either the possibility of death or outright death itself. In addition, all of these meanings imply a kind of violence often associated with destruction, deadly harm, or fatal injury. So the Latin **nex** meaning "violent death" is not so far off after all.

> *Context:*   Cigarette smoking is a **pernicious** habit and should be avoided.

nostrum: *noun*

A quack remedy or medicine is often referred to as a **nostrum**. The word comes from the Latin **noster**, which means **our**. Years ago medicine men, as they were called, traveled across the countryside peddling their secret cures for anything that might ail a person: cancer, bunions, a cold, anything! They would shout "our own" meaning, of course, our own drug. No one else can provide it, only us. Today the meaning has taken on a different significance, although nostrum still refers to a quack remedy. This other designation is that a nostrum is a cure for all the ills of mankind, the embodiment of a panacea: economic, political, humanitarian, social, whatever. The nostrum will cure it.

Context: Television commercials during election campaigns are filled with **nostrums**—reducing the debt, balancing budgets, fighting crime, the never-ending drug problem, and ad infinitum.

epitaph: *noun*

Epitaphs are either carved or written inscriptions found on gravestones in memory of the persons buried beneath them. Many epitaphs are quite humorous. For example, there is an inscription that reads, "Here lies Ezra Scoggins who thought he was the fastest gun in the West." The word is built on the Greek **epi**, "upon" + **taphos**, "tomb." In addition to their being commemorative inscriptions, epitaphs can also appear as writing in praise of a deceased person, though this usage is not common. Be careful not to confuse the words **epitaph, epithet,** and **epaulet**. These are the source of Archie Bunker's more widely known malaprops.

Context: Most **epitaphs** include the dead person's date of birth and death and not much else except, of course, the deceased's name.

feckless: *adjective*

The Scots also contributed to the richness of language. The word **feckless** is one such case in point. It is an abridgment of two words: **effective** + **less**. Rather than use the cumbersome tandem **effectiveless**, the Scots shortened (truncated) it to form one word—**feckless**. Its meaning should be obvious—"lacking in purpose or vitality, ineffective, careless, or irresponsible." All imply an **ineffectiveness** of one kind or another.

Context: The father complained that he had reared a **feckless** son who did not merit an inheritance.

splenetic: *adjective*

Splenetic is the adjective form of **spleen**, a noun. The spleen, a part of the body's lymphatic system, acts as a filter for the body's blood. At one time long ago it was believed that the spleen was the seat of human emotions or passions. From the Greek **splèn** its English counterpart **spleen** was derived. It is but a short journey to get from spleen to splenetic, a word that carries with it a rather disagreeable meaning: ill-tempered, peevish, spiteful, or irritable. Splenetic individuals are not those one would seek out for companionship. Dictionaries also list the word **melancholy** as an archaic meaning of splenetic, i.e., one no longer in current use. Melancholy, as you may recall, was presented in another lesson under the word **humor**, which at one time meant **fluid**. In this context it was suggested that the word humor might be tied to beliefs concerning the body's lymphatic system. **Melancholy** was derived from the Greek **melas**, "black" + **cholē**, "bile." It also may have been held that the spleen was one source of black bile that caused "black moods" or nasty dispositions. All of this is, of course, speculation. It does, nonetheless, afford the reader an opportunity to journey along less traveled paths in search of word origins that are no less than fascinating.

> *Context:*   The elderly man's **splenetic** demeanor made him the target for many mischievous pranks.

pusillanimous: *adjective*

While the word **pusillanimous** is forbidding in appearance, its meaning is not at all difficult to understand. The Latin **pusill(us)**, which means "petty, very small," and **anim(us)**, which means "mind or spirit," make up the word. The current meaning of pusillanimous is as one might expect—"to be lacking in courage or resolution"—in a word, "cowardly." This corresponds nicely with the Latin **petty in mind or spirit**.

> *Context:*   The young soldier was cited for his **pusillanimous** conduct in the face of the enemy.

EXERCISES

A. Match the definition in Column B with the word it defines in Column A.

Column A	Column B
1. ecumenical	a. hatred; antagonism
2. nostrum	b. before noon
3. splenetic	c. universal; all-encompassing
4. animosity	d. anguish; suffering
5. travail	e. destructive; toxic
6. feckless	f. potion; remedy
7. pusillanimous	g. commemoration for a deceased person
8. epitaph	h. ineffective; incompetent
9. antemeridian	i. irritable; spiteful
10. pernicious	j. cowardly; apprehensive

B. Choose the sentence in which the boldface word is used correctly.

1. a. The most **ecumenical** way to pay your monthly bills is to adhere to a planned budget.
   b. The three churches of different faiths in our neighborhood agreed to hold an **ecumenical** service to honor the heroes and heroines of the Vietnam War.
   c. Joe and John were called **ecumenical** twins because they didn't look alike.

2. a. The author of the mystery book preferred **animosity**, so he wrote under an assumed name.
   b. The **animosity** between my two brothers assured us of a peaceful home.
   c. No one could have predicted that the **animosity** between the man and his wife would result in homicide.

3. a. We regarded the kittens as **pusillanimous** because they never grew any bigger than they were at six weeks.
   b. Bert Lahr made famous the role of the **pusillanimous** lion in the movie version of "The Wizard of Oz."
   c. Alfred was awarded a medal of honor for his **pusillanimous** actions during the hostage crisis.

4. a. The **epitaph** was made of solid marble and tapered to a point six feet above the grave of the fallen soldier.
   b. Ben Jonson wrote beautiful verses in praise of Shakespeare as a fitting **epitaph** to a man who was his rival in life.

    c. After the two cars crashed, the driver of one jumped out of his auto hurling **epitaphs** at the other driver.

5. a. My father was saving for his retirement years, "because," he said, "**travail** is the one thing I've never had time to do, and now I'm planning to see all of America."
    b. Martin said he was planning to go by **travail** to the West Coast because he was afraid to fly.
    c. It is difficult today to comprehend the **travail** suffered by the Pilgrims during their first winter in New England.

6. a. Hatred is a **pernicious** emotion that can lead to the breakup of family or friends or even start a war.
    b. "A **pernicious** law will guarantee that all the neighbors will live in harmony," promised the mayoral candidate.
    c. That was truly a most **pernicious** gesture—paying for your friend's hospital bill.

7. a. My uncle had a strange **nostrum** that aliens were sleeping in his bedroom every night.
    b. Ella's grandmother prescribed a **nostrum**, the ingredients of which were known only to her, that always seemed to cure Ella's colds.
    c. The Latin teacher was so exasperated with Murray's ignorance of the day's translation assignment that he said sarcastically, "And I suppose you think that **nostrum** is Nostradamus' son?"

8. a. When David asked Jenny to go steady, she said, "Yes, I'd love to; you are the most **feckless** boy that I have ever known."
    b. After spending a sunny day at the beach, Joe's face was covered with bright **feckless** spots.
    c. "Don't marry that young man," Jane's father advised her. "He is the most **feckless** admirer you have ever brought home."

    C. Choose the word or phrase that best defines the boldface word in each sentence.

1. When he fired Monty, the boss said, "You are the most **feckless** worker I have ever hired."
    (a) frenetic   (b) irresponsible   (c) fickle

2. Rob's **splenetic** outburst characterized him as (a) splendid
   (b) spiteful (c) gracious.

3. When Alonzo said he couldn't concentrate in the **antemeridian**,
   he was referring to (a) afternoon (b) morning (c) vespers.

4. The rabbi who taught the class in "Near and Far Eastern Relig-
   ions" had an open, **ecumenical** point of view.
   (a) universal (b) calumnious (c) inimical

5. So far, the idea of turning swords into plowshares has not
   proven to be a **nostrum** that will insure enduring peace.
   (a) remedy (b) command (c) ultimatum

6. The **animosity** between the two neighbors was manifested daily
   in their constant arguing.
   (a) anguish (b) hostility (c) alliance

7. The ticking crocodile in "Peter Pan" turned Hook into a **pusillanimous** pirate.
   (a) courageous (b) spirited (c) timorous

8. Many people are titillated by the humorous **epitaphs** they find
   on old gravestones.
   (a) sagas (b) memorial inscriptions (c) epics

9. The **pernicious** rumor started by the scandal-mongering newspaper ruined the actor's reputation.
   (a) false (b) malignant (c) unreliable

10. Citizens in war-torn countries experience such **travail** in daily
    life that they despair of ever being happy again.
    (a) hunger (b) thirst (c) anguish

   D. Choose two of the following words: animosity, travail, epitaph,
   splenetic. Use your words in your own sentences.

Lesson

15

venial: *adjective*

The Latin **veni(a)** means "indulgence," a benign kind of permissiveness. The Roman Catholic Church has a special designation for a venial sin. It is a sin against the law of God that does not deprive the sinner of grace. This is explained in the following manner: A venial sin is one that the sinner does not fully understand in terms of its severity, or the sinner did not participate in the sin with full consent. In contrast to the **venial sin**, there is the **mortal sin**, which could endanger one's very soul. In any case, the Roman Catholic Church indulges or overlooks venial sins and in this regard relaxes its spiritual authority. In a secular setting, the word venial means "a petty offense, one that is pardonable." There is a word from Spanish that has about the same meaning as **venial**—the Spanish word used in English is **peccadillo** from the diminutive of **pecado**, meaning "a small sin." On the other hand, there is another English word that looks much like venial, and that word is **venal**, but its meaning is 180° distant from venial's meaning. It derives from the Latin **venalis**, meaning "capable of being bought, or sold." A venal person will sell his or her honor, country, or principle, if the price is right. Judas committed a venal sin against Christ, as did Faust, who committed a venal sin when he sold his soul to the Devil for power. These figures and others who have been corrupted by money or power fill many pages of literature.

Context: The judge remanded the youth into the custody of his parents because his offense was of a **venial** kind.

officious: *adjective*

Who has not met a meddlesome busybody, one who butts into business that should be of no concern to that person? This **officious** individual is not a likable person because he or she is too forward, too "pushy." The word comes from the Latin **officios**, meaning "obliging, dutiful." The current definition is "objectionably forward in offering unrequested and unwanted aid or advice." In a word, officious individuals interfere. The current meaning does not agree with the Latin **officios** ("obliging, dutiful"). The rub is that while officious individuals may think they are being obliging and dutiful, they are in fact quite the opposite. They are a pain in the neck.

> *Context:* The matronly looking woman was berating in an **officious** manner a young mother whose child was misbehaving.

droll: *adjective*

The word **droll** comes from the Middle French **drolle**, and it means "a pleasant rascal." The word has a special characteristic that makes its use tricky. Droll means "amusing," but "amusing in an odd way." It is a kind of whimsy, a waggish humor. Will Rogers, raconteur extraordinaire, had a droll sense of humor. Incidentally, the Middle Dutch **drol** means "a fat little man." Insofar as the English version of the word is concerned, they were dead wrong: a droll person need not be fat, little, or a man.

> *Context:* His **droll** conversations oftentimes went unappreciated as is so often the case with whimsical humor.

altruism: *noun*

The Italian word **altrui** means "someone else." It is a borrowing from the Latin etymon **alter**, meaning "other," which is entirely consistent with the phrase **someone else**. The English word **altruism** is built on these borrowings, and it means "concern for the welfare of others; selflessness." The connection among the words **alter, altrui,** and **altruism** is obvious. An altruistic person is concerned with someone else, someone other than the self.

> *Context:* Mother Teresa's **altruism** is known by people in all corners of the world.

machination: *noun*

The word **machination** has an unusual pronunciation: the **ch** is pronounced as a **k**. It finds its origin in the Latin **machinat**, which means "to design, to invent, or skillfully contoured." The current meaning of machination is "an artful device or action, generally with evil intent as a goal." It is a form of plotting to achieve a sinister end. The machinations of Brutus and Marc Antony to bring about the death of Julius Caesar succeeded in their goal.

> *Context:*   The **machinations** of most despots are aimed at furthering their own selfish interests.

tsunami: *noun*

The word **tsunami** is derived from **tsu**, "harbor" + **nami**, "wave." The word means "an unusually large wave produced by a seaquake or undersea volcanic eruption." When a tsunami reaches land, it destroys everything in its path, which can include entire cities in the worst cases. The word appropriately comes from the Japanese language since Japan is an island nation sitting atop a string of undersea volcanoes which are the origin of catastrophic seaquakes. These quakes spawn the tsunami. It is a word heard on newscasts that report on quakes, either sea or land.

> *Context:*   The **tsunami** engulfed the harbor city killing hundreds of people and destroying almost all of the buildings.

attrition: *noun*

Attrition is built on the Latin etymon **atterere**, and it means "to rub against." Its current meaning is "the act of weakening, exhausting by constant harassment or abuses." The Latin **atterere**, meaning "to rub against," is quite accurate linguistically. A constant rubbing against, much like the natural consequences of erosion, will weaken, exhaust, or wear down. Bear in mind that the rubbing against is to be taken figuratively.

> *Context:*   The company's decision to downsize would not impact its employees; rather, **attrition** would account for reduction in its labor force—deaths, resignations, illnesses, retirements, etc.

vitiate: *verb*

To **vitiate** is "to impair the quality of, to invalidate, to corrupt or to pervert." Pretty strong stuff, but this is the message **vitiate** sends.

It is built on the Latin **vitiare**, and it means "to spoil." In a figurative sense, the meanings listed for the word **vitiate** imply a kind of spoiling. To invalidate is to spoil the validation; to pervert is to spoil or change for the worse, and so on. The spoiling is used more as a metaphor for the words corruption, invalidation, and perversion.

> *Context:*   The sexual harassment charge leveled against the mayor **vitiated** the likelihood of his winning the next election.

cenotaph: *noun*

A **cenotaph** is a tomb or a monument erected in honor of a person whose body is buried elsewhere. It is derived from the Greek etymons **kenos,** "empty" + **taphos,** "tomb." Do you recall the etymon **taphos** in the word **epitaph**? In any case, there are many such monuments to be found throughout the world. One of the more famous cenotaphs in the United States is the Washington Monument.

> *Context:*   **Cenotaphs** are quite common in our nation's capital, Washington, D.C.

inveterate: *adjective*

The word **inveterate** means "habitual, firmly established over a long and persistent period of time." One can almost see the word **veteran** built into inveterate, and the former is essentially what the word implies. A veteran smoker is an inveterate user of tobacco. One who is a veteran liar is an inveterate prevaricator. The word inveterate is built on the Latin **invetare**, meaning "to age," which in turn was derived from the Latin **veter**, meaning "old." An inveterate thief is an **old** hand at stealing. This explanation provides the connection between the old and the new.

> *Context:*   He was an **inveterate** consumer of con games, scams carried on over the phone, and it cost him a pile of money.

EXERCISES

A. Match the definitions in Column B with the words they define in Column A.

Column A   Column B

1. droll   a. pardonable
2. machination   b. interfering; meddlesome
3. cenotaph   c. humanitarian; unselfish
4. officious   d. scheme; conspiracy
5. vitiate   e. tidal wave
6. altruistic   f. abrasion; wearing away
7. tsunami   g. invalidate; corrupt
8. inveterate   h. whimsical; offbeat
9. venial   i. monument to honor someone whose body is
10. attrition   buried elsewhere
                            j. habitual; inured

B. If the boldface words are used correctly in the sentences, write
C; if not, write N.

1. My mother said, "When the Morrisons come to dinner, I think
   I'll have roast **venial** with snow peas and applesauce."

2. My Irish grandfather always said that Robin Goodfellow was a
   droll little elf.

3. The high school teachers dreaded Parents' Night because the **officious** Mrs. Xavier always came to criticize them and tell them
   the correct ways to teach.

4. The **machinations** of the candidate's campaign workers almost
   ruined his chances of being elected.

5. My grandfather was an **inveterate** of World War II and often
   told me stories of his years in the U.S. Navy.

6. When my Aunt Jane went to the **tsunami** wrestling matches
   with my uncle, her only reaction was, "My goodness! They do
   eat well, don't they?"

7. The school board managed to stay within its budget by not filling the teaching positions left vacant by normal **attrition**.

8. The star football player was expelled because he took bribes and
   had, therefore, **vitiated** the reputation of the school.

9. The assassinated king was buried in a subterranean chamber directly beneath the **cenotaph** erected in his memory.

10. The winner of a vast lottery fortune became known for her **altruistic** gifts of scholarships for worthy students.

C. Using the clues below, write the words defined. The letters corresponding to the shaded squares will spell a friendly word.

1. meddlesome

2. whimsical

3. a monument

4. pardonable; trivial

5. erosion; abrasion

6. to invalidate

7. a tidal wave

8. habitual

9. generosity; selflessness

D. Choose two of the following words: droll, altruism, tsunami, attrition. Use your two words in two sentences of your own.

Lesson

16

gambit: *noun*

Gambit finds its origin in the Italian word **gambetto,** which means "the act of tripping." It refers to a calculated move intended to score a point; in chess it is a move to gain an advantage by risking one or more minor pieces. The express purpose of a gambit is to gain an advantage, whether at chess or conducting foreign policy. The object is to trip someone by allowing him or her to believe an advantage can be had by taking the bait so carefully placed for enticement.

> *Context:* The financier's **gambit** to raise the price of his stock worked like a charm.

caldron: *noun*

A **caldron** is a very **large kettle**. It comes from the Late Latin **caldaria** and means "warm bath." While one would not normally bathe in a caldron, it should be noted that in many instances it would be possible. Some caldrons are large enough to accommodate a person who is so inclined. Perhaps the most notable caldron in literature is the one used by the three witches in Shakespeare's *Macbeth.*

> *Context:* The workers dumped a 50-gallon drum of dye into the **caldron** and mixed it together with several other chemicals.

tyro: *noun*

The Latin **tyro** means "recruit" and is the origin of the English word **tyro**. Obviously a recruit is a beginner, no matter what his aspirations. The word **tyro** currently means "a beginner, a novice, an initiate." This is not too far removed from the Italian **tiro**, meaning "recruit."

> *Context:*   The **tyro** Indy race driver miscalculated the turn, crashed into the wall, and killed himself.

dissipate: *verb*

The Latin word for "to scatter" is **dissipare**, from **dis**, "apart" + **sipare**, "to throw." One sense of our word **dissipate** is "to scatter, dispel, or disperse." If something is scattered widely, it tends to disappear. Thus we dissipate our money, time, and energy if we are wasteful of them. If we squander good health by indulging in rich foods, late hours, or excessive use of alcohol, we dissipate our health. We most often use the word to mean that a person is dissolute, or has wasted himself in some manner, thereby bringing harm to himself. **Dissipate** can, however, be used without implying intemperance, meaning simply "to scatter" as in the case of gas or odors which do dissipate themselves over time.

> *Context:*   Taking drugs can and does **dissipate** one's health.

deprecate: *verb*

To **deprecate** is "to express serious disapproval, to depreciate, to belittle." One can almost see the word **depreciate** in the word **deprecate**. The stretch is not a very long one. To deprecate is "to lessen the value of," and this is precisely the word's meaning. It is built on the Latin **deprecāt(us)**, and it means "pray against." While the word **pray** in the Latin is an overstatement in terms of the word's current meaning, the negative **against** fits in nicely with "depreciate, belittle, or earnest disapproval."

> *Context:*   The prosecutor **deprecated** the testimony given by the witness and charged the defense with subornation, "taking false information from a witness."

attenuate: *verb*

The word **attenuate** has its origin in the Latin etymon **attennāre**, which means "to make thin." Bear in mind that the thinness alluded to is not of a physical nature. One cannot attenuate his or her weight, for example. The thinness is figurative: "to reduce in force, intensity, quality, or value." This is the kind of thinning that is implied—"a reduction, a lessening." For example, one can attenuate bad behavior by suggesting anger as an excuse.

> *Context:*   The federal government in an effort to **attenuate** the negative economic forecasts indicated that a reduction in personal income taxes was forthcoming.

accolade: *noun*

The word **accolade** is built on the Latin **collum**, meaning "neck." During the romantic period of history when knights roamed about in quest of deeds of daring, the honor of knighthood was bestowed upon those who performed acts of honor and bravery. Knighthood was conferred upon these individuals by tapping the shoulder just below the neck with a sword. An accolade today is any form of public praise not unlike that accorded knights of old.

> *Context:*   **Accolades** are heaped upon those who garner Nobel prizes, not to mention a one-million-dollar cash award.

supplicate: *verb*

To **supplicate** is "to make humble and earnest entreaty, to implore, to beg." A second definition is more in the spiritual realm. It is "to pray humbly to." The word is built on the Latin **supplicāre**, "to kneel," which is a position consistent with prayer. The first meaning requires the supplicant to be humble while imploring. It does not impose prayer in any way. This is the major difference between the two meanings. A felon, for example, may supplicate the judge before sentencing; a cancer patient may supplicate his or her god for a miracle cure, more in the nature of prayer. The distinction can be subtle.

> *Context:*   On bended knee the **supplicant** implored his king to spare his life.

maelstrom: *noun*

Neither Latin nor Greek had anything to do with the origin of the word **maelstrom**. It comes from the Dutch **malen**, "to whirl" + **stroom**, "stream"—"a whirling stream, a whirlpool." A maelstrom is a restless, tumultuous state of affairs, topsy-turvy, if you will. Some folks, for example, are caught up in a maelstrom of hate, bigotry, and violence. Neo-Nazi groups are a case in point. Bear in mind that a maelstrom may be taken quite literally to characterize a large, violent whirlpool, a vortex.

> *Context:* Seven candidates were vying for the party's endorsement, which created a political **maelstrom** that clouded the issues.

myriad: *adjective*

In English the word **myriad** means countless or innumerable. It is built on the Greek **myrioi**, meaning **ten thousand**. Ten thousand is by no means countless, but it is a substantial number—especially if you are counting beans, blades of grass, stars, or other objects occurring in great numbers and difficult to count precisely. There is an alternate meaning that does not suggest the idea of countless or innumerable. For instance, the President of the United States has **myriad** responsibilities imposed upon him by the Constitution. This certainly does not suggest that the responsibilities are countless; rather, it implies that they are diverse and numerous, but much fewer than ten thousand.

> *Context:* There were **myriad** points of light filling the star-studded evening sky.

EXERCISES

A. Match the definition in Column B with the word it defines in Column A.

Column A

1. caldron
2. dissipate
3. myriad
4. gambit
5. tyro
6. accolade
7. maelstrom
8. supplicate
9. deprecate
10. attenuate

Column B

a. a novice; beginner
b. to implore; to beg
c. award; citation
d. whirlpool; uproar
e. large kettle
f. adulterate; make slender
g. ploy; ruse
h. a great number, as stars in the sky
i. squander; dispel
j. disapprove; belittle

B. Select the item in which the boldface word is used correctly.

1. a. Caught up in the **maelstrom** of public emotion, the protestors began throwing rocks, or anything else that came to hand, at the police.
   b. We had at least seventy-five **maelstroms** to go before we could sleep.
   c. The TV weatherman referred to the **maelstrom** as the great calm and quiet of the eye of the hurricane.

2. a. We couldn't bathe our miniature poodle because the only **caldron** we could find was too small to hold him.
   b. The Mad Hatter in *Alice in Wonderland* tried to stuff the dormouse into a **caldron**.
   c. After a torturous ride through rain and sleet and fog, the Pony Express rider was happy to get himself into a **caldron** of hot, steamy water for a bath even though his knees hit his chin when he folded himself in.

3. a. Avery spent all afternoon in the chair by the window admiring the **gambits** of the girls walking by in the street.
   b. Pretending to have an upset stomach was a **gambit** that Charlie hoped would keep him home from school on the day of the final exams.
   c. The children played Chinese checkers on a colorful **gambit** board.

4. a. A seasoned golfer like Arnold Palmer can teach many techniques to aspiring **tyros**.
   b. If you had better **tyros** on the wheels of your racing car you might stand a chance of winning a race once in a while.
   c. The tsar was an absolute **tyro** of whom all the people were afraid.

5. a. "You can **supplicate** your income by getting a second job," Josh told his friend.
   b. How can you even begin to **supplicate** that Ezra stole the money from your wallet?
   c. "I will be a **supplicant** for Portia's hand," declared Bassanio, "and pray that I choose the casket that will make her my wife."

6. a. "I am so fond of my cousin," said Julia, "that I **dissipate** her visit impatiently and can hardly wait for her to arrive."
   b. After forty-eight hours the noxious fumes from the wrecked tank car were **dissipated** and the citizens returned to their homes.
   c. The local music critic disliked the organist's rendition of "Rhapsody in Blue" because he used the **dissipate** pedal too loudly.

7. a. The neighborhood children were selling fruit **accolade** on a hot summer's day for five cents a glass.
   b. The architect's use of a series of **accolades** made a unique facade at the front of the courthouse.
   c. The bandmaster received a standing ovation, a well-deserved **accolade**, for his creative use of the brass instruments in his presentation of "76 Trombones."

8. a. The chef **attenuated** the thin white sauce by adding both cornstarch and flour to the mixture.
   b. As I watched, the spider spun out a long, **attenuated** filament to add to its web.
   c. The whole neighborhood **attenuated** the meeting when the town council announced it was raising property taxes.

C. Unscramble the jumbled words and match each to its correct definition.

1. roty	a. violent whirlpool
2. nuatatete	b. to implore; to plead
3. stomalerm	c. trick; ploy
4. nordacl	d. public praise or honor
5. cuplispate	e. a novice
6. tibamg	f. squander; scatter
7. locadace	g. belittle; disapprove
8. passidite	h. spin out; diminish
9. precedeat	i. countless in number
10. yrmiad	j. large kettle

D. Choose two of the following words: gambit, accolade, maelstrom, sincere. Use your words in sentences of your own.

REVIEW OF LESSONS 1 - 16

A. All the words listed below are needed to complete the passage. Choose those that correctly make sense in the passage.

dotage	carnal	manifest
adamant	dissipated	asinine
caldron	pastiche	specious
inveterate	virulent	avuncular
inimical	vestiges	

Indoor vs. Outdoor Gardens

The last ___1___ of polite conversation are ___2___ when persistent, ___3___ gardeners discuss the pros and cons of raising houseplants or growing plants outdoors only.

The "outdoor gardener only" argues that indoor environment is ___4___ to plants, whereas the proponents of raising houseplants claim that this is a ___5___ argument; they are steadfastly ___6___ about their belief that houseplants show, or ___7___ only beneficial auras. They maintain that a windowsill filled with flowering plants is a ___8___ of color, making everyone happy.

Some gardeners go overboard. Some cultivate a ___9___ Venus's flytrap to devour bugs that they snatch out of thin air. One friend planted an avocado seed that grew into a tree and required a ___10___ to contain it.

Despite the gardener's ___11___ attitude toward them, some houseplants do not respond to loving care and are subject to ___12___ diseases that kill them.

The gardeners may grow old, but even in their ___13___ they maintain that any point of view except their own is ___14___.

B. Write the word that completes the meaning of the sentence.

1. A purging, a cleansing, or a spiritual purification can best be characterized as a (a) catharsis (b) caprice (c) caveat.

2. A trace or visible sign of something vanished or lost is a (a) penchant (b) vestige (c) foible.

3. To remove that which is morally offensive is to (a) explicate it (b) calumniate it (c) expurgate it.

4. That which is hazy, vague, or indistinct is (a) nebulous
   (b) inimical   (c) frenetic.

5. Persons who lead people for their own selfish reasons are
   (a) trucklers (b) demagogues (c) pedagogues.

6. A silly, stupid, or unintelligent remark is which of the following?
   (a) asinine (b) virulent (c) idiosyncratic

7. A caustic, biting, or sharp remark is best characterized as
   (a) vicarious (b) mordant (c) morbid.

8. That which is easily understood by the senses, especially sight,
   is (a) manifest (b) decadent (c) implacable.

9. To be good company, to be friendly and agreeable, is to be
   (a) indomitable (b) contumacious (c) convivial.

10. To deprive of strength, to weaken, is to (a) emasculate
    (b) exult (c) explicate.

   C. Write F if the statement is false or T if it is true.

1. **Feckless** persons are generally admired by their peers.

2. To display one's **animosity** in debate will score points.

3. A **pusillanimous** person would be likely to **truckle** to those
   who treat him or her in a heavy-handed manner.

4. **Splenetic** persons might well exhibit animosity in their behavior.

5. A **venial** sin is one that the Catholic church chooses to forgive.

6. A **tsunami** is a destructive hurricane.

7. To **vitiate** is to improve the quality of a thing.

8. **Capricious** behavior is entirely predictable.

9. The **penchant** for gambling has gotten many people into deep
   trouble.

10. An **eponym** is a sword used in fencing.

11. Most people look forward to their **dotage**.

12. To engage in **badinage** is to be mean-spirited in intent.

13. A **parochial** view is one that is universal in its scope.

14. To **explicate** matters is to provide additional detailed information.

15. A **foible** is a glaring character fault.

Dimension One
Part Two

"Our next hymn will be Kinkering Congs." ("Conquering Kings")
spoonerism

Words from Proper Nouns

Lesson

1

Janus-faced: *adjective*

Janus was the Roman god of doorways, of beginnings, and the rising and setting of the sun. It was held that Janus, while having but one head, had two bearded faces opposite each other, one looking backward, the other looking ahead. No more appropriate name could have been given to the month of **January**, a time when most people look back at the old year and look forward to the new. As for a Janus-faced person, one need only remember the meaning "hypocritical, two-faced, deceitful."

> *Context:*   Because he agreed first with one point of view, then changed to the opposite, the political candidate was termed **Janus-faced** by the newspapers.

milquetoast: *noun*

A **milquetoast** is "a person who does not have a strong backbone"—easily dominated and even more readily intimidated. The word comes from a character in a cartoon, "The Timid Soul," by H.T. Webster, a 20th-century American cartoonist. The character's name in the comic strip was Casper Milquetoast, and he epitomized the very essence of meekness, timidity, and a shyness that had no bounds.

> *Context:*   Henry appeared to be afraid of his own shadow, so his friends called him a **milquetoast**.

jabberwock: *noun*

The word **jabberwock** comes from a poem "Jabberwocky" by Lewis Carroll (1832-1898). It appears in his work THROUGH THE LOOKING-GLASS. Oddly enough, the poem has no meaning in itself since it was nonsense writing that Lewis Carroll designed to give the appearance of making sense. For example, the grammar and syntax are consistent with standard English. But in every other respect it is pure gibberish. The letters and symbols have no meaning. Carroll no doubt borrowed from the English word **jabber**, meaning "to speak rapidly and indistinctly, almost incomprehensibly." Who has not heard a teacher's admonition, "Stop all that jabbering and get to work". You no doubt can't count the times. The following stanza has been excerpted from Carroll's "Jabberwocky."

> 'Twas brillig, and the slithy toves
> Did gyre and gimble in the wabe;
> All mimsy were the borogoves,
> And the mome raths outgrabe.

Context: Allison spoke so rapidly that her words oftentimes were incomprehensible, a kind of **jabberwocky**.

Shangri-la: *noun*

Shangri-la comes from **Shangri-La**, a hidden paradise in James Hilton's novel LOST HORIZON (1933). It has two meanings. The first is "a remote paradise," so inaccessible that it is not known to any living being outside its borders. This is the Shangri-La depicted by Hilton. The second meaning is more general. It is "an area whose name and location are kept secret," and this place though very special is not a paradise. An inveterate fisherman who found a special place to fish for bass, large in both size and number, might think of this place as his Shangri-la. The words **utopia** and **Shangri-la** are very close in meaning.

Context: Because Jim had four older sisters, he retreated often to the secret solitude of his tree house, which he called his **Shangri-la**.

Lothario: *noun*

Nicholas Rowe (1674-1718) wrote a tragedy titled THE FAIR PENITENT. In it, there is a young seducer of women who seem not to be able to resist his charm or wiles. Of course he takes full advantage of this power over women. Today a **Lothario** (sometimes lower case) is "a charming young man who seduces and deceives women," many women, one might add.

> *Context:* Thinking of himself as an irresistible **Lothario**, Frank couldn't understand why he didn't have a date for the junior prom.

braggadocio: *noun*

Edmund Spenser's epic poem "Faerie Queen" (1552-1599) is the source of the word **braggadocio**, which means "empty boasting." **Braggadocchio** is a character in Spenser's poem who personifies this kind of behavior: a swaggering manner; cockiness; pretentious bragging. He was all of these. It must be obvious that the words **brag** and **braggart** come to English from the same source.

> *Context:* Falstaff, a character in Shakespeare's comedy, *Merry Wives of Windsor*, was a man of huge physical proportions who was also noted for his excessive **braggadocio**.

lethargy: *noun*

Lēthē was a mythical river of Hades whose water according to legend caused **forgetfulness** of the past in those who drank it. Today the word lethargy takes on a more subtle meaning. A lethargic person is "one who is sluggish, indifferent, apathetic," all of which have little to do with forgetfulness. But there is a second meaning that is more in keeping with the word's etymology, and that definition is "abnormal drowsiness resembling deep sleep." One can make a case here that in a state of abnormal drowsiness the first sensibility to abandon a person is his ability to think and therefore to remember. The adjective form of lethargy is **lethargic**.

> *Context:* After they had eaten a meal consisting of several courses of meat, vegetables, and dessert, the whole family slumped into a **lethargic** stupor.

bacchanalia: *noun*

The Roman **Bacchanali** was a festival of **Bacchus**, the god of wine. It was celebrated with dancing, song, and revelry in general. In the course of celebration, many revelers imbibed more than they should have. It was not uncommon during these feasts that their behavior degenerated in drunken orgies. Today the word has taken on a meaning generally associated with drunkenness or an excessive indulgence in an activity that could be described as orgiastic, and it might well be sexually oriented.

> *Context:*   We picked so many quarts of sun-ripened strawberries that eating them with cream became a **bacchanalian** feast.

pyrrhic victory: *noun*

King Pyrrhus (319-272 B.C.) of Epirus defeated the Roman legions in battle at Asculum in 279 B.C. While the victory belonged to Pyrrhus, his own armies suffered such staggering losses he was never again considered a major player in the struggle for military power. Today a **pyrrhic victory** is one too costly to the victor. One might consider the North's victory over the South after the Civil War a pyrrhic victory at best.

> *Context:*   Winning the marathon race was for David a **pyrrhic victory** since his closest friend had collapsed at the finish line and had to be rushed to a hospital.

chauvinism: *noun*

The word derives from a legendary soldier Nicholas Chauvin who was extremely devoted to Napoleon. He had a fanatical patriotism, a military devotion to the glorification of one's country. Obviously the current meaning is much broader than this, especially with reference to men and the provincial belief in a male-dominated society. **Chauvinism** (SHOW-vin-izm) now means "a prejudiced belief in the superiority of one's own group," whatever this group may be.

> *Context:*   The diplomat's **chauvinism** made him intolerant of other countries represented at the United Nations.

Exercises

A. Match the definition in Column B with the word it defines in Column A.

Column A

Column B

1. Lothario
2. milquetoast

a. gibberish; nonsense language
b. an ideal place

3. lethargy   c. a victory at tremendous cost
4. chauvinism   d. unscrupulous rake; seducer
5. Janus-faced   e. apathy; torpor
6. braggadocio   f. overzealous patriotism; undue partiality
7. bacchanalia   to any group or place
8. jabberwocky   g. two-faced; hypocritical
9. Shangri-la   h. a meek or timid person
10. pyrrhic victory   i. empty boasting; pretentious bragging
                         j. wild celebration

B. Write the word from the list below that best completes the meaning of each sentence.

Shangri-la	braggadocio
lethargy	pyrrhic victory
jabberwocky	chauvinism
milquetoast	Janus-faced
Lothario	bacchanalia

1. The swaggering confidence and _____ of the boxer sent the spectators into raucous laughter when he was counted out by a knockout in the second round of the bout.

2. Accused of seducing his leading lady, the handsome actor proved to be a _____ in his private life as well as in the movie roles he played.

3. "I can't put this bookcase together," mourned my husband. "As far as I'm concerned, these directions that are supposed to tell me how to do it are so much _____."

4. My younger brother's room, although a cluttered mess, was his _____, a fantasyland filled with unbounded joy and dream fulfillment.

5. There are those who contend that Richard Nixon during the Watergate incident behaved in a _____ manner, saying one thing for public consumption and quite another behind closed doors in his oval office.

6. In Somerset Maugham's novel OF HUMAN BONDAGE, the protagonist, Philip Carey, is badgered into being a _____ by Mildred, the waitress who takes over his life for a while.

7. Hovering around 90° for five days, the temperature plus the humidity accounted for the _____ of the workers on the highway construction project.

8. Mildred felt that if she continued smoking while admonishing her children not to smoke, she could be termed _____.

9. Mardi Gras in New Orleans and Carnival in Rio de Janeiro are popular examples of modern-day _____.

10. The litigant in the celebrated divorce case eventually realized that losing his wife, the love of his children, and the regard of all his friends had turned his winning in the courtroom into a _____.

   C. Choose the word or phrase that best conveys the meaning of the boldface word or phrase.

1. Some of the parents had a **chauvinistic** attitude toward girls being allowed to play on the school's soccer team.
(a) prejudice   (b) favorable   (c) indifferent

2. Aunt Prudence's idea of a **bacchanalia** is a birthday party with cocoa, cake, and sparklers instead of candles.
(a) musical   (b) backwash   (c) orgy

3. Henry David Thoreau found his **Shangri-la** was to live for a time in the wilderness surrounding Walden Pond.
(a) downfall   (b) ideal place   (c) misfortune

4. I was half asleep during the lecture on the Battle of Hastings, so my notes were absolute **jabberwocky** when I tried to transcribe them for studying.
(a) intellectual   (b) nonsense   (c) jaundiced

5. The Union's eventual victory over the Confederacy was at best a **pyrrhic victory** since what remained of the United States after the conflict was a nation divided by ideology and devastated by the ravages of war.
(a) disappointment   (b) celebration   (c) success at great cost

6. Many times politicians are accused of being **Janus-faced** because they support whatever cause seems at the moment to be the popular one.
(a) hypocritical   (b) judicious   (c) greedy

7. "Don't be such a **milquetoast**," Jenny said when her sister screamed at the sight of a mouse running across the floor.
   (a) noisy girl   (b) timid soul   (c) crusty person

8. Except for my brother who went jogging, the rest of the family collapsed into a **lethargic** state after devouring the huge Thanksgiving dinner.
   (a) hilarious   (b) frenetic   (c) torpid

9. The **braggadocio** of Pinocchio usually resulted in the lengthening of his nose.
   (a) humility   (b) empty boasting   (c) gibberish

10. Ambrose considered himself to be a veritable **Lothario** because many of the girls he dated thought he was a good catch.
   (a) dancer   (b) ladies' man   (c) conversationalist

   D. Choose two of the following words: milquetoast, lethargy, Janus-faced, chauvinism. Use your two words in two sentences of your own.

Lesson

2

Babbitt: *noun*

George F. Babbitt is the main character in a novel by Sinclair Lewis (1885-1951). The title of this work quite appropriately is BABBITT (1922). In it Sinclair Lewis had Babbitt personify the American middle class and its mundane attachment to business and social ideals. Lewis made Babbitt the typically ideal model for narrow-minded and smug self-satisfaction. Today the word suggests these same qualities, a conforming person who adopts ready-made values of the middle class. There are reasons to suppose that the YUPPIE generation of the 1970s and 1980s were indeed Babbitts in every sense Sinclair Lewis intended. Wearing a three-piece suit and driving a BMW were the hallmarks of a successful life.

> *Context:* Janet broke her engagement to Gerry because she found him to be a dull, unthinking **Babbitt**.

malaprop: *noun*

Mrs. Malaprop is a character from the play *The Rivals* (1775) by Richard B. Sheridan (1751-1816). In the comedy Mrs. Malaprop has a penchant for substituting a sound-alike word for the intended word. The end result was a ludicrously humorous misuse of language, and this is what the word means today. Be mindful that the humor derived from a **malaprop** depends on making the connection between the word used and the word that was intended. For example, Archie Bunker's malaprop, "He's here to collect his pound of fish" takes on a humorous meaning only when there is a recognition that what he meant was not **fish**, but **flesh**, a reference to Shakespeare's *Merchant* *of Venice.* Bunker is a malapropist non pareil: "the immaculate connection"; "he yelled 'pig' and other epaulets"; "perversion is nine-tenths of the law."

> *Context:*   To say that a great musician was a child "progeny" is to label him falsely with a **malapropism**.

pandemonium: *noun*

John Milton's epic poem *Paradise Lost* is the source of the English word **pandemonium**. The word's current meaning is "confusion, uproar, din, chaos." In Milton's narrative poem there is a place he called Pandemonium, the capital of Hell. Milton coined the word; actually it was the name of a place for Milton, because there were no names or words in the language that could convey his impressions of this place in Hell, this place that housed all the devils and Satan himself as well. So he needed a new word. Milton went to the Greek **pan**, "all" + **demon**, "devil" + **ium**, "a place for," and from them **pandemonium** is born. This hellish place in the netherworld could not have been named more aptly. Currently the word has nothing at all to do with devils or demons. It simply denotes uproarious noise and confusion.

> *Context:*   The minute the teacher left the room, **pandemonium** reigned.

spoonerism: *noun*

W.A. Spooner (1844-1930) was an English clergyman noted for slips of the tongue. A **spoonerism** requires a transposition of letters from two words. For example, the use "of queer old dean" for "dear old queen" is a spoonerism. So too is "crooks and nannies" used in place of "nooks and crannies." Finally, he "hissed my mystery lesson" for "he missed my history lesson," and "a high White Souse horse" for "a high White House source." When concluding a wedding ceremony, Rev. Spooner advised the groom, "It is kisstomary to cuss the bride."

> *Context:*   **Spoonerisms**, transpositions of letters in words, are humorous only when listeners know what the speaker really intended to say.

philistine: *noun*

At one time a native of Phystia, an ancient country southwest of Palestine, was known as a **Philistine**. It was also common knowledge that Philistines were antagonistic to cultural and artistic values. Phystia was devoid of anything resembling an artistic bent. Today the word has taken on an added dimension: "ignorant, especially middle-class people with no cultural values." One must be mindful that Philistines had an almost inbred **antagonism** for cultural pursuits, and it is this antagonism that is missing from the word's current meaning which is rather harsh in its characterization. Some people have not assimilated cultural values because they were never instilled in them through no fault of their own. The word should be used with care to insure that its application is justified.

Context: Surprisingly, the professor was a **philistine** when it came to an appreciation of modern art.

sadistic: *adjective*
The word comes from the name of a French soldier and novelist named Comte Donatien de Sade (1740-1814) who delighted in inflicting extremely cruel and painful perversions upon others. Herein lies the crux of the meaning applied to the word **sadistic**: "one who must derive pleasure from inflicting pain on others." From the surname **de Sade** comes the word **sadistic**. Ted Bundy, whose placid outward demeanor masked his **sadistic** nature, was a killer of many young women.

Context: Judged a **sadistic** serial killer, the prisoner was condemned to life imprisonment by the jury.

Panglossian: *noun, adjective*
The word comes from the novel CANDIDE by Voltaire, a French satirist. In it can be found a character named Pangloss, who embodies the essence of an optimist. Pangloss can find good in evil. All will be well because to Pangloss this is the best of all possible worlds. Voltaire was, of course, presenting a parody of the optimism of a German philosopher named Leibnitz. Today the word means "blindly expecting a favorable outcome or naively dwelling on hopeful aspects." Neville Chamberlain, England's Prime Minister prior to World War II, made a pact with Hitler that he believed would bring peace in his time. This turned out to be a Panglossian view of Nazism and Adolf Hitler. There is another word that closely approximates Panglossian—the word is Pollyanna, which will be presented in another section of this book. It means a person who is blindly optimistic.

Context: Blithely **panglossian** about his final grade in chemistry, Bill was crushed by the reality of his "D" exam paper.

martinet: *noun*

Jean Martinet was a 17th-century French army officer who was known far and wide for his rigidly conformist insistence on unquestioning discipline and unquestioning compliance with orders given by superior officers. Today the word has application beyond the military, and it means "a person who demands absolute adherence to rules." An example of such usage is: Teachers who are **martinets** seldom win the respect of their badgered students.

> *Context:*   Teachers who acquire the reputation of being **martinets** are feared by prospective students.

cross or pass the Rubicon

The Rubicon is a river in Italy, a river which when crossed by Julius Caesar and his army left him no alternative but to press on forward. This precipitated a civil war in 49 B.C. Today crossing or passing the Rubicon has a less restrictive meaning: "a limit when passed or exceeded permits no return." Napoleon Bonaparte's Rubicon turned out to be the frozen tundra of Russia. Once committed he could not retreat, and this signaled the eventual defeat of the French armies.

> *Context:*   Once having bombed Pearl Harbor, the Japanese had crossed the **Rubicon** leading to their ultimate defeat.

Machiavellian: *adjective*

The political doctrine of Machiavelli denies the relevance of morality in political affairs and holds that guile and deceit are justified in pursuing and maintaining political power. In short, the end justifies the means, the end being retention of power. Niccolò Machiavelli (1469-1527) was an Italian Renaissance statesman. He was a political writer widely read at the time, especially his work THE PRINCE, in which he argues that a politician can and should use any means at his disposal to retain power: deceit, cunning, lies, intimidation, or any other strategy that works toward that end. Adolf Hitler embodied the essence of **Machiavellian** politics and governance.

> *Context:*   The **Machiavellian** plot to destroy the reputations of all members of the diplomatic corps was, fortunately, unearthed in time.

EXERCISES

A. Match the definition in Column B to the word it defines in Column A.

Column A

1. spoonerism
2. sadistic
3. malapropism
4. Panglossian
5. Babbitt
6. crossing the Rubicon
7. pandemonium
8. philistine
9. Machiavellian
10. martinet

Column B

a. politically devious; amoral
b. taskmaster; drill sergeant
c. uproar; chaos
d. a materialistic person; indifferent to art, music, or dance.
e. deliberately cruel; taking pleasure in inducing pain in others
f. stereotype of the complacent American middle-class
g. naive; blindly optimistic
h. unintentional humorous misuse of a word or phrase
i. passing a limit that permits no return
j. transposition of usual initial sounds of two or more words

B. From the list of words below, choose the word or phrase that best completes the meaning of each sentence.

Babbitt	malapropism
pandemonium	crossing the Rubicon
Machiavellian	philistine
martinet	spoonerism
sadistic	Panglossian

1. The term "point of no return" used in World War II to alert pilots that once they passed a designated spot on an aircraft carrier they could not turn back is similar in meaning to the phrase _____.

2. Substituting for the phrase "barefoot boy with cheek of tan," the punch line to a popular joke back in the 1960's—"boyfoot bear with teak of Chan"—is called a _____.

3. When the girls' basketball team won the national championship _____ broke out in the college gym because everyone was cheering and yelling.

4. "Boss" Tweed's shrewd machinations and _____ strategies made him a powerful political figure in New York in the late 1800's, bringing the city to bankruptcy in only six years of his dominance.

5. Even when he failed three of his required courses, Jack's roommate remained so blithely optimistic about staying in college for the next semester that Jack said, "You are unbelievably _____."

6. Insisting on their wearing regulation outfits and shoes, the girls' gym teacher was secretly called a _____ by the girls in her classes.

7. The fictional character, _____, is a symbol of conforming American philistines.

8. "I think the professor gets a _____ thrill out of torturing us," Emma whispered to her friend as she read the questions on the final exam in history.

9. Because his only interests were making money and watching sports programs on TV, Jane told her father he was a _____ when he refused to go to the art exhibit at her school.

10. "I'm going to the beauty parlor to get my nails massacred," announced Angela with her usual penchant for coining a _____.

C. If the boldface word or words in the following sentences are used correctly, write C. If not, write N.

1. When the board of education decided to balance the school budget by cutting out all the art and music classes, angry parents called them **philistines**.

2. When the South American soccer team lost the title game, **pandemonium** in the crowd resulted in injury to many of the spectators.

3. Known for his pessimistic outlook on every aspect of life, Raymond was characterized as **Panglossian**.

4. In the United States Marines, especially, drill sergeants have a reputation for being **martinets** who expect recruits' blind obedience to orders.

5. When Alex made fun of the modern art exhibit that Gloria took him to see, she said, "You really are a typical **Babbitt**."

6. When the man next door (who had four dogs) complained of the "cold bats" in the neighborhood when he meant "bold cats," he was inadvertently creating a **spoonerism**.

7. The **sadistic** captain of the guards of the POW camp was well-liked because of his kindness and concern for prisoners.

8. **Crossing the Rubicon** is possible only if one hires a private yacht.

9. The **Machiavellian** conspiracy to assassinate the leader of the opposition by members of his inner circle was foiled by an alert bodyguard.

10. A **malapropism** refers to a poor structural supporting beam in the construction of a building.

  D. Choose two of the following words: malaprop, spoonerism, martinet, Machiavellian. Use your words in your own sentences.

Lesson

3

benedict: *noun*

Shakespeare made many contributions to language through his drama and poetry. Benedick is a character in *Much Ado About Nothing*. Note the spelling alteration from Benedick to benedict. A confirmed bachelor, he is very skillful at maintaining his single state. Eventually, however, he meets a woman more skillful than he, and at the play's end his state of single blessedness has changed. How this comes about is a hallmark of theatrical comedy. A **benedict** is a recently married man who was thought to be a confirmed bachelor.

Context: James lost his amateur standing as a confirmed bachelor when he married Lucille and took on the title of **benedict**.

nemesis: *noun*

Classical mythology has contributed an almost endless number of words to English. One of them is the word **nemesis**. It comes from the name of a goddess of divine retribution, and her name was **Nemesis**. Currently the word has nothing to do with being divine. It means "an opponent or rival whom a person cannot defeat." For example, Sherlock Holmes was Prof. Moriarty's nemesis. There is yet another meaning that has wider application: "that which a person cannot conquer or achieve." For many students test-taking is a nemesis. For others it might be cigarette smoking. For Richard Nixon it was Watergate.

Context: Until he escaped on the raft, Huck Finn's **nemesis** was his father.

serendipity: *noun*

THE THREE PRINCES OF SERENDIP is a Persian fairy tale about three princes who have the gift of finding valuable or agreeable things not sought after. Good things happen by chance, by accident, or by good fortune. Perhaps an example of a **serendipitous** occurrence might make the word's meaning clearer. Imagine being lost on some back road in New Hampshire. While attempting to get back on track, one comes upon a uniquely quaint village whose charm captivates the imagination, whose rustic beauty enchants the eyes. This happenstance would be **serendipitous**.

> *Context:*   We were warned to avoid a certain town on our journey from one state to another, but when we had a flat tire in this very town, we had a **serendipitous** experience, meeting people who were concerned, kind, and helpful.

charlatan: *noun*

In Italian **ciarlatano** is an alternate of **cerretano**, which literally designates "an inhabitant of Cerreta," a small village in Italy. It was rumored that **cerretanos** had for sale papal indulgences along with cures for every known malady afflicting mankind, ranging from the common cold to cancer. The **cerretanos** were, of course, frauds, quacks, fakers, and this is precisely the word's meaning today: "a pretender, especially a pretender to medical knowledge." In a more general context it refers to anyone who pretends to have expert knowledge or skill that he or she does not really have. For instance, mediums who claim to be able to communicate with the dead are **charlatans** just as those are who pretend to have a cure for incurable diseases.

> *Context:*   The doctor who took over a popular medical practice proved to be a **charlatan** with no accredited medical training.

quisling: *noun*

Vidkun Quisling (1887-1945) was a Norwegian army officer who was tried for and convicted of treason. Quisling during World War II cooperated with the Nazi invaders during their occupation of Norway. Today the word means "a traitor who serves as the puppet of the enemy occupying his country." There have been many such traitors over the years, and they are all known by the name taken by Vidkun Quisling.

> *Context:*   It appears that there have always been **quislings** who curry favor with enemy forces in return for preferred treatment.

nirvana: *noun*

The word **nirvana** has several meanings of specific religious significance, but for our purposes a general treatment would be more appropriate and certainly more useful. **Nirvana** comes from Sanskrit, and it is an almost perfect match for its English counterpart—**nirvana**. It means "a blowing out, an extinguishing." The "blowing out" can be described as extinguishing a lighted candle. If the **human will** is exchanged for the metaphor **lighted candle**, a meaning emerges that is clear and unambiguous. When one has reached a state of nirvana, there is an extinguishing of all care, pain, joy—all external reality. Individual consciousness is extinguished. The human will no longer exists, and the supplicant becomes one with the universe, a sublime state of being.

> *Context:*   Sometimes on a clear, star-studded night, one can experience a **nirvana**-like union with the universe.

Hobson's choice: *noun*

The phrase **Hobson's choice** means "a choice made freely that offers no real alternative." In other words, there is no choice. It comes from the name of an English liveryman, Thomas Hobson (1544-1631). He had a standing rule that applied to those who wished to hire a horse—"Take the horse nearest the stable door or none at all." It should be obvious that Hobson did not really offer his customers a choice at all, and this is the denotation that is attached to the phrase today.

> *Context:*   Scalpers who demand unreasonably high prices for tickets to the World Series offer only **Hobson's choice** to prospective buyers.

Armageddon: *noun*

The Bible makes reference to Armageddon (Rev. 16:14-16), a place where the final battle between the forces of good and evil will take place. The biblical reference undoubtedly is to the battlefield of Megiddo, an ancient city of Israel, the site of several great battles to which the Bible alludes. Today the word is used in a more secular sense—"any great and decisive battle." Not incidentally, this great battle between good and evil prophesied in the Bible will signal the end of the world.

Context: Mankind is constantly being warned, especially by clerics, that **Armageddon** is possible in the modern world.

gerrymander: *noun*

In 1812 Elbridge Gerry (1744-1814) and his political party redistricted Essex County, Massachusetts. When the newly formed districts were configured and shown on a map, it had a very odd shape. As a matter of fact, it was very similar to the form of a salamander, any tailed amphibian. So the latter part of sala**mander** and the name **Gerry** were wedded and the word **gerrymander** was born. The word currently denotes a division of an area into voting districts so that one party gains a distinct advantage over another. Another noun form is gerrymandering, a ploy to which the courts do not take too kindly.

Context: Political aspirants to powerful legislative jobs are willing to employ **gerrymandering** techniques in order to ensure a voting plurality in their favor.

macabre: *adjective*

A traditional feature of morality plays of the Middle Ages was the slaughter of the Maccabees, and from Maccabee the word **macabre** came into being. This aspect of the morality play presented the "danse de Macabre," or the "dance of death." The English word **macabre** has this rather gruesome lexical heritage, and the word currently denotes horror, gruesomeness, especially as they apply to death. In another context, the word is much less sinister. For example, one can have a macabre sense of humor. An American writer, Ambrose Bierce (1842-1914), exhibited a macabre sense of humor in his work, especially one titled THE DEVIL'S DICTIONARY. Another entertainment personality who is more contemporaneous was Alfred Hitchcock, a movie maker with a macabre bent.

Context: The children were frightened by the **macabre** costumes of the Halloween visitors at the door.

EXERCISES

A. Match the definition in Column B to the word it defines in Column A.

Column A

1. nemesis
2. quisling
3. Hobson's choice
4. gerrymandering
5. macabre
6. benedict
7. charlatan
8. nirvana
9. Armageddon
10. serendipity

Column B

a. accidental or chance discovery of agreeable things
b. a fake; a fraud
c. release from care and pain; bliss
d. a confirmed bachelor who gets married
e. a great and decisive battle
f. traitor
g. something unconquerable, impossible
h. a choice that is no choice
i. to manipulate voting districts
j. ghastly; dark humor

B. Choose the word from the list below that correctly completes each sentence.

gerrymandering   macabre
nirvana   charlatan
serendipity   Armageddon
nemesis   benedict
Hobson's choice   quisling

1. Aaron's friends teased him unmercifully by calling him a _____ when he returned from eloping with Clara.

2. "Ballroom dancing has always been my _____," Charlie mourned. "I think I have two left feet."

3. We had a feeling of pure _____ when having a flat tire in a charming country village resulted in everyone rushing to help us, feed us, and entertain us.

4. Madame Fiorenza was proven to be a _____ when the curtain behind her was torn, revealing an assistant manipulating sound and visual effects with hi-tech equipment.

5. As a member of the American Embassy in a foreign country, the diplomat was discovered to be a double agent and was branded a _____ by his own government.

6. The people coping with a blizzard in New England thought of south Florida as _____.

7. "Take it or leave it," the ticket scalper outside the stadium said, offering the buyer an option known as _____.

8. Believing that _____ would occur on February 10, the cultist group gave away all their worldly possessions and gathered atop a mountain to await the end of the world.

9. The political party in power, although accused of _____, managed to control the majority seats in the state legislature.

10. Some of the movies about aliens abducting people into outer space or coming to earth in assumed human forms are too _____ to be entertaining.

C. If the pairs of words below are synonyms, write T. If not, write F.

1. quisling—traitor

2. benedict—closing prayer

3. nirvana—nervous twitch

4. Armageddon—great, decisive battle

5. macabre—ghastly; eerie

6. gerrymander—salamander

7. nemesis—undoing; downfall

8. Hobson's choice—to hobble

9. charlatan—imposter

10. serendipity—serene

D. Choose two of the following words: serendipity, charlatan, gerrymander, macabre. Use your words in sentences of your own.

Lesson

4

mnemonics: *noun*

The word **mnemonic** means "assisting or intended to assist memory." Mnemonics (construed as singular) is the process or technique of improving or developing memory. For instance, should one want to commit to memory the names of the Great Lakes, an effective mnemonic device would be the word **HOMES**. From it come the lakes' names: Huron, Ontario, Michigan, Erie, and Superior. There are countless other such devices—**i** before **e** except after **c** or when **ei** is sounded like **ay**. Exceptions: Neither leisured foreign sheiks seized the weird heights. The word comes from the Greek goddess of memory whose name was Mnēmosynē. While there is not a perfect correspondence between the words, it is close enough to understand from where the word mnemonics was derived—mnemonics: Mnēmosynē.

Context: Taking a course in **mnemonics** will give one valuable techniques for remembering names, places, or ideas.

billingsgate: *noun*

Billingsgate is essentially the use of coarse and vulgar language. It comes from the name of a fish market located in London, which has been demolished recently. Fishermen toil in and around the sea, a stern taskmaster that requires seamen to lead coarse, rough lives. This spilled over into their use of language, which ended up being vulgar. Perhaps now the term **fishwife** takes on a new meaning. It is an extremely uncomplimentary appellation that characterizes these women much like their male counterparts. They too had foul tongues and even coarser manners.

Context: One of the memorable moments in MY FAIR LADY is the scene where the cockney folk banter in the coarse, vulgar language known as **billingsgate**.

cupidity: *noun*

The word **cupidity** denotes an "inordinate desire, an excessive eagerness, especially to gain material wealth." Oddly enough the word has its origin in the name of the winged cherub who carries bow and arrow. His name is, of course, Cupid, which comes from the Latin **Cupido**, and it means "eager, desirous." Cupid had in mind an eagerness, or a desirability, in matters of love. Somewhere the signals were botched, and English ended up with the word **cupidity**—meaning "avarice, inordinate desire for material wealth." **Cupidity** comes from the Latin **cupid(us)**, which means "eager, desirous," and this in turn has its origin in the name Cupid, god of love.

Context: In George Eliot's novel, SILAS MARNER, Silas' reputation for **cupidity** was completely changed when the child, Eppie, conquered his heart.

guillotine: *noun*

Not many would want to associate their name with a device having a very sharp blade that was used to behead people. Joseph Guillotin (1738-1814), who invented the guillotine, was accorded this somewhat dubious honor. While this infernal machine is seldom used today, if at all, it was used extensively during the late 1700s, especially during the French Revolution.

Context: Charles Dickens' TALE OF TWO CITIES paints for the modern reader the horror of death by the **guillotine**.

pander: *verb*

In Greek mythology **Pandarus** was the procurer of Cressida for Troilus. From Pandarus the word **pander** is born. It means "to provide gratification for another's desires," just as Pandarus provided Cressida for the pleasure of Troilus. Keep in mind that the desires alluded to are of a base nature, and the word is used pejoratively in all instances. Many television shows, for example, pander to an audience bent on two themes—sex and violence. In a broader context, one can pander to the vulgar tastes of others, or to their greed, or racist views, or sexist notions, whatever. The word has wide application.

Context: Gossip columnists **pander** to the public's fascination with the scandalous escapades of Hollywood celebrities, especially.

tenebrous: *adjective*

Tenebrae is a Roman Catholic celebration during which lauds are sung on the last three days of Holy Week. Accompanying this celebration is a ceremony of candles commemorating the suffering and death of Christ. The word is built on the Latin **tenebrae**, and it means **darkness**. During the celebration, the candles are extinguished progressively until none are lit and there is darkness. The darkness is more metaphor than real; it is in the nature of darkness oftentimes associated with **gloom** rather than **absence of light**. This is the darkness that relates to the crucifixion of Christ. Today the word **tenebrous** means "dark, gloomy," and it may be used in a secular context when appropriate.

Context: Rooted in religious ritual, the word **tenebrous** expresses a kind of gloomy, mystical darkness.

plutocracy: *noun*

The Greek **ploutos** means "wealth." When this etymon is combined with **kratos**, "rule or power," the word **plutocracy** is born. It means government by the wealthy. There are many examples of plutocracies, a few of which can be found in Latin American countries. In plutocracies there are two classes or divisions of people—the rich and the poor. Where there is no middle-class, plutocracies inevitably arise. **Plutus** in Greek mythology was the god of wealth. He is not to be confused with **Pluto**, the name given to Hades or the ninth planet in order from the sun.

Context: When a **plutocratic** government is formed by the wealthy ruling class, and there is no middle class, the poor people have no voice in the government.

gorgon: *noun*

Gorgon can be used in either upper or lower case. Without question the current usage of the word is mostly the latter. Equally undeniable is that the former (upper case) is far more interesting in terms of the mythology attached to it. Gorgon comes from the Greek lookalike word **gorgos**, meaning "terrible." This is the idea suggested in the word's current meaning: "an ugly, mean, repulsive woman, an absolutely terrible person." On the other hand, Gorgon (upper case) refers to any of three sisters, terrible monsters having snakes for hair, claw-like hands, and eyes that turned humans to stone when looked into. The most widely known Gorgon is Medusa, the only mortal one, who was beheaded by Perseus, son of Zeus. It is well worth mentioning that one of world's most celebrated sculptors, Benvenuto Cellini (1500-1571), did a work, a bronze statue of Perseus, that stands in Florence, Italy. It is a chilling sight to witness, Perseus clutching in one hand a bloodied sword and in the other, Medusa's head. Once again, Greek mythology breathes life into yet another English word. Finally, keep in mind that **gorgon** (lower case) simply means "a mean, ugly, repulsive woman."

> *Context:*   No woman, even though she might seem to be repulsively ugly to others, would welcome being called a **gorgon**.

limbo: *noun*

The word **limbo** has both a secular and a spiritual meaning. With reference to the latter, limbo is the abode of souls kept from heaven by extenuating circumstance, e.g., failure to be baptized. A second meaning of a secular nature is "a condition of oblivion or neglect." For example, one's promotion at work can be in a state of limbo in that it is uncertain. Finally, limbo is "an intermediate place or state." As in the case of souls, the stay in limbo is not for eternity. There is the distinct possibility of release. These meanings may parallel each other but their intentions are quite dissimilar—in one instance it was souls that were in limbo while in the other it was one's promotion. The word comes from the Latin **in**, "on" + **limbō**, "edge." The **edge** in a theological context refers to the border between heaven and hell. In a secular context, limbo is a temporary place or state to which one is assigned. How long is temporary? Who knows? It's certainly not for eternity; that's for sure.

> *Context:*   After he fell from his bike and hit his head on a rock, Jim said he seemed to be wandering in a kind of **limbo**, not knowing where he was.

procrustean: *adjective*

Procrustes was a legendary highwayman whose exploits were known far and wide. He not only robbed stagecoach passengers of their valuables, he also kidnapped some of them. They were taken to his castle (Procrustes was a rich crook) and in it he had a bed that came to be known as a **procrustean bed**. His victims would be placed on the bed and if they were too long for it, he would lop off the offending parts. On the other hand, if they were too short, he would with the aid of a rack type device stretch them until their bodies did conform to the dimensions of the bed. The meaning of **procrustean** today is "an arbitrary standard to which conformity is forced." The word also means "no regard for individual differences."

Context: Because of the **procrustean** demands made of those attempting to fit into the glass slipper, Cinderella's stepsisters must have emerged from the trial with really sore feet.

EXERCISES

A. Match the definition in Column B with the word it defines in Column A.

Column A

1. guillotine
2. tenebrous
3. cupidity
4. limbo
5. mnemonics
6. procrustean
7. pander
8. billingsgate
9. plutocracy
10. gorgon

Column B

a. coarse, vulgar language
b. memory aid
c. to act as a procurer; cater to
d. a repulsive-looking woman
e. ruthlessly enforced conformity
f. death machine
g. government by the wealthy
h. avarice
i. dark; gloomy
j. a state or place of uncertainty

B. From the list of words below, choose the one that best completes the meaning of the sentence.

procrustean
limbo
guillotine
cupidity
gorgon

pander
tenebrous
billingsgate
plutocratic
mnemonic

1. Showing little concern for the welfare of the poor, leaders of a _____ government may be fostering a rebellion.

2. Because he defied the _____ standards of the military school, Edgar was summarily expelled.

3. Because a hurricane warning had been issued, our plans for a three-day sailing vacation were consigned to _____.

4. Many people believe that TV programs _____ to the public's taste for violence as the gladiatorial games in the Roman arena did centuries ago.

5. The vulgar _____ of blowsy women have added much color and humor to musicals such as THREEPENNY OPERA.

6. _____ devices are good methods of recalling geographical place names.

7. The use of the _____ as a form of capital punishment was actually considered humanitarian in its day when compared to previous methods.

8. When I came home with my hair twisted into serpentine curls, my father took one look at me and laughed, "You make a remarkable _____."

9. Some cultist groups believe that the end of the world will be heralded by a foreboding, _____ cloud stretching over the land.

10. His all-consuming _____ known to all the townspeople made the real estate broker a suspect when the investment profits were reported missing.

    C. Choose the item that best conveys the meaning of the boldface word in each sentence.

1. Widely known for his **cupidity**, the miser was not pitied when his cache of jewelry was stolen from his safe.
(a) timidity   (b) greed   (c) sadism

2. Joshua took a course in **mnemonics**, but after the first lesson he forgot where the class was being held.
(a) memory assistance   (b) Greek grammar   (c) mythology

3. "Sentence them to be **guillotined**," shouted the crowd as the wealthy nobles were put on trial.
(a) imprisoned   (b) electrocuted   (c) beheaded

4. Looking at the greenish, **tenebrous** cloud approaching, the family raced for shelter, fearing it was a warning of an imminent tornado.
(a) dark   (b) thunderous   (c) tenuous

5. Because he used **billingsgate** when he thought the microphone was turned off, the mayoral candidate lost the election.
(a) infidelity   (b) vulgarity   (c) dishonesty

6. Alice's plans for gaining early college admission were **in limbo** because her final high school grades weren't ready for transcript.
(a) uncertain   (b) limited   (c) macabre

7. "What **procrustean** rules of society determine that I must wear a dress rather than slacks to the concert?" demanded Elsa.
(a) polite   (b) unwritten   (c) rigid

8. The artist stated, "I refuse to **pander** to the philistines of the world who have only tasteless middle-class values when it comes to appreciating contemporary art."
(a) truckle under   (b) disparage   (c) agree to

9. The old bag-lady shuffling into the alley seemed a veritable **gorgon** with her straggly, unwashed hair falling across her face.
(a) snake   (b) repulsive creature   (c) gardener

10. The **plutocratic** rulers of the small country decided to raise the taxes on every bag of grain harvested by the farmers.
(a) egoistical   (b) wealthy   (c) maniacal

D. Choose two words from the following: mnemonics, guillotine, pander, limbo. Use your two words in your own sentences.

Lesson

5

marathon: *noun*

Who has not seen or heard the word **marathon**? No one. It comes from an ancient Greek city named Marathon. A messenger was sent from the city of Marathon to announce the victory of Greece over the Persians in 490 B.C. The messenger's destination was Athens which, incidentally, was 26 miles plus 385 yards, the exact distance run by marathoners. Of course, it should be obvious that the messenger ran from Marathon to Athens, and this is how the word marathon found its way into English. One might be interested to know how other Olympic venues found their way into English: biathlon, triathlon, pentathlon, decathlon. Look them up in a collegiate dictionary and make your own word histories. Today any long contest with endurance as the primary factor is considered a marathon, as a "dance marathon" or for that matter the presidential primary race, a marathon of a different kind.

> *Context:* The popularity of **marathon** running seems to prove that both young and old today are making an effort to be physically fit.

stygian: *adjective*

The River Styx in ancient Greek mythology is one of the rivers of Hades, across which the souls of the dead were ferried. This is, if nothing else, a gloomy prospect. The word's current usage conveys "a sense of infernal gloom," and given the circumstances, who would not be filled with despair? History is replete with **stygian** tales—the holocaust is one such tragic episode. When referring to the word in the Greek context, it appears in upper case. In a broader more generic context, it requires the lower case.

> *Context:*   When we went down the stairway to explore the **stygian** depths of the old dungeon, I felt a shiver of dread go up my spine.

tawdry: *adjective*

Tawdry is a corruption of St. Audrey, a place where fairs were held at which neckpieces known as St. Audrey's laces were sold. These laces were indeed cheap and showy, lacking in any good taste. Today **tawdry** means exactly that—"cheap, showy, and lacking in good taste." Not only can goods be tawdry, but an incident, for instance, may well be characterized as tawdry if it is in poor taste. A husband and wife who bicker loudly at an exclusive restaurant and annoy other diners are engaged in a tawdry public display of bad manners—tasteless behavior.

> *Context:*   "You cannot go to church in that **tawdry** outfit," Lucille's mother exclaimed. "At least, press your skirt."

calliope: *noun*

The word **calliope** (ka-LIE-a-pea) has its origin in Greek mythology, an unending source of English words. It comes from the Greek Kalliope, the Muse of epic poetry. This is the origin of the English word **calliope**. Note the minor alteration in spelling. The **K** in Greek becomes a **c** in English. A calliope is "a keyboard instrument using steam to power whistles that play musical notes." It is generally associated with the circus. **Kalliope** is the Greek word for "beautiful voice." While the calliope is an unusual musical instrument, it does have a pleasing sound. Check the word **calligraphy**. It too takes the etymon **kallos**, meaning "beauty."

Context: I can still remember the excitement of the sound of the **calliope** music at the end of long circus parades my father used to take me to see.

apochrypha: *noun*

The word **apochrypha** may be used with either a singular or plural verb. Apochrypha are 14 books of the Vulgate, the Latin translation of the Bible done by Saint Jerome at the end of the 14th century A.D. Eleven of these books are accepted in Roman Catholic canon. Protestants, however, rejected this entire version of the Bible since these books were not a part of the Hebrew scripture. This is perhaps where the current meaning of "doubtful accuracy" comes into play. The word may be used in a secular sense: anything written which is of doubtful authorship is referred to as apochrypha. The adjective form is **apochryphal**.

Context: The story of George Washington cutting down the cherry tree is most probably an **apochryphal** account.

Byzantine: *adjective*

The word **Byzantine** has its origin in 5th-century A.D. architecture, an intricate art form made up of huge domes and intricate spires and minarets. It utilized a highly stylized and rich use of color. There were other identifying marks not relevant to our purposes. Suffice it to say that Byzantine architecture was complex in both form and color. Today the word denotes that which is highly complicated, intricate, and involved. Beyond this, Byzantine conduct suggests intrigue that is scheming and devious, not to mention its complex design. There are, for example, those who contend that John F. Kennedy's assassination had a more sinister, a more Byzantine backdrop than that which government officials will reveal.

Context: Trying to prove that the terrorist had been planning the bombing for months, the government uncovered a convoluted **Byzantine** plot.

mesmerize: *verb*

Franz Mesmer (1734-1815) was a German physician who first discovered the art of hypnosis, and in his honor the word **mesmerize** found its way into English. One meaning of the word is to hypnotize. It has another meaning that is also used widely, and this meaning is "to spellbind, to fascinate." For example, it is the opinion of many that outstanding criminal defense attorneys are able to mesmerize juries in behalf of their clients.

Context: The kitten seemed to be **mesmerized** by the lights on the Christmas tree.

Halloween: *noun*
What child beyond the age of 3 or 4 years is not intimately acquainted with **Halloween**? The word has special religious significance that many people do not know. All Saints' Day is celebrated on November 1. October 31 is the eve of this holiday. The word is derived from All-hallows Eve, which is the eve of All Saints' Day. Today Halloween has taken on another significance—trick or treat. Who has not delighted in seeing youngsters outfitted in costumes of various design—witches, goblins, and ghosts—bent on filling their pillowcases with sweets of infinite variety. How this delightful custom came into being is anyone's guess.

Context: **Halloween** costumes today reflect the popularity of T.V. characters.

vandal: *noun*
Vandals were a tribe of Germanic people who savaged both Gaul and Spain in the 5th century A.D. In 455 A.D. they sacked Rome. This is what Vandals were noted for—plundering, destroying anything in their path. Rome was never again to be a city of comparable grandeur, the cultural capital of the Roman Empire. Today **vandal** (lower case) has a far less menacing denotation: mischievous or malicious destruction or damage to property. Halloween is an occasion that sometimes prompts malicious damage to property—**vandalism**?

Context: No one could understand why the fifth-grade bulletin board had been ruined by **vandals**.

bowdlerize: *verb*

To **bowdlerize** is "to expurgate, to edit (as a piece of writing) by prudishly omitting parts considered indelicate." The key word is **prudishly**. Thomas Bowdler (1754–1825) took it upon himself to **expurgate** dialogue from Shakespeare's plays. Hardly anyone today would consider Shakespeare's works in need of expurgation. In fairness to Bowdler, however, it should be noted that he did his work at a time when prudish behavior was not all that uncommon. In any case, this is how the word **bowdlerize** found its way into English. One wonders what he would have had to say about X- and R-rated movies and novels replete with four-letter words. Bowdler would have been like a "kid" in a penny-candy store. He wouldn't know where to begin.

Context: Ironically, those critics who **bowdlerize** certain passages in books often, in their ignorance, delete passages that are perfectly innocent of any objectionable meaning.

EXERCISES

A. Match the definition in Column B with the word it defines in Column A.

Column A

1. apochrypha
2. mesmerize
3. stygian
4. bowdlerize
5. calliope
6. marathon
7. vandalize
8. Byzantine
9. Halloween
10. tawdry

Column B

a. eve of All Saints' Day
b. cheap; tasteless behavior
c. steam-powered musical instrument
d. writings of doubtful authenticity
e. to expurgate prudishly
f. intricate; involved
g. a contest of endurance or inordinately long competition
h. to spellbind; to fascinate
i. gloomy; infernal
j. do malicious damage to

B. If the boldface word in each sentence is used correctly, write C. If not, write N.

1. "That music you are playing so loudly on your CD player is less melodious than the **calliope** that used to be in circus parades," complained Jack's grandmother putting her hands over her ears.

2. The brilliant neon lights turned the parking lot into a **stygian** nightmare.

3. The deer crossing the highway at night was **mesmerized** by the headlights of our car, and we nearly ran into it.

4. It is difficult to trace the route from **Halloween's** genesis as a religious celebration to a celebration of witches, ghosts, and trick-or-treats.

5. The **marathon** scheduled for Thanksgiving morning seemed longer than the prescribed 26 miles and 385 yards because the snow made running so difficult.

6. An investigation into the affairs of the supposedly reputable firm revealed a convoluted, **Byzantine** scheme to defraud all the investors of their money.

7. Four boys in the eighth grade were accused of **vandalizing** the school's cafeteria because they hoped the authorities would have to allow them to go off campus to get lunch.

8. Only **tawdry** costumes were available for the Halloween dance, but everyone was delighted with them because they were so elegant and obviously expensive.

9. My teacher was rudely surprised when—after explaining in great detail a passage from HAMLET—she found it had been **bowdlerized** from the school textbook.

10. After the experts had studied the book reputed to be a long-lost novel by Jane Austen, they declared it to be **apocryphal** because the paper it was printed on post-dated Austen's lifetime.

C. Unscramble the words in Column A and match with the correct definition in Column B.

Column A   Column B
  1. enbyantiz   a. to spellbind
  2. plicolae   b. cheap; sleazy
  3. niagyst   c. steam-powered musical instrument
  4. woderbizel   d. trick-or-treat night
  5. thomrana   e. of spurious authorship
  6. wolelehan   f. intricate; complicated
  7. waydrt   g. a perpetrator of malicious damage
  8. charypphoal   h. gloomy; foreboding
  9. lavnda   i. expurgate prudishly
 10. meremizes   j. a competitive race of endurance

D. Choose two words from the following: marathon, tawdry, mesmerize, vandal. Use your words in your own sentences.

REVIEW OF LESSONS 1 - 5

A. Write T if the statement is true or F if it is false.

1. **Spoonerisms** and **malapropisms** are different in kind, but they
   have the same general effect on those who hear them.

2. A **Babbitt** is much the same type person as a **milquetoast**.

3. **Jabberwocky** and **babble** are pretty much the same thing.

4. A **Lothario** would more than likely be given to **braggadocio**.

5. A **pyrrhic** victory is a total victory.

6. A **Janus-faced** person would probably do well serving in a
   Machiavellian-run political system.

7. **Pandering** is done for many base reasons, but **cupidity** is is not
   among them.

8. **Calliopes** are most often found being played at Broadway per-
   formances.

9. The word **stygian** evokes feelings that can best be described as **tenebrous**.

10. The words **Shangri-la** and **utopia** are very close in meaning.

    B. Which word was derived from each of the literary references? Write your answers in a list.

1. from the cartoon "The Timid Soul" by H. T. Webster
    (a) Janus-faced   (b) milquetoast   (c) jabberwock

2. Lewis Carroll's *Through the Looking Glass*
    (a) jabberwock   (b) braggadocio   (c) Babbitt

3. Spenser's *Faerie Queen*
    (a) Lothario   (b) braggadocio   (c) milquetoast

4. James Hilton's novel *Lost Horizon*
    (a) Shangri-la   (b) pandemonium   (c) benedict

5. from Shakespeare's *Much Ado About Nothing*
    (a) nemesis   (b) charlatan   (c) benedict

6. from the River Styx from Greek mythology
    (a) tawdry   (b) stygian   (c) Sisyphean

7. from Voltaire's work *Candide*
    (a) Panglossian   (b) quisling   (c) Babbitt

8. from a Roman god of doorways who could look both forward and backward
    (a) milquetoast   (b) June   (c) Janus-faced

9. from a novel by Sinclair Lewis about a middle-class, narrow-minded, smugly satisfied character
    (a) rodomontade   (b) Lothario   (c) Babbitt

10. a play by Richard B. Sheridan, *The Rivals*
    (a) jabberwock   (b) malaprop   (c) solecism

    C. Using the clues, write the words defined on page 150. The letters corresponding to the shaded squares will spell a turbulent word.

1. Person with no cultural values

2. Unintentional humorous misuse of language

3. Strict disciplinarian

4. Deliberately cruel

5. Undefeatable enemy

6. Ghastly

7. Empty boasting

8. Fake; fraud

9. Chance discovery of agreeable things

10. Traitor

11. Overzealous loyalty to a group or place

Lesson

6

protean: *adjective*

In Greek mythology Proteus was a sea god who had the power to **change** his shape at will. The current meaning is pretty much what the myth suggests—"changeableness." There is, however, an essential difference between the two. Proteus had the power to change the shape or form of his own body. Protean refers to changeability or variability in, for example, one's beliefs or point of view. In the case of some politicians it is one of the hallmarks of a successful bid for office. Say one thing today and something quite different tomorrow. Mood swings can be characterized as protean—from happiness to moroseness. To repeat, **changeability** is the key.

> *Context:* Depending upon whether or not he took his medicine, Earl's **protean** behavior sometimes made him seem to be an entirely different person from the one we knew.

Cassandra: *noun*

The word Cassandra can be used only with an upper case letter **C**. It finds its way into English via the classical Greek mythology. Kassandra, according to myth, was the daughter of Priam, King of Troy, and Hecuba, his wife. Kassandra was said to be a prophetess who managed to incur the wrath of Apollo, ancient Greek and Roman god of light, healing, music, poetry, and most important in this instance, prophecy. It is further suggested in legend that Apollo cursed Kassandra so that her prophecies would go unheeded despite the fact that they were true, and therein lies the irony. Today the word carries the same meaning: a person who prophesies doom or disaster; one who utters unheeded prophecies. Note the minor alteration in spelling from Kassandra to Cassandra.

> *Context:*   We always called Janice a **Cassandra** because, no matter what plans we made, she always said, "Oh! That will never work."

maudlin: *adjective*

In the Gospel of Saint Luke mention is made of a tearfully penitent sinner who, to demonstrate her love for Christ, bathed his feet using her tears. The woman's name was Mary Magdalene. The incident was so widely known about that soon artists portrayed her in their work with tear-filled eyes. In time her name became synonymous with "tearfully sentimental." The word itself is a corruption of Magdalene—**maudlin. Maudlin** means "crying at the slightest provocation, overly sentimental." Bear in mind that tears play a much lesser role in the word's usage today. One needs only to be in an overly sentimental frame of mind. Tears are not essential.

> *Context:*   The final scene in the movie must have been **maudlin** because all the people coming out of the theater were surreptitiously wiping their eyes.

Parthian shot: *noun*

Parthia was a country in western Asia near the Caspian Sea. It had an army that was noted for an unusual tactic when in battle. It was the custom of the Parthian army, which was made up mostly of horsemen, to shoot arrows in a rearward direction as they rode off in flight. Sometimes the flight was real and at other times it was feigned. Today the phrase means "to make a sharp telling remark or point as one is leaving"—a Parthian shot?

> *Context:*   Turning just as he reached the door, Alfred hurled one last **Parthian** shot at the school board because the members would not listen to his argument.

argonaut: *noun*

The word **argonaut** can be used with an upper or lower case letter **a**. When the former is used, Argonaut refers to sailors who sailed with Jason aboard the ship Argo in classical mythology. The legend recounts Jason's odyssey to return to his father the "golden fleece," a coat of pure gold taken from the "golden ram." When used with a lower case **a**, the word means an adventurer, someone on a quest to find a thing of great value which ultimately leads to great danger. The word comes from **Argo**, "the ship" + **nautes**, "sailors," sailors aboard the ship Argo. One can find other words that owe their origin in part to this same etymon: **astronaut, cosmonaut, nautical**. Check them out in a collegiate dictionary.

> *Context:*   Vikings were Scandinavian **argonauts** who plundered the coasts of northern and western Europe during the 8th, 9th, and 10th centuries.

Utopia: *noun*

Utopia is a fictional island created by Sir Thomas More in his work *Utopia* (1516). Sir Thomas More envisioned his creation as one that epitomized perfection—in law, politics, social conventions, etc. On occasion the word appears with a lower case letter **u**, carrying about the same denotation as the utopia envisioned by Sir Thomas More—a place of perfection in every aspect.

> *Context:*   The class assignment was to describe in some detail a global **Utopia**, one that would make it an ideal world in which to live.

tantalize: *verb*

The word **tantalize** is taken from classical Greek mythology. There is a fable concerning a king whose name was Tantalus. He committed many misdeeds and was ultimately condemned for all time to stand in a pool of clear water neck deep with fruit-laden trees above his head. This may not sound too bad until the details become known. Whenever Tantalus would bend his head to drink the cool spring water, it receded out of reach. When he reached up to pluck a succulent fruit, it too would move out of the reach of his grasp. This was to go on for all eternity. The word **tantalize** currently means "to torment, tease by heightening expectations that cannot be reached or attained." This is pretty much the situation that Tantalus got himself into.

> *Context:*   No scent is so **tantalizing** as homemade bread just out of the oven.

Pharisee: *noun*

Pharisees were members of an ancient Jewish sect that emphasized strict observance of Mosaic law. This procrustean view of Mosaic law led many Jews, more liberal in religious matters, to look upon the

Pharisees as hypocritical, self-righteous. They charged that the Pharisees observed scrupulously the letter of Mosaic law without regard for the spirit of the law. This led to another meaning of the word **pharisee** (lower case): "sanctimonious." Today the word means for the most part "sanctimonious," and most people who wish to express this idea of being self-righteous or hypocritical choose it rather than the word **pharisee**. The words are not synonyms. Pharisee is a noun and sanctimonious is an adjective.

> *Context:*   People are often characterized as **Pharisees** if they insist that their interpretation of the meaning of life is the only correct one.

quixotic: *adjective*

Don Quixote (kee HO tay) was the impractical, idealistic hero of the novel written by Miguel de Cervantes (1547-1616). Appalled by the poverty, starvation, and injustice so prevalent at the time, Cervantes created in the early 17th century *Don Quixote de la Mancha.* The work was a comedic satire of a society that was devoid of ideals, gallantry, compassion, and honor. Thus into our language the word **quixotic** was born, and it means "impractically idealistic or foolishly chivalrous." When we say that someone is the kind of person who would tilt at (charge against with lance at the ready) windmills, we refer to one of Quixote's misadventures in his gallant but somewhat impractical quest. Be that as it may, humanity embraces quixotic people who will "fight the unbeatable foe" and "dream the impossible dream." Quixote's odyssey in the final analysis was as gallant as it was foolish.

> *Context:*   James had the **quixotic** idea that if everyone in the world had the same amount of money there would be no famine or war.

roentgen: *noun*

Wilhelm Conrad Roentgen was the discoverer of the x-ray in 1895. He was awarded the Nobel Prize for his discovery in 1901. His discovery is too complex to explain here. Suffice it to say that radiation is measured in units known as roentgens. Perhaps in light of what we know today about radiation, the distinction is at best a dubious one. There is an amusing anecdote attached to the discovery of the x-ray. When Roentgen first made known his discovery, women became incensed. They thought the x-ray could unclothe them, leaving women at the mercy of unscrupulous users of the x-ray. At the time it was a very serious matter until women could be convinced that the x-ray had no such power.

Context: The comet surprised all the scientists because it gave off radiation that was measurable in **roentgens**.

EXERCISES

A. Match the definition in Column B with the word it defines in Column A.

Column A   Column B

 1. tantalize   a. sharp remark made as one is leaving
 2. Parthian shot   b. changeable
 3. Cassandra   c. a measure of radiation
 4. pharisaic   d. overly sentimental
 5. Utopia   e. to torment; to tease
 6. protean   f. impractically idealistic
 7. argonaut   g. self-righteous; sanctimonious
 8. roentgen   h. unheeded prophet of doom
 9. maudlin   i. adventurer on a dangerous quest
10. quixotic   j. a society with ideal laws and social
                        conditions

B. From the list below choose the word that best completes the meaning of each sentence.

protean   Parthian shot
Utopia   Cassandra
argonauts   tantalizing
roentgen   quixotic
Pharisee   maudlin

1. "That was a cheap _____ you made to Jake at the end of the party; you didn't give him a chance to reply," Arnie said to his friend.

2. In spite of his _____ portrayals of deathbed scenes, Charles Dickens is regarded as an outstanding English author.

3. Alex could never keep up with his fiancée's _____ and unpredictable moods.

4. Alice fantasized about winning a huge sweepstakes prize and creating a _____ for all the poor and homeless people in her city.

5. The _____ as a measure of radiation has been mainly supplanted by new high-tech methods.

6. Modern _____ may not be in search of gold, but they are usually on some potentially dangerous quest that they cannot abandon—such as Jane Goodall's study of gorillas in the wild.

7. Stephanie's friends nicknamed her _____ because she was always predicting the most pessimistic outcome to anything they anticipated doing.

8. Philip branded himself a holier-than-thou _____ because he told the principal the names of all the boys who had skipped school for the fun of it.

9. As he passed the bakery store, John was assailed by the most _____ odors he had yet experienced in his attempt to stay on a diet.

10. Trying to create a utopian world is the dream only of _____ persons; the realists are too cynical to believe such a world could ever be possible.

    C. If the boldface words in the sentences below are used correctly, write C. If not, write N.

1. If the **tantalizing** odors emanating from my aunt's kitchen were any indication, she was a super cook.

2. Because no one listened to any of **Cassandra's** prophecies, she became unbearably depressed.

3. James was elected president of the student council because his **protean** nature made him so dependable.

4. **Roentgens** are used to measure radon in the cellars of private homes.

5. The teacher said that Alicia's theme was not worth a high grade because of its **maudlin** sentimentality.

6. "Your view of the benefits promised by a new government is somewhat **utopian**," remarked the politician to his adversary.

7. John won first prize at the rifle range for coming nearest to the target with his **Parthian shot**.

8. Martin had the **quixotic** idea that if everyone in the world had the same amount of money there would be no more war.

9. My ten-year-old brother wanted to build a birch-bark canoe so he could explore the river in back of our summer camp as a true **argonaut** would do.

10. The judge was characterized as **pharisaic** because he was willing to allow any interpretation of the law that was offered by the defendant.

    D. Choose two words from the following: maudlin, Utopia, tantalize, quixotic. Use your words in two sentences of your own.

Lesson

7

myrmidon: *noun*

The word **myrmidon** is derived from classical mythology. Legend has it that Myrmidons were a class of people of ancient Thessaly who accompanied their king Achilles to the Trojan War. They were very faithful followers who did their king's bidding without question. Today the word means "a person who executes his master's orders without scruple." One might reasonably expect to find myrmidons in the military where unquestioning obedience to orders is expected of all personnel. The question then arises: at what point does one's conscience override this kind of thinking? What happened at Nuremberg where war criminals were tried in 1945-1946 is a case in point.

> *Context:* An ant colony is a perfect example of the word **myrmidons**, since each ant religiously carries out its assigned task even though this obedience may lead to its death.

peripatetic: *adjective*

Peripatetic (upper case) has to do with Aristotle, a Greek philosopher, and pertains to the Aristotelian school of philosophy. While teaching at the Lyceum in Athens, Aristotle would walk about constantly, and it became a kind of trademark. The word **peripatetic** comes from the Greek **peripatein**, and it means "to walk about." It is also used with a lower case **p**, and it essentially means what it did originally but in a more extended way. The traveling about was no longer restricted to walking. A plane, a ship, an auto would do just as well. So long as one moves from place to place, the word **peripatetic** can apply. Secretaries of State are peripatetic by the very nature of their jobs. On the other hand, a hobo may be characterized as peripatetic in that he moves from place to place without ever rooting himself to one location.

> *Context:* Elmer's mother said, "I can't stand this family's **peripatetic** lifestyle: your father travels constantly; your sister belongs to ten different school clubs; and you are off to football, basketball, or soccer practice every day."

narcissism: *noun*

Narkissos was a beautiful youth who, it is said in Greek legend, pined away for love of his own image as he saw it reflected in a pool. He prayed that his beauty would outlive him. Gradually he wasted away, but in his place grew the lovely flower we know today—the narcissus. Today the word means "excessive love or admiration for oneself." Many people believe that Hollywood is filled with narcissists. They may be right.

> *Context:* Just because I was admiring myself in the full-length mirror to see how good my Easter outfit looked on me, my brother accused me of being **narcissistic.**

tarantella: *noun*

Tarantella is the name of a dance, which has as its origin the city of Taranto in the south of Italy. From this city's name, the word **tarantula** was born, a hairy rather formidable appearing spider, which was not uncommon to the region. It was held that the bite of this spider caused tarantism, an uncontrollable urge to dance. To combat tarantism a dance was devised, a dance made up of whirling steps and lively music called the tarantella. It was supposed to cure tarantism, which swept through the area from the 15th through the 17th centuries. Actually tarantism had nothing to do with the tarantula. Rather it was a disease that medical science now believes to have been St. Vitus' Dance or Huntington's disease. It afflicts the nervous system and victims suffer uncontrollable bodily movements (like a dance), one obvious manifestation of the disease. These movements were what inhabitants of Taranto believed to be a dance—tarantism. This is, of course, a fanciful view of a disease that still persists to this day. A great deal remains to be done by medical researchers to combat such diseases of the central nervous system.

> *Context:* The **tarantella**, a very fast dance, was thought to protect one from tarantism, a malady resulting from the bite of a spider.

panacea: *noun*

The name of the ancient goddess of healing was Panacea (pan-a-SEE-a) from **pan**, "all" + **akos**, "cure." Today the word is for the most part used with lower case **p**, and it means "a cure-all, a remedy for all ills." Many purported panaceas can be found in the advertising slogans created by Madison Avenue ad men and women. There are panaceas to lose weight, panaceas to make us stronger, better looking, younger—you name it and it's there somewhere. All are touted as panaceas, but should one have used any of these products, they were probably big disappointments. There are other uses of the word, less frivolous. For example, there are those who would contend that there are no panaceas to eliminate wars, hunger, poverty, and injustice. The word is as you can see quite versatile. There are precious few panaceas that are in fact what they claim to be.

> *Context:* Ellen agreed to take part in an experiment designed to prove that a new medical miracle pill was not the **panacea** claimed by the company advertising it.

stentorian: *adjective*

Stentor was a Greek herald, a character in Homer's epic the *Iliad*. Heralds carried important news events and proclamations from place to place. Since there were no means of vocal amplification, they were required to have lusty voices that would carry the news events which were delivered in open squares, places not conducive to acoustical enhancement. **Stentorian** currently refers to "those who have loud, deep, resonating voices." Bear in mind that when used in this context, the word is not capitalized.

> *Context:* Rachel knew that Martin was right behind her in the crowd because she could identify his **stentorian** voice no matter where he was.

Sisyphean: *adjective*

From Greek mythology the word **Sisyphean** is born. Sisyphus was the despotically cruel king of Corinth who was condemned for all eternity to roll a large stone to the top of a steep hill in Hades. The catch was that as Sisyphus approached the hill's apex, the stone would somehow slip away from him and roll back down the hill. This went on and on and on for all time. An example might make the meaning of Sisyphean more clear. There are those who contend that drug rehabilitation is a Sisyphean task. The word means "requiring continued effort oftentimes without results that can justify the resources put into that effort." Don't lose sight of the fact that Sisyphean is always capitalized.

Context: All the work the dance committee did decorating the gym turned out to be a **Sisyphean** effort because the gym still looked like a gym when they got through.

Sword of Damocles: *noun*

Damocles according to Greek legend was an attendant at the court of a despotic ruler named Dionysius. Legend has it that Damocles in an effort to flatter the sovereign extolled Dionysius' happiness. Dionysius had other ideas. He sat Damocles at a banquet table with a sword suspended over his head, a sword that was secured by a single strand of hair. This was to demonstrate to Damocles the perilous nature of happiness and good fortune. Neither is to be taken for granted. Today the word denotes "an impending disaster or threat of a calamitous happening." Dionysius' point is well-taken, but perhaps he carried the exercise a bit too far.

Context: The possibility of terrorists defeating their efforts is a **Sword of Damocles** hanging over the heads of the delegates at the peace conferences.

bedlam: *noun*

The word **bedlam** finds its way into English via the Hospital of St. Mary of Bethlehem located in London, England. It served as an asylum for the mentally ill. Bedlam is a corruption of Bethlehem. One can almost hear the word bedlam in Bethlehem. The sounds are remarkably close. This hospital existed before psychiatric care was available to the insane. Patients were crowded into too small living quarters, oftentimes without medical care or a proper diet. It was not unheard of that patients spent their entire lives at this hospital once having been committed there. In any case, imagine the din, the confusion, the uproar that would emanate from such a place. The word bedlam means "a place or situation of noisy uproar and confusion."

Context: The announcement that there were no more tickets available for the concert turned the area near the box office into **bedlam**.

Pandora's box: *noun*

Pandora means in Greek "all-gifted." This is clearly a reference to Jupiter's "gifting" Pandora with exquisite beauty among a host of other human attributes that made her someone very special. This, of course, made Pandora very happy. Jupiter also gave her something else—a box that was never to be opened no matter what. Well, Pandora being human had an unrelenting urge to take a peek inside the box. Eventually her insatiable curiosity got the better of her, and she did open the box, only to loose a multitude of miseries not yet known to humankind, not ever. Hunger, pestilence, envy, hatred came streaming out of the box. Of course Pandora was devastated by what she had done and slammed shut the lid to the box, but, alas, it was too late. She did, however, manage to salvage one or two items in the box, and one of them was **hope**—humankind's salvation! Today the phrase "Pandora's box" means "that which is the source of many difficulties, none of which could have been foreseen." Albert Einstein, perhaps unwittingly, opened a Pandora's box when he discovered his now famous equation: $e = mc^2$ (energy = mass $\times$ the speed of light squared). Surely he did not envision Hiroshima.

Context: When public buildings and private homes were required to be insulated with asbestos, no one dreamed of the **Pandora's box** of problems that would ensue.

EXERCISES

A. Match the definition in Column B with the word it defines in Column A.

Column A

1. narcissism
2. Sisyphean
3. bedlam
4. myrmidon
5. Pandora's box
6. Sword of Damocles
7. peripatetic
8. panacea

Column B

a. obeying orders without question
b. moving from place to place
c. whirling, lively, or frenzied dancing
d. a cure-all; a solution for all ills
e. loud, deep voice
f. endless effort accomplishing nothing
g. source of insoluble problems
h. excessive self-love

9. stentorian   i. impending disaster
10. tarantella   j. place of noise and confusion; madhouse

B. If the boldface word(s) are used correctly in the following sentences, write C. If not, write N.

1. The autobiography of the adulated actor was so **narcissistic** that he lost his popularity with his once adoring public.

2. When **Pandora's box** was opened all the lovely flowers and beneficial insects were let loose upon the world.

3. The final exam in trigonometry was a **Sword of Damocles** hanging over my head.

4. To the mother of a large busy family, laundry, housekeeping, and shopping are **Sisyphean** tasks.

5. Completely ignoring the orders of the Green Beret leader, Arnold was termed a **myrmidon** by his mates.

6. His **peripatetic** pacing up and down the hospital corridor marked Jerome as a new father-to-be.

7. Once it was commonly believed that dancing the **tarantella** was a cure for the poisonous bite of a tarantula.

8. "Speak a little louder," the voice teacher instructed Barney, "your voice is so quiet and **stentorian** that we cannot understand a word you say."

9. Many people in the country thought that electing a new president would be a **panacea** for all the current ills of government.

10. **Bedlam** is a word derived from the name of the hospital St. Mary's of Bethlehem, which was a tranquil, quiet place specializing in short-term care for elderly people.

C. Choose the phrase or word below each sentence that best conveys the meaning of the sentence.

1. One of the show-stopping numbers in the musical revue was a version of the **tarantella** presented by the Italian Club.
(a) a chorale   (b) a dance   (c) a comedy skit

2. When Erwin's father was summoned to an audit by the income tax auditors, he said, "Until this is ironed out, I have the **sword of Damocles** hanging over my head."
(a) good fortune   (b) promise of protection   (c) threat of calamity

3. Classmates called Morris a **myrmidon** for stealing the midterm exam questions from the teacher's desk because the leader of his gang told him to do so.
(a) a person trying to overthrow a leader   (b) a person obeying orders without question   (c) a person obeying initiation requirements

4. The psychiatrist diagnosed Frank's **narcissism** as the reason for his lack of friends and inability to function in social situations.
(a) love of self   (b) love of flowers   (c) love of eating

5. Astronauts in the early space flights were not allowed to mingle with other people afterwards until they were thoroughly examined by medical experts for fear that outer space might prove to be a **Pandora's Box** of contaminating diseases.
(a) panacea   (b) source of unanticipated problems   (c) bedlam

6. Sitting at a desk from nine to five every day was not Lemuel's idea of a great career; so he decided to become a traveling salesman, which suited his **peripatetic** lifestyle.
(a) thoughtful   (b) questionable   (c) wandering

7. Touting his miraculous liquid tonic, the charlatan proclaimed it as a **panacea** for all kinds of aches and pains.
(a) cure   (b) soothing lotion   (c) herbal concoction

8. In **stentorian** tones the travel guide announced that our next stop on the trip would be Washington, D.C.
(a) modulated   (b) hoarse   (c) resonating

9. The argument between two of the hockey players resulted in **bedlam** when the whole crowd in the arena took sides.
(a) uproar   (b) fist fight   (c) order

10. The cleanup task following the tornado's wreckage of the neighborhood seemed like a **Sisyphean** endeavor to everyone.
(a) beneficial   (b) unending   (c) pitiful

   D. Choose two words from the following: peripatetic, panacea, Sisyphean, bedlam. Use your words in your own sentences.

Lesson

8

philippic: *noun*

Demosthenes in the 4th century B.C. delivered speeches harshly critical of Philip II of Macedon. From the name Philip the word **philippic** is derived. Later the word broadened its scope to include orations of Cicero against Antony in 44 B.C. The word **philippic** currently is "any strong verbal denunciation characterized by bitter invective." Demosthenes was a prominent Athenian orator and statesman (384-322 B.C.).

> *Context:* After the presidential primaries were over, candidates who had previously been delivering bitter **philippics** against each other suddenly became friends again.

draconian: *adjective*

The word **draconian** is also derived from a man's name. Draco was an Athenian statesman and lawmaker. Draco's laws were proverbially harsh and pitilessly severe. They were both known and feared far and wide. Draconian measures more likely than not can be found in autocratic forms of governance where leaders have unlimited power to enact any laws they choose. The word has wide application. A judge, for example, can sentence a defendant to a severely harsh prison term which could be characterized as draconian.

> *Context:* Students protested what they considered to be a **draconian** dress code required by the school administration.

165

rodomontade: *noun*

Italian literature provides the lexical backdrop for the word **rodomontade**. Matteo Biardo (1434-1494) authored a work *Orland Inamorata* in which a character named Rodomonte appeared. He was a blustery fellow caught up in his perception of self-importance—a conceited braggart. From Rodomonte the word **rodomontade** emerged, and it currently reflects precisely those characteristics and traits attributed to Biardo's Rodomonte. Another lesson already studied presented a word very similar in meaning. Perhaps you might recall the word—**braggadocio**, which means "pretentious cockiness, empty boasting."

> *Context:* The school bully intimidated the younger boys by keeping up a constant **rodomontade** about his fighting ability, a trick he never used again after Jason proved him to be nothing but a noisy braggart.

epicure: *noun*

Epicurus was a Greek philosopher (circa 342-270 B.C.) whose philosophy embraced pleasure as the highest good. Today the word's meaning is more restricted in that the pleasure alluded to so broadly in Epicurus' philosophy is more pointed in the direction of art, music, drama, literature, and food and drink. **Epicures** are connoisseurs having cultivated a refined taste for the arts and culinary pursuits. Several words come close to the meaning of epicure: gastronome, gourmet, and gourmand. However, there is a distinction to be made. The three words mentioned suggest eating fine food and imbibing the most expensive spirits. That's it: food and drink are the only concerns of gourmands, gourmets, and gastronomes. This is, of course, not the case with epicures, whose tastes run far beyond food and drink. One other point. Gourmands, gourmets, and gastronomes eat heartily, sometimes excessively. Again this is not true of epicures.

> *Context:* Invited to dinner at the home of their new neighbors, my parents were almost overwhelmed by the **epicurean** feast they were served.

Pollyanna: *noun or adjective*

The novel *Pollyanna* (1913) is a fictional creation of Eleanor Porter. Pollyanna is a character in Porter's work who was an irrepressible optimist, finding good in everything and everybody. It is this quixotic, almost slavish, commitment to optimism that makes the word carry with it a less than complimentary image. Its current meaning suggests that only a fool could be so dotingly optimistic and not see a dark side to human nature.

Context: Ella was such a **Pollyanna** that it was impossible to have a serious discussion with her in any controversial subject.

caesarean section: *noun*

A **caesarean section** is a method of delivery that removes the fetus from the mother's uterus by cutting through the abdominal walls and the uterus. As one might guess, it bears the Caesar name, specifically Julius Caesar, who was said to have been born in this manner. It might be worth mentioning that the Caesars have contributed other words to the language: July for Julius; August for Augustus; and the Julian calendar for Julius once again. Let us not forget the words **kaiser, tsar**, and **czar**, all of which are derived from the Caesar family name.

Context: Delivered by **caesarean section**, the twins were healthy and noisy from the moment they were born.

sybarite: *noun*

Sybaris was an ancient Greek city located in what is now the south of Italy. It no longer exists, having been destroyed in 510 B.C. Sybaris had a reputation for its vast wealth and the luxurious life style of its inhabitants. They wanted for nothing. The word **sybarite** is the only remaining legacy of the city Sybaris. It is currently used almost exclusively with lower case **s**, and it means "a person who is devoted to luxury, opulence, and pleasure in general." This pretty well sums up what the ancient people of Sybaris expected of life. The word currently carries an uncomplimentary connotation. Most people would agree that there is more to life than material wealth.

Context: With the death of Dorian Gray (in the novel by Oscar Wilde), his portrait revealed the ravages of the **sybaritic** life he had led.

shylock: *noun*

The word **shylock** currently means "a lender of money at unlawfully exorbitant interest rates." In a word, shylocks are usurers, those who charge excessive interest rates on loans. Shylocks are generally ruthless in the conduct of their business, and the word business is used loosely. It is common knowledge that mobsters engage in this practice, and they have been designated as shylocks. The origin of the word is a play by William Shakespeare, *The Merchant of Venice*, in which a money lender named Shylock plays a pivotal role. From Shakespeare's Shylock the word **shylock** was born.

> *Context:*   Rick realized that in order to pay his debts he would have to deal with money lenders who in fact were no more than unscrupulous **shylocks**.

somniloquy: *noun*
Somnus was the ancient Roman god of **sleep**. From this the word **somniloquy** is derived, and it means "talking in one's sleep." The Roman god **Somus** + **log**, "to talk," go to make the word. There are other derivatives of this word that have the same origin: **somnific**, **somnolent**, and **somnambulate**. Check a collegiate dictionary or un-abridged dictionary to determine their meanings, especially the word somnambulate. Which do you think has to do with sleep walking?

> *Context:*   Arnold didn't know he was a **somniloquist** until his tent-mates at summer camp said, "Wow! You'd be surprised at the things you say when you talk in your sleep."

Lilliputian: *adjective or noun*
An Irish writer by the name of Jonathan Swift (1667-1745) wrote a satirical novel called *Gulliver's Travels* (1726); in it there was an imaginary place called Lilliput, and of course the inhabitants were **Lilliputians**. What set them apart from all other humans was their diminutive size—they were small, actually tiny people. Gulliver had an exciting encounter with Lilliputians that makes very interesting reading. The word's current meaning is "small," but small in the sense of being petty or narrow. It also characterizes those people who have very little influence. (See the word **feckless**, Lesson 14, Dimension One, Part One.)

> *Context:*   Amy decided she could not marry Joe because he was always preoccupied with such **lilliputian** details that he was extremely boring.

EXERCISES

A. Match the definition in Column B with the word it defines in Column A.

Column A

1. Pollyanna
2. sybarite
3. philippic
4. Lilliputian
5. somniloquy
6. caesarean section
7. epicure
8. draconian
9. shylock
10. rodomontade

Column B

a. fastidious connoisseur
b. severe; rigorous
c. surgical delivery of a fetus
d. incurable optimist; Panglossian
e. pretentious bragging; bluster
f. one devoted to pleasure and luxury; hedonist
g. verbal denunciation; tirade; jeremiad
h. talking in one's sleep
i. narrow-minded; petty
j. a relentless creditor; demanding one's pound of flesh

B. From the words listed below, choose the word that best gives the meaning of each sentence.

somniloquy   shylock
philippic   Lilliputian
rodomontade   draconian
epicurean   Pollyanna
sybarite   caesarean section

1. "Boy! are you a _____," Daniel exclaimed when his brother refused to lend him ten dollars unless he repaid the money with interest.

2. In his public _____ castigating his political opponent, Zachary gave vent to all his hatred of the man.

3. Given to _____, Alice never knew whether to believe us or not when we told her what she had unknowingly revealed to us.

4. Denise was such a _____ that she found something positive to say about every disaster that befell, however traumatic.

5. Because he was wealthy enough to live the life of a _____, no
one could understand why Richard Cory (in Edward Arlington
Robinson's poem) ended his own life.

6. Sentenced by _____ law to be a galley slave for stealing a loaf
of bread, Jean Valjean, protagonist of *Les Miserables*, was transformed by the bishop's kindness.

7. First impressed by Erik's _____, the students in speech class
soon learned that he was none of the things he proclaimed to be.

8. The surgical technique of performing a _____ has saved the
lives of many a mother and child.

9. Accepting an invitation to dine at Marcel's home meant that one
would experience an _____ feast surrounded by his latest eclec-
tic purchases of modern art.

10. "My opponent's diminutive stature is paralleled only by his
_____ mind," commented the incumbent senator to the members of the press.

C. Choose the definition that is most correct for each word.

1. draconian
(a) dragon   (b) harsh   (c) deacon   (d) con man

2. shylock
(a) barber   (b) locksmith   (c) heartless moneylender
(d) Godfather of the mob

3. Pollyanna
(a) eternal optimist   (b) name of a parrot   (c) many-sided geo-
metrical form   (d) polygamist

4. rodomontade
(a) sermon   (b) braggadocio   (c) merry-go-round   (d) robot

5. lilliputian
(a) narrow-minded   (b) huge   (c) flowerlike   (d) captive

6. philippic
(a) nickname   (b) priestly   (c) denunciation   (d) famous artist

7. somniloquy
   (a) sleepwalking (b) drowsiness (c) sleeping pill (d) talking in one's sleep

8. sybaritic
   (a) ascetic (b) hedonistic (c) puritanical (d) suicidal

9. epicure
   (a) philosopher (b) connoisseur (c) Spartan (d) author's name

10. caesarean section
    (a) part of an army (b) microscopic slide (c) method of delivering a child (d) part of a calendar

   D. Choose two words from the following: epicure, sybarite, somniloquy, Lilliputian. Use your words in two sentences of your own.

Lesson

9

hades: *noun*

In classical mythology **hades** (lower case) was the netherworld or, put less euphemistically, hell. **Hades** with upper case **H** was the god of this underworld. Since Hades was the dispenser of worldly goods and riches, he was able to arrange deals with many sinners by providing them with whatever they wanted most in life. This, however, was a **quid pro quo** arrangement. In exchange for his favors, one had to give his or her soul to Hades, and consequently was consigned to hades for all eternity. There is a popular saying: "Give the devil his due." Well, he has done quite well linguistically. Many words in English are derived from his or her name or a derivation thereof: Satan, Pluto, Devil, Mephistopheles, Prince of Darkness, and Beelzebub, a word coined by John Milton in his epic poem "Paradise Lost." Other phrases are also references to Hades—"between the devil and the deep blue sea" (between two undesirable alternatives), or "raise the devil" (to cause a commotion); finally, there is the expression "devil of a . . ." as in "he had a devil of a time . . ." (hellish or extremely difficult). In this context Hades has done quite well, better perhaps than he rightly deserves. Incidentally, one of his names, Pluto, given to him by the Romans, is not to be confused with a planet in our solar system by the same name. They have nothing whatever to do with each other.

Context: The mythical **hades** of Greek mythology seems more humid and stygian than the hell of Jonathan Edwards' philosophy.

jacquard: *noun*

Jacquard is a fabric that is made on a loom, a Jacquard loom, invented by a Frenchman, J.M. Jacquard (1752-1834). The fabric is elaborately designed as in a brocade, a heavy cloth with a raised design, or damask, a reversible fabric with patterns. Incidentally, the word **damask** comes from the name of a city in Syria. Can you guess its name? No matter, the city is **Damascus**, where damask was first made. Jacquard is to this day a popular fabric used in making furniture coverings and also women's apparel.

> *Context:*   My mother went shopping the minute she saw that **jacquard** comforters were going on sale at the local department store.

odyssey: *noun*

The Greek poet Homer wrote an epic work, the *Odyssey*. In it Homer recounts Odysseus' ten-year journey in his attempt to return to his home in Ithaca following the Trojan War. Homer describes the adventure, the dangers that Odysseus faced, and from this the current word **odyssey** is born. It means "any series of wanderings or journeys that put the traveler in situations of extreme hardship and noteworthy experiences." Admiral Peary's trek to the North Pole is a classic example of an odyssey. This use of the word appears in lower case always. Only references to Homer's epic appear in upper case.

> *Context:*   Ralph hoped to complete an epic **odyssey** in his hot air balloon, but he was forced down by the weather only ten miles from his starting point.

gargantuan: *adjective*

A French writer named Rabelais wrote a novel *Gargantua and Pantagruel* (1532). In it appears a character named Gargantua, an amiable king who was enormously large with an even larger appetite for food and drink. From Gargantua, the king, the word **gargantuan** originates. It currently means "of enormous, gigantic size or proportion." In Japan sumo wrestlers are gargantuan in size, oftentimes weighing four hundred pounds or more. Keep in mind that one can have a gargantuan appetite for such things as life itself. Epicures, for instance, might have gargantuan appetites for the pleasantries in life: good food, music, and art. They can't get enough of them.

Context: The **gargantuan** "papier-mâché" sculpture that Lester had made for the art show collapsed of its own size only minutes after he was awarded the first prize.

stoicism: *noun*
Zeno was an ancient Greek philosopher who lived before the birth of Christ. He founded a school and an accompanying philosophy which promoted a complete repression of emotion. One should not be moved by either joy or grief, especially to those occurrences that are unavoidable—death, for example. Generally the word is used to characterize those who are able to endure grief or pain without complaining or demonstrating emotion. The word comes from the Stoic school of philosophy founded by Zeno. The adjective form is **stoical**.

Context: Milton's **stoic** acceptance of the death of his 16-year-old dog kept the rest of us from being maudlin.

herculean: *adjective*
Greek fable celebrates a hero named Hercules who was said to possess exceptional strength, courage, and size. He was the son of Zeus. Hercules won immortality by performing twelve tasks put before him by Hera, wife of Zeus and queen of heaven. The word currently denotes that which possesses extraordinary strength, unstinting courage, and gargantuan size. The words **gargantuan, titanic**, and **herculean** are quite close in meaning, although they are not actually synonyms. There are shades of difference. These differences are both denotative and connotative in kind.

Context: When Ray spent a month at his uncle's riding school, earning his way by cleaning the stables, he said, "Now I know why this is called a **herculean** task."

Kafkaesque: *adjective*
Kafka was an Austrian writer with a bent for the surreal, a 20th-century literary and artistic movement that attempts to express the workings of the subconscious mind by fantastic imagery, oftentimes taken from dreams. The more bizarre the images the better. The word **Kafkaesque** relates to that which is surreal and usually accompanied by a sense of impending danger. In Kafka's "Metamorphosis" the main character awakens one morning to find that he has been transformed into a loathesome insect. This personifies surrealism. This is Kafkaesque!

Context: Our whole adventure of exploring the underground caves was so unreal as to be **Kafkaesque**.

halcyon: *adjective*
The genus **Halcyon** included various kinds of birds, especially the kingfisher, which was said to have the power to calm winds and waves at sea. Ancient legend has it that the halcyon nested at sea and calmed the sea during the time of winter solstice. In classical Greek mythology this bird was known as **Alcyone**, not too far removed from **halcyon**. Its contemporary meaning extends to almost anything: **halcyon** weather or the **halcyon** days of one's youth. Calm, peaceful, prosperous, carefree, joyous, and tranquil are a few synonyms for the word **halcyon**.

Context: The **halcyon** days of an unusually warm autumn gave way suddenly to a snowstorm in October.

mercurial: *adjective*
The Roman god Mercury served as messenger for all gods. One can suppose that gods wished their messages delivered swiftly, so Mercury had to move quickly in order to placate them. This is one meaning of **mercurial**—"swift." The word also means "changeable," which implies **swiftness**. The change must be quick. For example, a person who has mood swings from unbounded joy to the depths of utter despair in relatively short periods of time may be said to have a mercurial emotional bent. One can have a mercurial temper, or the stock market can reflect mercurial changes in performance. The word can be used in a wide variety of ways.

Context: His **mercurial** changes of allegiance made it difficult to know where the politician stood on party policies.

Junoesque: *adjective*
Juno in Roman mythology was the goddess of the Pantheon, a temple erected in honor of all gods: **pan**, "all" + **theos**, "god." She was the patroness of marriage and the well-being of women. Currently the word embraces the idea of stately bearing, a beauty that is both imposing and esthetic. Upper case **J** is required in all uses of the word **Junoesque**.

Context: Fred fell madly in love (for the umpteenth time) with the new girl in school because, as he constantly babbled, she was so **Junoesque**.

EXERCISES

A. Match the definition in Column B with the word it defines in Column A.

Column A

1. Kafkaesque
2. jacquard
3. mercurial
4. Junoesque
5. hades
6. gargantuan
7. herculean
8. halcyon
9. odyssey
10. stoicism

Column B

a. repression of emotions
b. hell
c. gigantic; enormous
d. of exceptional strength, size, or courage
e. brocade; heavy cloth
f. series of journeys or wanderings
g. swift; changeable
h. stately; imposing beauty
i. surreal; bizarre
j. peaceful; prosperous

B. From the list of words below, choose the one that best completes the meaning of each sentence.

jacquard   hades
herculean   gargantuan
odyssey   Junoesque
Kafkaesque   halcyon
mercurial   stoicism

1. Impressed by Everett's _____ while the fishhook was being removed from his cheek, the doctor praised him for being helpful during the operation.

2. Frances kept a fascinating journal of her _____ from New England to Japan, detailing all the trauma, laughter, and learning along the way.

3. Janet's mood changes were so _____ that none of her friends could predict her behavior from one minute to the next.

4. Woven into the rich pattern of the _____ drapery was the symbolic emblem of the family coat of arms.

5. The committee members who volunteered to clean up the gym after the junior prom looked at each other in despair, wondering if they would ever accomplish the _____ task.

6. Kirk made his snowbound classmates indescribably envious when he wrote postcards about the _____ weather in Florida during spring break.

7. The judges agreed enthusiastically in their choice of Miss America because of her _____ stature and sophisticated philosophy of life.

8. The _____ of Greek mythology was not nearly so frightening as the hell of Dante's *Inferno*.

9. Once they watched Freddie satisfying his _____ appetite, the campers realized why he weighed over two hundred pounds.

10. The movie had such a _____ quality that we couldn't throw off the unreality of it even though we stopped for hamburgers on the way home.

C. If the boldface word is used correctly in the sentence, write C. If not, write N.

1. Only five feet tall and chunky as a butterball, Esmerelda was popular because of her **Junoesque** stature.

2. Esther remembered the **halcyon** days of her childhood as the happiest time of her life.

3. **Hades** is a mythical place where—as in *The Mikado*—"the punishment fits the crime."

4. Because of his **stoical** philosophy, Andrew always raged and ranted whenever his plans miscarried.

5. Elaine's evening gown, fashioned from a richly embroidered **jacquard**, was as light and diaphanous as silk.

6. Lisa's **mercurial** temperament made her decisions about her life completely impossible to understand.

7. The wind was so strong that holding the balloons in check was a **herculean** effort as the Macy's Thanksgiving Day paraders defied the elements.

8. When we recited the **odyssey** of our nightmarish auto trip through the worst blizzard of the year, our friends sympathized with us for the travail we had undergone.

9. The Lilliputians described in Gulliver's first account of his travels were **gargantuan** people.

10. My dream had such a **Kafkaesque** quality that I awoke in complete confusion, frightened by the grotesque images I held in my memory.

   D. Choose two of the following words: odyssey, stoicism, herculean, mercurial. Use the words in two of your own sentences.

Lesson
10

Achilles' heel: *noun*

Achilles was the most formidable Greek warrior of the Trojan War and hero of Homer's epic the *Iliad*. He was slain when Paris, a Trojan prince and abductor of Helen of Troy, wounded him in the heel, the only vulnerable spot on Achilles' body. The phrase **Achilles' heel** means "an area, or a part, perhaps even a feature that is exclusively or at the least especially vulnerable." Today the weakness alluded to is seldom associated with anything physical. Rather, it is to character or emotional make-up that the word applies. For example, one's Achilles' heel may be an obsession with gambling, or it may be having too large an ego. In either instance, one is made susceptible to criticism or attack. Incidentally, there is a large tendon, the Achilles tendon, that runs from the foot to the calf muscle in the leg, which if damaged can incapacitate a person. It is, in a word, the most vulnerable part of the foot. Sound familiar?

Context: My aunt had eight cats because her tenderness for stray animals was her **Achilles' heel**.

titan: *noun*

In Greek mythology there was a family of giants, the offspring of Uranus and Gaea. These giants were known as Titans. When used in this context, upper case is required. When the word is used with a lower case letter **t**, it has a much broader reference: "a person or thing of colossal dimensions, strength, or influence." For example, Henry Ford is looked upon as a titan of the automobile industry. There are titans in the political arena, technological, and educational fields. In terms of a thing, consider the proposition that IBM is a titan among manufacturers of business machines.

Context: The **titans** of the sports world tried to agree on where and how they should build a new multi-sports arena.

galvanize: *verb*

To **galvanize** is "to arouse to awareness or action." **Galvanize** is also used in a scientific context: "to shock or stimulate by using an electrical current." An example of the former usage is a group of people who are galva-.ized to action; it is as though they were subjected to an electrical charge. An idea may be substituted for the electrical charge, an idea such as the attack on Pearl Harbor that galvanized the American people to work together to defeat a common enemy. The word is derived from an Italian named Luigi Galvani who discovered the principle of galvanism, electricity produced by chemical action.

Context: The football team was **galvanized** into action by the cheering fans.

flora and fauna: *noun*

Flora was the Roman goddess of flowers. Currently the word includes much more than flowers. All plants of a particular region are referred to as **flora:** "vegetation of all kinds." **Fauna**, on the other hand, comes from the Roman goddess Faunus, an ancient Italian woodland deity, and it includes all the animals of a given region. Together these words just about cover anything that can be found on earth, excluding minerals, ores, etc. Oftentimes these words are used as a pair—the **flora and fauna** of the region provided scientists with new information about prehistoric beings who inhabited this part of the world.

Context: One of the most gratifying experiences of traveling is becoming acquainted first-hand with the **flora and fauna** of other climates than one's own.

euthanasia: *noun*

The ancient personification of death was **Thanatos**. When **thanatos** is combined with the Greek etymon **eu**, "good; well," the word **euthanasia** is formed. Literally in Greek it means "a good death," which appears to be an oxymoron, a phrase in which one word contradicts another as in "almost perfect." However, in this instance neither word contradicts the other. "Good death" relates to those suffering terminal illnesses accompanied by extreme and chronic pain. Might not death under these circumstances be welcomed? Euthanasia takes on two forms: active and passive. The former requires an overt act that precipitates the patient's death—injecting a lethal dose of drug into the patient. The latter, passive euthanasia, is indirect. For example, life-sustaining support is withheld from the patient. The patient is then allowed to die a natural death. To remove intravenous feeding tubes from a patient is one form of passive euthanasia. **Active euthanasia** is unlawful in any form. **Passive euthanasia** is permitted if specific conditions are met: a patient's living will indicating this is his or her wish; a physician's assessment of the patient's illness, and family concurrence.

> *Context:*   The question of whether or not **euthanasia** for human beings is ethical has become a prominent issue in society.

boycott: *verb*

The word **boycott** has a history dating back over 100 years—to 1880. At the time there was an organization known as the Irish Land League headed up by its founder Michael Davitt. One of the goals was reduced rental charges. Captain Charles Cunnigham Boycott (1832-1897), British estate manager in County Mayo, refused to accept the reduced rental fees, holding out for what he thought were fair rental charges imposed by his employer. He was the very first to suffer the consequence of not complying with the League's aims—ostracism. He was shunned by all; he was villified by the tenant farmers. From this, the word boycott was born. It was first used by the Irish as far back as 1880, and the word caught on and was used in both Europe and the United States. The current meaning of the word boycott is "to join in refusing to deal with or patronize a seller, employer, or any other person or group." In effect, to boycott is to do what the Irish Land League did as a protest—complete ostracism. Words take strange paths in order to find their way into English, and this is one such case.

> *Context:*   The powerful countries agreed to **boycott** trade with those countries whose politics they thought to be threatening.

laconic: *adjective*

Laconia was a region inhabited by Spartans and located in the southwest peninsula of Greece. Its capital city was Sparta. Spartans, a stoic people, acquired the reputation for using speech sparingly, saying only what was vital to communication. From Laconia the word

laconic is derived, and it means essentially what was attributed to Spartans—"the sparing use of language." There is an anecdote that might help you to remember the word. President Calvin Coolidge was said to have been one of America's most laconic statesmen. One evening at a banquet given in his honor, a comely young reporter bet her coworker that she could get President Coolidge to say more than two words. The wager having been made, the young reporter approached the president and whispered that she had just made a wager that she could get him to say more than two words. Coolidge looked up at her and replied laconically, "You lose."

> *Context:*   Generally, my father's **laconic** reply to my request to use the family car was, "No."

colossus: *noun*

One of the Seven Wonders of the World was a 100-foot-tall bronze statue of Apollo, ancient Greek and Roman god of light, healing, music, and manly beauty among other things. It is believed to have been located in the harbor of Rhodes, a Greek seaport, and built between 292 and 280 B.C. The statue was destroyed by an earthquake in 224 B.C. Eventually what was left of the statue was sold as scrap metal. Legend has it that Apollo stood astride the entrance to the harbor, and all ships entering or leaving Rhodes sailed between his outstretched legs. The word **colossus** comes from the Greek **kolossōs**, "giant statue." When referring to the statue, upper case is required—**Colossus**. In all other instances, lower case is appropriate. Today the word means "anything of gigantic size or power." The adjective form is **colossal**. Finally, **gargantuan** and **titan**, words already studied, are close enough in meaning to be considered synonyms.

> *Context:*   When we finally finished the first draft of the class yearbook, we found that we had put together such a **colossal** amount of material that we had to start editing carefully.

solecism: *noun*

A **solecism** violates the conventions of acceptable grammar. Solecisms are common to language use, perhaps too common. For example, the phrase "between you and I" is a solecism. (The pronoun should be **me**, not **I**.) **Solecism's** lexical heritage is quite interesting. It comes from the name of a city in ancient Greece, Soli, an Athenian colony, where a substandard dialect was spoken. From Soli the word solecism came into being, "an incorrect use of language."

Context: Because of common usage, especially noticeable on TV programs, many **solecisms** in the American language have been admitted as acceptable by grammarians.

babble: *noun*

The Bible has made a number of contributions to English, and the word **babble** is one of them. The Book of Genesis contains a parable, a story designed to convey a moral lesson, concerning the ancient city of Babel (note the different spellings). Its inhabitants believed that the easiest way to heaven was to build a tower and simply climb one's way to heaven. This tower came to be known in the parable as the Tower of Babel. The parable continues by telling of God's displeasure with this effort. There were no easy ways to the Gates of Heaven. One had to work hard at it for a lifetime, and towers were not a part of the scheme. God punished the tower builders by having each inhabitant of Babel speak a language that was unknown to any other person. The result was, of course, a great deal of incomprehensible gibberish, and this is precisely the word's current meaning—"unintelligible language, gibberish, or confusion of sounds or voices," all of which are consistent with the biblical reference to Babel. The word Babel comes from the Assyrian and Babylonian, and it means "gate of god."

Context: **Babbling** incoherently, the stranger at the door seemed to be incredibly frightened by something out there in the dark.

EXERCISES

A. Match the definition in Column B with the word it defines in Column A.

Column A

1. titan
2. flora and fauna
3. babble
4. laconic
5. Achilles' heel
6. solecism

Column B

a. vulnerable spot
b. to arouse to awareness or action
c. painless death
d. a person or thing of gigantic strength, size, or achievement
e. someone of enormous stature or power

7. euthanasia   f. vegetable and animal life
8. galvanize   g. terse, concise; sparing of words
9. colossus   h. a nonstandard or incorrect use of language
10. boycott   i. ostracize; blackball
                       j. unintelligible language

    B. Choose the word or phrase below each sentence that best conveys the meaning of its boldface word or phrase.

1. The shipwrecked sailors spent many days exploring the island for edible **flora and fauna** because they had no idea when or if they would be rescued.
(a) ferns   (b) fawns   (c) plants and animals

2. Because the lecturer was **laconic**, the students found it easy to outline the main topics of the lecture.
(a) concise   (b) learned   (c) lazy

3. Although Gerald was so good-looking and had such a resounding voice that he was cast as the juvenile lead in the play, we soon discovered that acting in front of an audience was his **Achilles' heel**.
(a) strength   (b) obsession   (c) vulnerable point

4. Paul Bunyan and Babe, his big blue ox, are among the most **colossal** figures in American folklore.
(a) beloved   (b) gigantic   (c) colorful

5. Is it possible that the *Titanic* was so named because it was built to be a **titan** among the luxury liners of its day?
(a) giant   (b) beacon   (c) Lilliputian

6. Frank was not hired to be a guide through the museum because his spoken English was peppered with **solecisms**.
(a) imprecations   (b) grammatical errors   (c) tasteless comic comments

7. Medical leaders and religious leaders continue to debate about the ethical propriety of allowing **euthanasia** to be practiced on human beings.
(a) mercy killing   (b) eulogizing   (c) experimentation

8. The student body was **galvanized** into frenzied cheering when the home team beat the visitors by one point in the basketball tournament.

(a) lulled (b) electrified (c) forced

9. Sitting in the theater near people who **babble** constantly throughout the film makes me so angry that I cannot enjoy the movie.
   (a) eat (b) fidget (c) prattle

10. The student union voted to **boycott** the intramural games because they felt that the underclass members had been ignored when the teams were chosen.
    (a) underwrite (b) blackball (c) advertise

C. Using the clues, write the words defined below. The letters corresponding to the shaded squares will spell a terse, concise word.

1						
2						
3								
4					
5						
6				
7					

1. nonstandard use of language

2. prattle; jabber

3. vulnerable spot

4. vast in size

5. to arouse to action

6. something great in power, size, or achievement

7. to ostracize

D. Choose two of the following words: Achilles' heel, flora and fauna, euthanasia, boycott. Use your words in two sentences of your own.

REVIEW OF LESSONS 1 - 10

A. From the list of words below the selection, choose the word that best completes the meaning of the sentences.

Making a list of all the words that have come into the English language from Greek or Roman mythology would be a ___1___ undertaking, requiring a ___2___ effort.

A reporter, for instance, writing a description of the winner of a beauty contest might characterize her as ___3___, comparing her to a goddess. The reporter might go on to say that another contestant lost the title because her ___4___ was her inability to express herself coherently in front of an audience.

When America sent voyagers to the moon, the crew members were on an ___5___ as adventurous as the original journey of Odysseus.

Once the spaceship was airborne the astronauts had ___6___, so to speak. They were successful, however, in spite of possible unknown dangers more threatening than anything that came flying out of ___7___.

In spite of ___8___-like prophecies of doom and failure, the moon voyagers became ___9___ of space travel; they were not ___10___ about their adventures when giving interviews; on the other hand, they showed no signs of ___11___ even though they were being honored by the whole world.

titans	Sisyphean
Achilles' heel	narcissism
herculean	crossed the Rubicon
Pandora's box	odyssey
stoical	Junoesque
Cassandra	

REVIEW OF LESSONS 1 - 10

B. Which word fits into the context of the sentence preceding it?

1. A football game caused the crowd to lose control and to do untold damage to the stadium, including ripping down the goalposts.
   (a) tenebrous   (b) pandemonium   (c) serendipity

2. The gruesome movie depicted cruel and inhuman torture being inflicted on innocent women and children and was characterized by movie reviewers as "too horrific for teens."
   (a) macabre   (b) procrustean   (c) sardonic

3. The mayor's position on the matter was harshly inflexible, so much so that the entire Town Council voted against it.
   (a) tawdry   (b) procrustean   (c) saturnine

4. Although she believed her attire fashionable, in truth it was plain for all to see that it was lacking in good taste.
   (a) serendipitous   (b) draconian   (c) tawdry

5. The plot that was hatched by the military junta was both complex in its design and devious in its intent.
   (a) Byzantine   (b) stoical   (c) mercurial

6. The patron in the restaurant devoured a meal that would fill an elephant's stomach, and his waiter marveled at such an enormous appetite.
   (a) Kafkaesque   (b) gargantuan   (c) herculean

7. His companies when combined made the business magnate a true colossus in the field of electronics; he had no peer.
   (a) titan   (b) draconian   (c) panderer

8. James, aside from his narrow-mindedness, had not an original thought in his entire life.
   (a) procrustean   (b) benedict   (c) Babbitt

9. Steve had a penchant for changing his position on company matters, so much so that he was referred to by his coworkers as the "company chameleon."
   (a) a Pharisee   (b) an argonaut   (c) protean

10. The candidate's plan for the city's future was so impractically idealistic that it was rejected out of hand by the voters at the polls.
(a) narcissistic   (b) quixotic   (c) peripatetic

   C. Write T if the boldface word(s) contributes correctly to the meaning of the sentence. Write F if it does not.

1. **Malapropisms** are humorous language mistakes and their use should be encouraged at school.

2. The word **Babbitt** carries with it a positive frame of reference.

3. A **charlatan** according to Webster is one who lives in a town in Italy named Cerreta.

4. A **Panglossian** view of the world is much like that held by **quixotic** persons.

5. Those whose approach to life is **maudlin** seldom have many friends.

6. To **bowdlerize** a piece of writing is to edit it prudishly.

7. A cloth called **jacquard** is a **damask** made in Damascus.

8. The **halcyon** days of the Vietnamese War are remembered vividly by those who fought in it.

9. Any woman, or at least most women, would be pleased, overjoyed to be described as **Junoesque**.

10. Most English teachers when reading student themes are on the lookout for **solecisms** of one kind or another.

   D. Below you will find short passages followed by 4 word choices. You are to determine which of them fits into the context of the passage. Keep in mind that there may be more than one response. There may be two, three, or all four that are correct.

1. Brian met his wife Miriam for the first time at, of all places, a baseball game between the N.Y. Mets and the St. Louis Cardinals. He was immediately struck by her statuesque beauty graced by an equally enchanting personality. It was indeed a fortunate happenstance that they both chose to attend that game,

or they might otherwise have never met. Brian might still be the confirmed bachelor that he made out to be. They were married in less than six months after they first met.

Which of the following characterize or name either Brian or Miriam? There is also a reference to their chance meeting in one of the words.
(a) benedict   (b) bedlam   (c) Junoesque   (d) serendipitous

2. Mrs. Brown's melancholy and sullen disposition did little to encourage her students to learn. As a matter of fact, her temperament deteriorated to the point that the class came together as one and brought their complaint to Mr. Newall, principal of the school. After hearing the students' lament, Mr. Newall replied briefly, "You're here to learn, not to be entertained." End of discussion. The students then decided to try another approach. They rebelled! Mrs. Brown's instructions were ignored, and life became pretty unbearable for her. She finally got the message and her attitude changed dramatically. With this the class settled down, and learning once again became the order of business.

Which of the following words fit into the context of the passage?
(a) halcyon   (b) galvanized   (c) boycott   (d) laconic

3. The judge sentenced the defendant to a stiff prison term, so severe that even the prosecutor felt it unfair. In addition to this, the justice before sentencing delivered a scathing lecture denouncing the defendant in the strongest language. This judge made it plain that this was his court and he could do as he pleased.

Which words fit into the context of the passage?
(a) Parthian shot   (b) philippic   (c) draconian   (d) narcissistic

4. To take another's life is in the eyes of many persons wrong, no matter the intent. There are, on the other hand, many people who believe that patients suffering terminal illnesses accompanied by excruciating pain should be relieved of such agony by inducing in them a painless death. There is of course merit on both sides of the issue which presents an exceedingly intricate social, legal, and religious dilemma. The solution seems not to be in the offing, which is for many advocates of mercy killing a gloomy

prospect especially, they contend, for the patients' loved ones who must bear witness to their suffering.

Which words describe or name this issue?
(a) euthanasia   (b) Stygian   (c) tenebrous   (d) tawdry

Dimension Two
Part One

Automat

Word Families

Since the English language itself is derived from a combination of other, older languages, it follows that the etymologies of most English words may be traced back to words or word elements in other languages. Both Latin and Greek have made major contributions to English, and, therefore, this section deals with primary borrowings from these two venerable languages.

The lessons that comprise Dimension Two of your book focus on **word families**. This approach is very different from the work you did in Dimension One. Specifically, words are grouped into families or communities having a common lexical background. Most often a primary etymon joins with a secondary etymon to form an English word. A specific case in point should prove helpful. There is in English a

191

word **cephalopod**. It is built on the Greek **cephalo**, "head" + **pod**, "foot." Knowing the meanings of these etymons is useful, but what the word **cephalopod** means still escapes you. What possibly can be all head and feet? Another cue is needed, and that cue is context. Words are not used in a solitary way; they work together in order to communicate ideas. The following context cue should make clear the meaning of **cephalopod**.

"One of the most fearsome creatures living in the briny ocean depths is surely the **cephalopod** with its snake-like tentacles protruding from what appears to be its head."

Perhaps now the word's meaning crystalizes. In a real sense, is not the octopus ostensibly all head and feet—tentacles? It seems to have no middle part. So a cephalopod is an octopus. But it doesn't end here. There are other words that use the etymon **cephalos**, meaning "head":

hydrocephalous   cephalic index
encephalitis   encephalograph

The other etymon, **pod**, means "foot," and oftentimes it is used interchangeably with the Latin **ped**, meaning "foot." Together they form a large family of words:

pedestrian   pedal   podium   podiatry
pedicure   pedicab   pedometer

One might argue, and with merit, that this is well and good, but it doesn't provide the meaning of **hydrocephalous**, for example. Again, another cue is needed—context. If we know that **hydor** in Greek means "water," a context sentence will fill in the gaps:

"The young boy's head was patently enlarged due to a **hydrocephalic** condition."

Essentially the boy's head was filled with a fluid (water?) that made it distended, swollen. This basically is how the approach works: meanings of etymons + context = word meaning.

Each of the lessons is followed by exercises to provide you with an opportunity to put to use what you have learned. The word that appears in the exercise is not always in the same grammatical form as the one presented in the lesson. The purpose of the exercises is not to test for such specific forms. It is, rather, to test your recognition of the etymons from which a word is derived.

In brief, you will learn not *about* words in this section; you will learn *from* words. The totality of human knowledge can be reduced to words. They can teach us about ourselves and the world in which we live.

Lesson

1

AUTOS: *"self"*

The word element **autos** comes from the Greek language, and it means "self." A number of words that are part of the English language owe their origins to this etymon: autograph; autotroph; autosuggestion; autohypnosis; autoplasty; and others. Two words that belong in this exercise will appear in subsequent lessons and will be given fuller treatment. The words are **autocracy** and **autogenous**. (See Lessons 4 and 6 of this dimension.)

autobiography: autos + graphein, *"to write"*   *noun*

The biography of a person that is written by the person him- or herself is an **autobiography**. A biography, on the other hand, is one's life written by another person. Two commonly used etymons accompany autos—**bio** and **graphein**. They appear in many other words: biology; biopsy; biodegradable; biogenesis, and many others. Graphein is even more common to English words: graphite; graphic; photograph; bibliography. Such word elements are important to building one's vocabulary. Remember them; they will come up again and again in future lessons.

autograft: autos + graft *(origin unknown)*   *noun*

The origin of **graft** in the word **autograft** is uncertain. It has been suggested that its original meaning was "to unite," which is consistent with autograft's meaning. In any case, it is a surgical procedure that involves grafting tissue from one part of the body to another. Keep in mind that the tissue being grafted must come from the patient, not an outside donor. This procedure is also known as **autoplasty**, and one of the more popular procedures is rhinoplasty—plastic surgery of the nose. Autografts are common since the body's immune system tends to reject tissue from foreign bodies or at least bodies foreign to it.

autogamy: autos + **gamos,** *"marriage"* *noun*
Autogamy relates to fertilization of flowers by their own pollen. Literally the word means "married to the self." In a manner of speaking this is true of autogamous flowers. They do not require a partner in order to reproduce themselves. It is in this context that the word's etymology makes sense—they are married to themselves. Another word that means the same thing is **gynandrous—gynē,** "woman" + **andros,** "male." Gynandrous flowers are also capable of self-reproduction.

Automat: auto + **matos** *"move"* *noun*
The word Automat designates an eating establishment where food can be purchased by inserting coins into slots after which customers may lift a plastic door and help themselves to the food behind it. There is no human contact in the procedure—it is automatic. There were a number of Automats in New York City some years ago, and they were quite popular, too. The best known Automats in New York were the Horn & Hardart chain, a name that became synonymous with such eateries. They went out of business years ago. The word Automat itself is a telescoping of the word **automat**on.

autonomic: auto + **nomos,** *"law"* *adjective*
The word **autonomic** is most often used to name part of the body's nervous system—the autonomic nervous system. It is this collection of organs, nerves, and ganglia that regulate involuntary action such as the beating of one's heart. The will is not involved. One cannot, for example, willfully make the heart stop beating. It is part of the body's autonomic nervous system.

autopsy: autos + **opsis,** *"sight"* *noun*
An **autopsy** is a postmortem—**post,** "after," **mortem,** "death"— examination. A doctor dissects the cadaver to determine the cause of death. Literally the word from the Greek means **"seeing with one's own eyes** the cause of death."

autonomous: autos + **nomos,** *"rule; law"* *adjective*
Autonomous means "self-contained or independent from external rule." Such autonomous entities are essentially self-governing, and this meaning is consistent with the word's etymology: **autos,** "self,"

nomos, "rule." The noun form is **autonomy** and the adverb, **autonomously**.

automaton: autos + matos *"acting"*   *noun*
The word **automaton** need not be restricted exclusively to robots; it can also be used to characterize human behavior if it is mechanical or automatic. In a word, if one acts like a robot, the word automaton may be used to characterize such a person's behavior—robotic in fashion. The word's etymology is self-explanatory: **autos,** "self," + **matos,** "acting."

autogenous: autos + genos *"birth"*   *adjective*
See Lesson 4, Dimension Two, Part One

autocracy: autos + kratein, *"power"*   *noun*
See Lesson 6, Dimension Two, Part One

EXERCISES

A. Match each definition in Column B with the word it defines in Column A.

Column A

1. automaton
2. autonomy
3. autobiography
4. autogamy
5. Automat
6. autopsy
7. autonomic
8. autograft

Column B

a. life story written by the subject
b. procedure to determine cause of death by seeing for oneself the dead body
c. transplanting tissue or organ from one part of the body to another part of the same body
d. self-operating mechanism
e. acting independently of volition or by reflex
f. independence; self-rule
g. self-fertilization
h. restaurant without servers

B. Complete each sentence by writing the appropriate word from the list below.

autopsy   autobiography
autonomy   automatons
autonomic   autografts
automatic   autogamous

1. Thanks to my _____ nervous system, I drew my hand back from the flame in time after I spilled cooking oil on the gas burner.

2. When her husband collapsed at the controls, Mrs. Smith put the plane on _____ pilot until she could get landing directions from the tower.

3. When the _____ was completed the coroner said the man had died from natural causes.

4. The _____ of Benjamin Franklin has become an American classic because it is also an historical record of events in the late 18th century.

5. Many British colonies were granted _____ after World War II.

6. Because the flower seeds I planted were _____, they soon sprouted plants that covered the entire area.

7. Some factories use _____ instead of people to perform repetitive, mechanized tasks.

8. _____ are usually necessary when a person is severely burned.

C. Complete each word by writing the required word fragments derived from one of the etymons you have studied.

1. auto_____ = reflex or involuntary

2. auto_____ = self-originating

3. auto_____ = movement without human help

4. auto_____ = seeing for oneself to determine the cause of death.

5. auto_____ = transplanting tissue or organs from one part of body to another part of same body

6. auto_____ = story of one's life (self-written)

7. auto_____ = self-rule

8. auto_____ = self-operating mechanism

D. Choose two of the following words: autobiography, autopsy, automaton, autonomous. Use your words in two sentences.

Lesson

2

A; AN: *"no; not; without"*

The Greek prefix **a**, or **an**, conveys the idea of negation. For example, the word **atom** is built on two Greek word elements: **a**, "not" + **tom**, from the Greek **temnein**, which means "to cut." Improbable though it may seem, the first "atomic theory" dates back to Greek antiquity and a school of philosophers known as "atomists." These men proposed that there existed a particle of matter (which they called **atomos**) that was not capable of being further cut or divided. The atom and the original meaning from the Greek no longer fit: it (the atom) has been split. The following words in Lesson 2 make use of this negative Greek prefix.

anodyne: an + **dyne**, *"pain"*   *noun*

The origin of **anodyne** is found in the Greek **an** + **odynē**, "pain." In a literal sense, anything that will relieve pain may be referred to as an anodyne: aspirin and morphine, among other drug compounds. The word, however, is used more in a figurative sense. For example, the student who failed a test for the second time is told by his teacher, "If you don't succeed at first, try, try again." This is meant to lift the student out of despair, and in this sense is a pain reliever. In brief, an anodyne may be used in both a literal and a figurative context.

anesthesia: an + **aisthesis**, *"feeling"*   *noun*

An **anesthesia** is "a drug that will cause general or local insensibility to pain and other sensations." A local anesthesia affects only a specific body part—a dentist's injecting novocaine to deaden the nerve endings in a tooth. A general anesthesia renders the patient unconscious. A physician may then work on the patient whose entire body is free of pain.

anarchy: an + **archos**, *"ruler"*   *noun*

Anarchy means "absence of rule or political authority." Lawlessness and social disorder are rife. The word has a meaning that is more generic than this. In a broad context **anarchy** means confusion, chaos, disorder of any kind. For example, "The angry group of strikers rampaged through the city streets creating an aura of anarchy—confused disorder."

achromatic: a + **chrōma**, *"color"*   *adjective*

Achromatic designates "colors having zero saturation" and, therefore, no hue or color. The family of neutral grays are achromatic. The word is built on **chrōma**, "color." Perhaps an example might be useful for our purposes: "Dark, desolate winter days of Maine are said to be **achromatic**—having little color."

agnostic: a + **gnostos**, *"known"*   *noun, adjective*

An **agnostic** suspends belief in a supreme being. Inasmuch as there is no proof to support the existence or nonexistence of a god, agnostics say it would be premature to make such judgments. Agnostics place a question mark after the word **god**. Keep in mind that agnosticism and atheism are quite different. The next word for study is **atheism**.

atheism: a + **theos**, *"god"*   *noun*

Atheists, unlike agnostics, contend that there is no god. God is a fiction. The Communist Party, especially under the iron hand of Stalin, was essentially atheistic. Churches and other houses of worship were closed for many years. The opposite word for atheism is **theism**; simply remove the negative. Theists believe in a personal God who is creator and ruler of the world.

anonymous: a + **homalos**, *"even"*   *adjective*

That which is **anonymous** is "without a name acknowledgment." Some writers, for instance, prefer not to sign their names to works they have done. There are others who donate large sums of money to worthy causes, and who prefer to remain anonymous. A crank call or a hate letter both may be anonymous in that the caller or writer refuses to identify himself or herself. Think about other words that use the etymon **nym: homonym; antonym; patronym; synonym.**

atrophy: a + **trephein,** *"to nourish"   noun*

To **atrophy** is "to waste away," especially tissues and organs of the human body. For example, a leg that is not used for extended periods of time will atrophy—wither or shrink in size. There are other forms of atrophy. Take for example those who do not use their brain power to the fullest will in time suffer an intellectual atrophy. Cystic fibrosis and multiple sclerosis are diseases that manifest a weakening or degeneration of the muscles. These disorders are classified as **dystrophic—dys,** "bad," + **trephein,** "to nourish."

anomaly: a + **homalos,** *"even"   noun*

An **anomaly** is "that which deviates from a norm or a rule," and in this sense embraces the Greek meaning of **homalos,** which suggests an unevenness. Anything odd, peculiar, or strange that results from not following a customary behavior is an anomaly.

EXERCISES

A. Write T if the boldface word is used correctly in the following sentences; if not, write F.

1. I am an **atheist** because I firmly believe that God is omnipresent and all-powerful.

2. A person who is confined to a wheelchair must do some kind of exercise to prevent **atrophy** of the leg muscles.

3. Jane's twin sister was so predictable about acting like all the "normal" high school sophomores that we called her an **anomaly.**

4. Jerome complained of the throbbing pain caused by the infected tooth, but he said that thanks to the **anesthetic** given by the dentist, he was able to bear it.

5. The hilarious comedy on TV served as an **anodyne** for Francesca's mood of depression.

6. Following the assassination of the president, a calm and disciplined state of **anarchy** prevailed in the government.

7. Whenever we got into a discussion about religion, Lila said, "I don't believe and I don't not believe, so that makes me an **agnostic**, I guess."

8. Because the room was decorated in shades of gray, varying from a barely perceptible gray to a wild, dark gray, I found the result too **achromatic** for my taste.

9. The **anonymous** phone call was disturbing enough to make John decide to alert the police.

B. Select the correct definition of each etymon.

1. chrōma
   (a) time   (b) color   (c) pain   (d) name

2. homalos
   (a) smell   (b) sound   (c) even   (d) known

3. onyma
   (a) cut   (b) name   (c) color   (d) pain

4. archos
   (a) even   (b) nourish   (c) color   (d) ruler

5. odynē
   (a) god   (b) cut   (c) pain   (d) even

6. theos
   (a) feeling   (b) time   (c) sound   (d) god

7. aisthesis
   (a) pain   (b) nourish   (c) feeling   (d) sound

8. trephein
   (a) nourish   (b) feeling   (c) name   (d) ruler

9. gnostos
   (a) feeling   (b) name   (c) known   (d) even

C. Match the definition in Column B to the word it defines in Column A.

Column A

1. anodyne
2. atheist
3. atrophy
4. anarchy
5. agnostic
6. anomaly
7. anonymous
8. anesthesia
9. achromatic

Column B

a. something abnormal
b. without a name
c. pain reliever
d. lacking color
e. person who does not believe in any god
f. drug that frees from pain or causes numbness
g. to waste away
h. lawlessness; absence of government
i. one who does not believe or disbelieve in a god.

D. Choose two of the following words: anesthesia, anarchy, anonymous, atrophy. Use your words in two sentences of your own.

Lesson

3

PATHEIA: *"feeling; disease"*

Lesson 3 deals with the Greek etymon **patheia**, and it means "feeling or disease." Which of these meanings applies in a given circumstance will generally be made clear by the context in which the word is found. What follows are words that have their lexical origins in the Greek **patheia**. Beside each word is listed the meaning(s) of the etymon(s) that make up the word. Learn these word parts. They are essential if you are to enlarge your vocabulary.

apathy: a, *"no; not"* + **pathein,** *"feeling"*   *noun*

Two commonly used Greek prefixes are **a** and **an**. When either is affixed to another Greek word element, it changes a positive to a negative: moral–amoral; symmetric–asymmetric; typical—atypical. The word **apathy** has prefixed to it the negative **a**, and it means "indifference; absence of concern; no feeling one way or another." While the Greek **patheia** means "feeling," the negative turns this around, and what apathy suggests is "no feeling." The word has a less than positive connotation since there are so few things in life so casual, so mundane that an absence of concern can be justified: voter apathy, parental apathy, political apathy, and a range of social apathies that are uncaring about the poor and homeless, crime in the streets, and on and on. Too many of us who live in microcosms of our own don't have the time or the inclination to devote to these needful causes.

pathology: pathein, *"disease"* + **logos,** *"study of"*   *noun*

The word **pathology** refers to **disease**. It is combined with the Greek **logos,** "science or study of." In very few instances **logos** means "word" as in **eulogy** and **etymology**. These will be covered in subsequent lessons. Specifically, pathology is "the study or science relating to the origin, nature, and course of diseases." It also means "any deviation from a normal, healthy, or efficient condition." In this latter sense, cancer is a **pathology** best treated by an oncologist, a cancer specialist. Pathologists are doctors who examine tissue, viruses, bacteria, etc., to determine the nature of diseases.

osteopath: osteon, *"bone"* + **pathein,** *"disease"*   *noun*
    An **osteopath** practices **osteopathy,** "a therapeutic system based on the notion that restoration and maintenance of good health can best be achieved by manipulating skeletal bones and muscles." In this regard osteopaths and chiropractors are much alike. Keep in mind that osteopaths are not accredited by the American Medical Association—they are not licensed physicians in the same sense that a medical physician is. There are other words that make use of the Greek **osteon** meaning "bone": osteomyelitis; osteotomy; osteoplasty; osteoid. Incidentally, the medical practice that treats bone infirmities is orthopedics. It will be studied in a subsequent lesson.

hydropathy: hydor, *"water"* + **pathein,** *"disease"*   *noun*
    Hydor is the Greek word for **water.** There are several medical terms that make use of this Greek etymon: hydrocephalous; hydrophobia; hydrothorax; hydropathy. These words have in some way something to do with water. **Hydropathy** is the treatment of disease by the use of water, externally or internally. Many persons who suffer a bone disease seek out such therapeutic treatments to alleviate chronic pain. Franklin Delano Roosevelt, who suffered from the ravages of polio, often visited sulfur springs which were believed to have a value in pain abatement. Finally, there are those words that employ the etymon **hydor** which have nothing whatever to do with illness: **hydrogen, hydraulic; hydrophone; hydroplane**; and others.

psychopath: psyche, *"mind"* + **pathein,** *"disease"*   *noun*
    Psychopaths are mentally deranged to the extent that they are aggressively antisocial. Psychopaths come in many different guises: psychopathic killers; liars; abusers of women and children; and so on. Psychopathic killers who sometimes commit mayhem upon others with no palpable reason are without question the most lethal of the lot. A Charles Manson is a classic case in point. There are those who would argue that psychopaths should be more pitied than condemned since

they are mentally ill, while others would recommend long prison sentences as being a more appropriate therapy.

pathos: pathein, *"feeling"*   *noun*
The word **pathos** means having the quality or the power to evoke feelings of pity or compassion, especially in expressive forms such as music, literature, speech, and sometimes art. It has already been brought to your attention, but it bears repeating: when an etymon has multiple meanings, context is required in order to determine which meaning is intended. Take, for example, this sentence: "Victor Hugo's novel *Les Miserables* engages the reader in a bittersweet tale that evokes pathos." The context should make clear that **pathos** in this case means "feeling." So too will context help you with other etymons that have multiple meanings.

antipathy: anti, *"against"* + **pathein,** *"feeling"*   *noun*
Anti is a prefix that means "against, opposite, or opposed to." For instance, the words **antidepressant, antidote, anticoagulant**, and **antibodies** all carry the idea of opposition in some sense. There are literally scores of words having **anti** as a prefix, and **antipathy** is one of them. It is built on the prefix **anti,** "against," + **pathein,** "feeling," and it means "a basic or habitual repugnance, an aversion." In short, one's feelings are dead set against whatever or whoever is the object of your antipathy. The adjective form is **antipathetic**.

empathy: em, *"with"* + **pathein,** *"feeling"*   *noun*
The word **empathy** is made up of two parts: **em,** "with" + **pathein,** "feeling." To empathize is "to identify with, to experience vicariously the feelings of another person." One must appreciate the difference between the words **sympathy** and **empathy**. The former is quite objective—the person doing the sympathizing is always him- or herself. There is the sense of detachment, albeit a concerned detachment. Not so with the word **empathy**, a very subjective state of being. The empathizer transfers his or her consciousness to another person. One vicariously shares the feelings of another—feels the anguish, participates in the experience. **Empathy**, therefore, is a much more powerful word than is **sympathy**. It should be used with care.

telepathy: tele, *"afar"* + **pathein,** *"feeling"*   *noun*
The dictionary defines **telepathy** as "communication between minds by some means other than sensory perception." A more conventional phrase "mind reading" is often used to refer to this phenome-

non. The Greek etymons suggest that a mind can communicate with another mind while they are far apart. Much of what passes as mind reading is the work of charlatans, but there is too much in the way of documented occasions during which some kind of communication took place in some unconventional manner. It is a claim that needs a lot more investigation. Finally there is a host of words that use the etymon **tele: telephone; telekinesis; teleprompter; telemetry**; and many others.

EXERCISES

A. Complete the words below by providing the missing etymons.

1. _____ pathy: indifferent; absence of concern

2. _____ path: a doctor who manipulates bones and muscles

3. _____ path: one who is mentally deranged

4. _____ pathy: a basic dislike; a repugnance

5. _____ pathy: identification with another's feelings

6. _____ pathy: "mind reading"

7. _____ pathy: treatment of disease through use of water

8. path_____: science relating to origin and nature of disease

9. path_____: feelings of pity or compassion

B. Write T if the statement is consistent with the meaning of the boldface word, or write F if it is not.

1. Voter **apathy** is one of the main reasons that Americans do not participate in the electoral process.

2. Mineral spas are one form of **hydropathy** used to lessen the pain of arthritis.

3. An **osteopath** is one who is mentally deranged.

4. A movie that evokes **pathos** in its audience is bound to generate a strong emotional response.

5. Most men and women of science scoff at the claims of **telepaths**.

6. To **empathize** with a friend requires the sharing of that friend's feelings.

7. Long-standing **antipathies** are the cause of many family feuds.

8. **Pathologists** study the nature, cause, and origin of disease.

9. **Psychopaths** can be a danger to both themselves and to others.

    C. Match the following items.

Column A

1. antipathy
2. osteopath
3. pathos
4. pathologist
5. psychopath
6. apathy
7. telepathy
8. empathy
9. hydropathy

Column B

a. a doctor who treats patients by manipulating bones and muscles
b. lack of feeling; indifference
c. one who has a deranged mind
d. communication at a distance without sensory perception; mind reading
e. an aversion; a dislike
f. evoking feelings of pity and compassion
g. specialist who studies the nature and cause of disease
h. therapy that uses water
i. sharing of another's feelings

    D. Choose two of the following words: psychopath, antipathy, empathy, telepathy. Use your words in two sentences of your own.

Lesson

4

GENOS: *"kind; race; family; birth; origin"*

The Greek word element **genos** has several meanings which could be the cause of some confusion. It's not really all that bad. Generally the context in which the word appears will indicate which of the meanings is intended. For example, "A congenital defect in the new-born's ability to hold down food concerned the pediatrician." It should be clear that in this context the meaning **birth** applies. The word in question must be seen in context, or it would be almost impossible to assign one of the multiple meanings to it. Familiarity and context are the keys to unlocking the meaning of the word element **genos**.

autogenous: auto, *"self"* + **genos,** *"origin"*   *noun*

Autogenous means "self-produced, self-generated." A good deal of the flora that you see is autogenous. Flowers, for example, have this reproductive capacity. Keep in mind that no living organisms have this same autogenous capability. The word is built on the etymons **auto,** "self" + **genos,** "origin." Many other words in English use the etymon **auto: automated; automaton; autocratic;** and others.

genesis: genos, *"origin"*   *noun*

Genesis means "a beginning, an origin." In a Biblical sense, it means "creation" and is the first book of the Bible—Genesis. There is another more frequently used context. For example, a novelist might suggest that an unexpected calamity was the **genesis** of the book he or she had just finished. Or racial prejudice finds its **genesis** in hatred. Keep in mind that genesis means "beginning or origin."

genocide: genos, *"race"* + **cadere** *altered to* **cide,** *"kill"*   *noun*

The Greek **genos** + **cide** are the origin of the English word **genocide,** which is essentially "the killing of an entire race or ethnic group." The most heinous of genocides is without question that perpetrated on Jews by the Nazis. In a more recent episode, it is said that Serbs are waging a genocidal war against Bosnians. It is euphemistically referred to by Serbs as "ethnic cleansing." The Latin **cide,** which is an alteration of **cadere,** is an important word element in English: patricide, homicide, suicide, regicide, fratricide, and others.

congenital: con, *"with"* + **genos,** *"birth"*   *adjective*

Congenital means "existing at or from one's birth." Synonyms for the word are innate, inborn, or inherent. It is also used in a more figurative context to indicate that something has been long-standing. For example, one may characterize a person as a congenital liar, indicating that the prevaricating has been going on for a long time—a born liar? This context is not to be taken literally, of course. These then are the two contexts: a congenital defect which does indeed take place at birth, and a congenital character trait of long-standing that seems to go back to one's birth. They are both used quite extensively.

eugenics: eu, *"good, well"* + **genos,** *"birth, race"*   *noun*

Eugenics is "the practice of improving a breed or stock by controlling the selection of parents." It has one overriding aim—to improve a species in very specific ways. The practice is quite common in animal husbandry to increase the amount of milk that a cow can provide, or to raise steer that will give more meat, etc. Purebreds—show dogs and race horses—are the result of eugenics. The practice has made inroads into human reproduction, but it is a young scientific endeavor that has not gained much support from the general public. The jury is still out in this socially delicate matter.

heterogeneous: heteros, *"other"* + **genos,** *"kind"*   *adjective*

A **heterogeneous** grouping "involves elements that are dissimilar, different." This is consistent with the Greek **heteros** meaning "other." That which is heterogeneous is not comprised of the same elements—there are other dissimilar elements. For example, student groupings in most schools are heterogeneous. They are dissimilar with regard to gender and ability. Again, the United States has undoubtedly the most heterogeneous population in the world.

homogeneous: homos, *"same"* + **genos**, *"kind"*   *adjective*
That which is **homogeneous** is "made up of elements of the same kind." If, for example, students in a particular school are grouped in terms of their ability, then the grouping is homogeneous. Were boys grouped together and girls the same, then the grouping would be homogeneous in terms of gender. The key word here, unlike in the word heterogeneous, is **sameness** or **uniformity**.

pathogen: path, *"disease"* + **genos**, *"origin"*   *noun*
A **pathogen** is that which "produces disease." Pathogens take many forms: bacteria, cigarette smoke, viruses, etc. Asbestos is oftentimes the pathogen causing lung disease; cholesterol is the pathogen causing occluded arteries. Doctors whose specialty is pathology are called pathologists—who determine the nature and cause of disease. Just keep in mind that pathogens are the ultimate source of a disease.

primogeniture: primo, *"first"* + **genos**, *"birth"*   *noun*
Primogeniture is the state of being the "firstborn child" to parents having more than one offspring. It is a term that is manifestly crucial in countries having a king or queen: monarchies. Primogeniture is the determining factor when succession to the throne is in question. In a more general usage, it is a reference to the firstborn son, which could be a determining factor in a contested inheritance, especially should the deceased have died intestate—without a will.

The law of primogeniture in Great Britain requires that a deceased's estate be left to the eldest son. This law is known as the "law of the first born." In America this is not the case. Gender has little to do with inheritance laws. Should the deceased die intestate (have no will), then the courts, not gender, decide who inherits what.

indigenous: indi, *"in"* + **gen**, *"born"*   *adjective*
The word **indigenous** has several meanings all of which are tied together by a common thread—all suggest the idea of "being inborn," as in the words **native, innate,** and **inherent**. These are precisely the definitions listed in a dictionary, **originating in a particular country, region, or locale**. Oftentimes the word indigenous is followed by the preposition **to**, as the plants were **indigenous to** an unnamed remote island located in the South Pacific. Specialty foods may be indigenous to certain cultures, speech patterns to specific regions, or for that matter cultural beliefs, such as those held by the Amish people are indigenous to localized areas of the United States.

psychogenic: psychē, *"mind"* + **genos,** *"origin"*   *adjective*

That which is **psychogenic** "originates in the mind." Many illnesses are psychogenic in nature. They exist in the mind only. At one time in Greek mythology the word **psyche** meant "soul," not "mind." **Psyche** was a maiden loved by Eros who, after overcoming the jealousy of Aphrodite, became the personification of the soul. Today psyche refers to the mind, although there may be one or two words that are vestiges of **psyche,** meaning "soul." One such word is **metempsychosis**—the transmigration of souls, which suggested that after one's death, the soul "migrated" and passed into the body of another living thing. The word is one of the very few that continues to use the ancient meaning of **psyche**—"soul."

genealogy: genea, *"family"* + **logos,** *"study of"*   *noun*

A **genealogy** is "a record," generally in the form of a table or other visual presentation, of the descent of a family, group, or person by tracing ancestral heritage. This lineage is referred to as a genealogy. It would not be too difficult to locate a genealogist who would undertake the study of your family background. If you knew enough background relating to your family, you could probably do your own genealogy.

hallucinogen: hallūcinārī, *"to wander in mind"* + **genos,** *"origin"* *noun*

Hallucinations are born in one's mind, and when the mind hallucinates, it wanders; and its perceptions do not comport with reality. A **hallucinogen** is that which "produces a hallucination;" it is the origin of that unreality. For the most part, hallucinogens are what are referred to as mind-altering drugs such as LSD. When taken, the mind hallucinates. There are mental conditions that are hallucinogenic—schizophrenia, which is characterized by a withdrawal from reality. There are others: manic depression, paranoia, psychoses, and senile dementia.

EXERCISES

A. The word element **genos** has several meanings: **birth, race, origin, kind,** or **family.** Determine which of these meanings fits the word element **gen** and write it in a numbered list. Then write the word for each numbered meaning.

1. psycho+gen (_____) = _____

2. primo+gen (_____) = _____

3. hetero+gen (_____) = _____

4. homolos+gen (_____) = _____

5. patho+gen (_____) = _____

6. auto+gen (_____) = _____

7. con+gen (_____) = _____

8. eu+gen (_____) = _____

9. geno (_____) + cide = _____

10. gen (_____) + esis = _____

B. Write a lesson word that fits each definition given.

1. a beginning; an origin

2. self-generated

3. that which causes a disease

4. first child born

5. of the same kind

6. originates in the mind

7. visual presentation of the descent of a family

8. practice that improves a breed

9. occurring with birth

10. killing an entire race

C. Write C if the meaning of the sentence is consistent with the meaning of the boldface word. Write I if it is not.

1. A **congenital** defect occurs only after birth.

2. Pandas are **indigenous** to China.

3. A **psychogenic** illness is induced by the mind.

4. **Eugenics** is practiced extensively in breeding race horses.

5. That which is capable of reproducing itself is **autogenous**.

6. **Genocide** is the killing of a large group of people.

7. Drugs, many of which are illegal, have the capacity to produce **hallucinogenic** results.

8. The Christian faith had its **genesis** with the birth of Christ.

9. A **genealogy** traces one's family origin for no more than one generation.

10. **Homogeneous** and **heterogeneous** are essentially antonyms, opposite in meaning.

    D. Choose two of the following words: congenital, heterogeneous, indigenous, genealogy. Use your two words in two of your own sentences.

Lesson

5

ANTHRŌPOS: *"human being"*
ANDROS: *"male; man"*
   Anthropos is a Greek word element that means "human being." It can also mean "man." **Andros** means "male" and in this sense "man" applies. Keep firmly in mind that **anthropos** means "human being," which embraces both genders—male and female. **Andros** is more exclusive. It refers to the male gender alone. The etymon for woman exclusively is **gynē.** Can you guess what the word **androgynous** means? That which is androgynous has both male and female characteristics in one. In botany it refers to flowers that have the ability to self-generate—autogenous? The Greek **gynē** will come up again in subsequent lessons.

anthropocentric: anthropos + **centrum**, *"center"* *adjective*
   An **anthropocentric** view of the universe places human beings at its center: reality can only be interpreted in terms of human values. Extending this notion, long ago people believed that they lived in a **geocentric** universe—**geo,** "earth"—and all things revolved around the earth, including the sun. This made humans the center of the universe if the idea is carried to its logical conclusion. Copernicus discovered otherwise. We live in a **helio,** "sun" + **centrum,** "center" universe. Does our sun revolve around yet another galactic sun? Who knows?

android: andros + **oid**, *"resembling"* *noun*
   An **android** possesses some human features but is itself not human. Androids abound in the sci-fi movie "Star Wars." There are in fact 25 different versions of androids, and they are referred to collectively as

214

"droids." The most well-known of them are C-3PO and R2-D2, both likeable "droids" possessing some human characteristics. Don't confuse the words **android** and **anthropoid**. An ape, for example, is an anthropoid, not an android. A robot is not an anthropoid; it is an android.

misanthropist misein, *"to hate"* + **anthrōpos** *noun*
philanthropist: philos, *"love"* + **anthrōpos** *noun*
    A **philanthropist** is one having an endearing affection for humankind which is manifested by charitable financial aid or donations of time and effort to worthy causes. A **misanthropist**, on the other hand, is one who has an abiding hatred of humankind. Fortunately for the human race the former far outnumber the latter. The adjective philanthropic can apply to groups as well as individuals. The Salvation Army, for example, is a philanthropic organization. Thankfully, there are many others.

anthropomorphic: anthrōpos + **morphē,** *"shape, form"*
adjective
    To attribute human form to that which is not human is a form of **anthropomorphism**, and this is especially true when a deity is involved. Many religions embrace some form of anthropomorphism—those that believe man is in the image of God. The etymon **morphē** is a commonly used etymon in English: **morpheme; amorphous; morphology; polymorphic**. In a lighter vein, animated cartoons such as Mickey Mouse, Donald Duck, and the Roadrunner are in a sense anthropomorphic. In these shows, human characteristics are attributed to animals, one form of anthropomorphism. They talk, walk, and have feelings much like humans.

philander: philos, *"love,"* + **andros,** *"male"* *verb*
    From the Greek **philandros,** "loving man," comes the word **philander**, which means "to engage in love affairs frivolously or casually." Gender attaches itself to the word in that only men can philander. To be referred to as a philanderer is not to be taken as a compliment. Quite to the contrary, it is a word that has become synonymous with duplicitous behavior.

polyandry: poly, *"many"* + **andros,** *"male, man"* *noun*
    The word means a marital state wherein a woman has more than one husband at a single time. The word for one marriage at a single time is **monandry** (**mono,** "one"). There are cultures in which **polyandry** is accepted practice. Therefore, there are no legal implications

attached to the word. The term bigamy is grounded in law. It is an unlawful practice. Keep in mind that either a man or woman can be a bigamist. Only a woman can engage in polyandry.

anthropoid: anthrōpos + oid, *"resembling"*   *noun; adjective*
  Anthropoid means "resembling human beings." Chimps, orangutans, and gorillas are anthropoids in that they do resemble man in several important ways. They are bipedal: **bi,** "two" + **ped,** "foot." All are able to walk on two feet in an upright position. The other noteworthy similarity is that they all have an opposable thumb which allows them to do work with their hands as can humans. Beyond these similarities, anthropoids do resemble the shape of humans in a general way.

anthropology: anthrōpos + logos, *"study of"*   *noun*
  Anthropology is a science that deals with the origin of humanity's physical, social, and cultural development. It is also concerned with humankind's development in an evolutionary context. When anthropologists are shown on television at work, they are seen digging in the earth for artifacts of one kind or another. Perhaps it might be a fossilized bone fragment. In any case, this is what they do for the most part—search for clues that will provide a better understanding of early human beings dating back to prehistoric times.

EXERCISES

  A. Fill in the missing word part to complete the word whose meaning is listed beside it.

1. _____ anthropist   has an abiding love of humankind

2. anthrop_____   science dealing with the origin of humankind

3. anthrop_____   a living creature resembling humans—an ape, for instance

4. _____ oid   possesses some features of humans but is not itself a living organism

5. _____ ander   to trifle with a woman's affections

6. _____ andry   practice of having one husband or male
                          mate at a time

7. _____ anthrope   one who despises humankind

8. _____ andry   having more than one husband at a time

9. anthropo_____   belief that humankind is at the center of
                          the universe

10. andro_____   having both male and female
                          characteristics in one, as in many plants

B. Match the word and the definition of each item below.

_____ 1. anthropoid   a. having the characteristics of
_____ 2. philanderer   both sexes in one
_____ 3. misanthrope   b. to attribute human form to that
_____ 4. anthropocentrism   which is not human
_____ 5. android   c. marital state where one woman
_____ 6. androgynous   has multiple mates
_____ 7. anthropomorphism   d. one who loves humankind
_____ 8. polyandry   e. belief that man is at the center
_____ 9. philanthropist   of the universe
_____ 10. anthropology   f. one who hates humankind
                               g. a man who trifles with the
                                  affections of women
                               h. resembling humans, as apes
                               i. study of the origin of the human
                                  species
                               j. possesses some human features
                                  but is not itself human, as a
                                  robot

C. Write C if the boldface word is consistent with sentence meaning, or write I if it is not.

1. Most people would agree that **philandering** is not generally accepted behavior.

2. **Polyandry** and philanderer have very little to do with each
other.

3. A **misanthrope** is very selective in his or her choice of friends.

4. **Anthropoids** and **androids** are similar in that they resemble humans, but they are unlike in that one is a living creature, the other is not.

5. Robotics play an important role in the development of **androids**.

6. Many plants exhibit **androgynous** characteristics.

7. Many religious teachings proclaim their god is **anthropomorphic** and that humankind is fashioned in his image.

8. It has taken centuries to prove the theory that humankind lives in an **anthropocentric** universe.

9. Many **anthropologists** search the ruins of dead civilizations hoping to unearth some unknown clue as to humankind's evolution.

10. Most **philanthropists** are "closet" misanthropes and have a deep hatred of humankind.

   D. Choose two of the following words: android, philanthropist, anthropomorphic, anthropology. Use your words in two sentences of your own.

REVIEW OF LESSONS 1 - 5

   A. Complete each word below by writing the missing etymon.

1. auto_____   a biography written by the subject him- or herself

2. an_____   absence of political rule; lawlessness

3. _____ pathy   no feeling; indifference

4. auto_____   self-generated; self-produced

5. andr_____   something that possesses some human features but is itself not human

6. _____ genital   occurring at birth

7. _____ pathy   to feel with; to experience vicariously

8. geno_____   killing off an entire race or ethnic group

9. psycho_____   originating in the mind

10. a_____   to waste away by disuse

11. a_____   belief that there is no god

12. auto_____   rule by one person; a dictatorship, for example

13. psycho_____   one whose mind is deranged

14. a_____   one who suspends judgment or belief in a god

15. eu_____   selection of parents for purposes of breeding

16. _____ geneous   of different kinds

17. an_____   a painkiller or a saying intended to make someone feel better

18. anthrop_____   in the form of humankind

19. path_____   that which causes disease

20. _____ anthrope   one who hates humankind

B. Write C if the boldface word is used in a way that is consistent with the meaning of the sentence, or write I if it is not.

1. **Autogamous**, which literally means "married to the self," is a synonym for the word autogenous.

2. **Genealogy** is a feeling of friendliness or conviviality.

3. One's leg, for instance, if not used over a long period of time will **atrophy**.

4. Cancer is a **pathology** best treated by an oncologist, a cancer specialist.

5. One might visit an **osteopath** for treatment of lower back pain.

6. The first book of the Bible is **Genesis**.

7. Humankind exists in an **anthropocentric** universe.

8. One example of an **anthropoid** is an ape.

9. **Empathizing** with another person is sharing vicariously his or her mental anguish.

10. To be **antipathetic** toward an idea is to oppose it.

C. Give the meaning of the following list of etymons.

1. auto	11. eu
2. bio	12. genos
3. graphein	13. dyne
4. gamos	14. heteros
5. patheia	15. homos
6. theos	16. philos
7. chroma	17. poly
8. a, an	18. oid
9. psyche	19. misein
10. tele	20. anthropos

Lesson

6

ARCHON: *"rule; power"*

KRATOS: *"power"*

The Greek word elements **archon**, "archy," and **kratos**, "cracy," are synonymous. They may not, however, be used interchangeably. For example, plutocracy cannot become plutarchy. What follows are words that have to do with either rule or power.

hierarchy: hieros, *"sacred,"* + **archon** *noun*

The word **hierarchy** comes from the Greek etymons **hieros** and **archon**. At one time in religious history, it was believed that there existed among angels a distinct line of command, or an echelon of importance. Therefore, angels were ranked from the lowliest to the supreme. It is within this religious context that the word **sacred** had become a part of hierarchy's etymology. A hierarchy is any system which ranks constituent parts in ascending order of importance. There are hierarchies within the church, among living things, in the army, etc.

autocracy: autos, *"self"* + **kratos** *noun*

One might think, judging by its etymology, that **autocracy** means "self-power or self-rule." Not so. Actually autocracy means rule by one person who has absolute power and is thus synonymous with despotism—rule by a tyrant. Incidentally, the word for self-rule is **autonomy**. Do you recall it from a previous lesson?

aristocracy: aristos, *"best"* + **kratos** *noun*

An **aristocracy** is a government ruled by an elite or privileged class. In South America vestiges of an aristocracy yet exist. The landed gentry have a great deal to say about how government is run. In democracies such as America, the word has a different meaning: "any group or class considered to be superior." The one aristocracy that stands out in America is that which is based on wealth. In Europe this is not the case. One's title or patronym determine whether or not the term **aristocrat** is appropriately used. In brief, the aristocracy in America is grounded in one's wealth; in Europe, the touchstone is bloodline. One is born an aristocrat.

It might be argued, and legitimately so, that in countries all over the world there exists another kind of aristocracy—intellectual. In America it is obvious. A case in point is a group calling itself MENSA. It is an exclusive club for brainy people. An IQ of 150 is a minimum requirement to join the club. Moreover, many "think tanks" found at all levels of government and industry place those who work in them at a premium. They are "special." In any case, there may well be an intellectual aristocracy both here and abroad.

monarchy: mono, *"one"* + **archon**

There are many **monarchies** that still exist in the world. Great Britain is a case in point. The word is built on the Greek **mono** and **archon**. Literally the word means "rule by one"—a king or a queen are both monarchs. The difference between an autocracy and a monarchy has already been pointed out, but perhaps it bears repeating. An autocracy has one ruler, but the ruler is a tyrant, a despot. A monarchy also has one ruler—a king or queen who may or may not be a tyrant.

patriarchy: pater, *"father"* + **archon**   *noun*

The word **patriarchy** means "rule by a father or a father figure." Many family units are made up of this kind of rule—the father is the dominant figure in the household and makes all decisions relative to family. There are in this same vein tribal units that abide by the rulings of an elder statesman who takes on the role of surrogate father for all tribespeople. In brief, a patriarchy is a political or a family structure that has as its head a father or a father figure. In a **matriarchy** the opposite is the case. The eldest female, generally, is in charge. This is by no means limited to governments. A family, for example, that has a woman as its dominant figure is a matriarchy. The word element **matr** means **mother**.

theocracy: theos, *"god"* + **kratos**   *noun*

A **theocracy** is "a form of government that recognizes God or another deity as the supreme civil leader." It can also be a form of government in which priests or ecclesiastics claim that theirs is a divine commission to rule. There are relatively few theocracies left in the world today. Mormons are still governed by ministers of God. The Vatican located in Rome is another such example. The pope is titular head of this governing structure.

anarchy: an, *"no, not"* + **archon**   *noun*

See Lesson 2, Dimension Two, Part One

democracy: demos, *"people,"* + **kratos**

A form of government which vests the supreme power in people who elect officials by means of the ballot. Do you recall other words using the etymon **demos**? In any case, they were **pandemic, epidemic**, and **endemic**. Each of these words will appear in greater detail in Lesson 8.

gynarchy: gyne, *"woman"* + **archon**   *noun*

The word **gynarchy** means "a governing structure in which women are the dominant political force." One would be hard pressed to identify such a governance. One example does come to mind. The fabled and no doubt apocryphal Amazon, a tribe of women who dominated their culture. Early Greeks believed such a tribe existed somewhere in Asia Minor. There is no evidence that would substantiate this claim.

plutocracy: ploutos, *"wealth"* + **kratos**   *noun*

A **plutocracy** is "a government controlled by the wealthy." There are few vestiges or pure plutocracies remaining in the world. Having said this, there are governments that come fairly close to being plutocracies. For example, in a few Central and South American countries the wealthy class have an inordinate say in how the government is to be run.

oligarchy: oligos, *"few"* + **archon**   *noun*

An **oligarchy** is government where the select few rule. In some cases the select few are families that hold sway over the populace. In other instances, the few are those in control of power—the military and the civilian police. The USSR after Stalin's death was an oligarchy. Of course since the dissolution of the USSR, it is the ballot that determines who will run the affairs of state. Stalin, incidentally, was an **autocrat**.

EXERCISES

A. Provide the etymon that will complete the words below.

1. _____ archy   ranked from low to high

2. _____ cracy   rule by one person having absolute power

3. _____ cracy   rule by those who believe god is the supreme civil leader

4. _____ cracy   rule by the people

5. _____ cracy   rule by the wealthy

6. _____ archy   absence of rule

7. _____ archy   rule by women

8. _____ archy   rule by one, a king or queen, for example

9. _____ archy   rule by the eldest male, generally

10. _____ archy   rule by the eldest female, generally

B. Match the etymon with its meaning.

1. ploutos   a. woman
2. aristos   b. wealth
3. pater   c. not; without
4. hieros   d. best
5. mono   e. father
6. oligos   f. sacred
7. theos   g. people
8. gynē   h. one
9. dēmos   i. few
10. a; an   j. god

C. Match the following words with their meanings.

Column A

1. rule by one person with
   absolute authority
2. rule in order of rank
3. rule by the best
4. rule by the wealthy
5. rule by select few
6. rule by ministers of God
7. rule by male elder
8. rule by women
9. government by the people
10. rule by one; a kingship

Column B

a. oligarchy
b. theocracy
c. patriarchy
d. monarchy
e. gynarchy
f. autocracy
g. democracy
h. plutocracy
i. hierarchy
j. aristocracy

D. Choose two of the following words: hierarchy, monarchy, democracy, matriarchy. Use your words in two of your own sentences.

Lesson

7

PSYCHĒ: *"mind; soul"*

To early Greeks the word element **psychē** meant, for the most part, soul, not mind. As language evolved, the meaning of **psychē** changed. The Greek meaning no longer applies, except for a few rare exceptions. One such exception is the word **metempsychosis**, whose definition is "transmigration of the soul—to be born again in another form or body." For our purposes, however, all words in this lesson in which **psychē** appears will convey the meaning "mind."

psychedelic: psyche + delos, *"visible"*   *adjective*

Psychedelic describes "whatever generates hallucinations, perceptual distortions, or psychotic states." The word is generally associated with hallucinogenic drugs, LSD most especially. Such substances are often referred to as **mind altering** drugs, and there are grave consequences attached to their use.

psychiatry: psychē + iatria, *"healing"*   *noun*

Psychiatry as you no doubt already know is "the medical practice that deals with disorders of the mind." It should be noted that psychiatrists are licensed physicians who practice a medical specialty which is approved by the American Medical Association. Psychologists, on the other hand, require no such license. They are allowed to study animal and human behavior, and cannot by law treat patients by means other than dialogue. One must be mindful of these distinctions when using the words.

psychic: psychē + ic, *"pertaining to"*   *noun, adjective*

Psychics in lay terms are "those who claim to have the ability to engage in telepathy or who claim to be able to see events to which they were not a part." Most psychics, it would be fair to say, are charlatans—quacks who pretend to have powers that they in fact do not have. Having said this, it must be pointed out that there are those few psychics who have demonstrated that under close scrutiny there is indeed something to their claims. Some psychics have worked with police departments and through these extraordinary powers have located missing persons in remote areas. How this was done scientists cannot say. There may be something to claims made by a few psychics—mediums or clairvoyants.

psychokinesis: psychē + kinetos, *"moving"*   *noun*

A working definition of **psychokinesis** is: "production of motion, especially in inanimate objects that are remote, by means of psychic power." The word suggests mystical powers that the scientific community rejects. As in the case relating to psychics, there have been many documented occasions during which psychokinesis has been legitimately demonstrated. The key to be mindful of is that there is movement, movement of inanimate objects. There is another word that describes such an action—**levitation**. The secondary word element is used in other words: **telekinesis; kinetic energy; kinetic art**. Look up their meanings. What does each have to do with movement?

psychodrama: psychē + dran, *"to do"*   *noun*

Psychodrama is a clinical technique that assigns roles to participants who must react spontaneously to a dramatic context that has been devised by a therapist. What is most important to psychodrama is spontaneity. To a trained clinician, participants reveal a great deal by their interaction with others. Psychodrama is used in other ways as well. For instance, there are college classes, especially psychology classes, in which the approach is used as a teaching tool. In any case, psychodrama is a kind of play-acting for a specific purpose and entertainment is not one of them; it is a serious business.

psychosomatic: psychē + soma, *"body"*   *adjective, noun*
psychogenic: psychē + genos, *"origin"*   *adjective*

The adjectives **psychogenic** and **psychosomatic** are essentially synonyms. The word psychogenic has already been presented in a previous lesson that dealt with the etymon **genos** (see Lesson 4). As for the word **psychosomatic**, it characterizes a person who experiences bodily symptoms which are primarily caused by the workings of the mind. This is the noun definition. When used as an adjective, psychosomatic describes as in "a psychosomatic illness." More on the word **psychogenic** can be found in Lesson 4 of Dimension Two, Part One.

psychosis: psychē + osis, *"abnormal condition"*   *noun*

A **psychosis** is "a severe mental disorder that may or may not be organic in nature." A severe traumatic experience may induce a psychosis among other non-organic causes. A psychosis deteriorates normal intellectual and social functioning. This abnormal behavior is generally accompanied by a complete withdrawal from reality. The person having the psychosis is referred to as a **psychotic** which can also be used as an adjective: **psychotic behavior**. Those suffering from a psychosis are in desperate need of psychotherapeutic treatment. They can be a danger to others as well as themselves.

psychopath: psychē + pathein, *"disease"*   *noun*

See Lesson 3 of Dimension Two, Part One.

EXERCISES

A. Add the etymon that completes each of the words below.

1. psych_____   hallucinogenic

2. psych_____   production of motion, especially in inanimate objects, by mind power

3. psych_____   clinical technique used by some therapists which calls for participants to role play

4. psych_____   experience bodily symptoms caused by the mind

5. psych_____   a synonym for #4

6. psych_____   one who has the power to engage in telepathy (ESP)

7. psych_____   medical practice that deals with disorders of the mind

8. psych_____   severe mental disorder that deteriorates normal intellectual and social functioning

9. psych_____   a person who has the disorder in number 8

10. psych_____   one who is mentally deranged and who exhibits aggressive social behavior

B. Match each etymon or word ending under Column A with its definition under Column B.

Column A

Column B

1. delos
2. iatria
3. ic
4. kinetos
5. dran
6. soma
7. genos
8. osis
9. patheia
10. otic

a. of or affect with (a word ending)
b. adjective ending meaning "pertaining to"
c. moving
d. to do
e. abnormal condition
f. body
g. origin
h. disease
i. visible
j. healing

C. Provide a word that you have studied to fit each definition.

1. medical practice dealing with mental disorders

2. a severe mental disorder

3. a person who has a psychosis

4. that which caused hallucinations

5. caused by the mind (referring to bodily symptoms)

6. has to do with mind altering drugs

7. one having the ability to engage in telepathy

8. a synonym for #5

9. production of motion, especially in inanimate objects, by the mind

10. clinical therapy that assigns role playing to participants

D. Choose two of the following words: psychiatry, psychic, psychosomatic, psychosis. Use your words in two of your own sentences.

Lesson

8

PAN: *"all"*

Lesson 8 has as its primary etymon the Greek **pan**, meaning "all." A word of caution is in order. All words that begin with **pan** do not carry with them this meaning. For example, the word **pantry** comes from the Italian **pane**, meaning "bread," and has nothing whatever to do with the Greek etymon **pan**. At one time a pantry was a place where bread was stored, among other things. A legitimate question arises: how will I know when **pan** is a Greek etymon? The answer is familiarity and context. You will see such words again and again. They will be seen in many different contexts. For example, "Early Greek thinkers, Aristotle and Plato among them, were **pantologists** inasmuch as there was so little knowledge for them to master that they were able to systemize all of it." The context makes abundantly clear that **pan** in the word **pantologist** is the Greek etymon **pan** meaning "all."

panegyric: pan + **agyris**, *"assembly"* *noun*

The word **panegyric** means "a laudatory or a praiseworthy commendation, either spoken or written." Generally but not always panegyrics are delivered at a public assembly. Oftentimes this public assembly is a gathering of friends and family of a deceased person. The laud or praise is intended for **all** who are **assembled** for the occasion.

panacea: pan + **akeisthai**, *"healing"* *noun*

A **panacea** is a cure-all. The cure alluded to here is not a cure in a medical context. It is more in the nature of a cure for such matters as social ills. For example, there are no panaceas that will eliminate the drug culture from the American scene. The problem is too complex to

230

submit to simplistic solutions. This is the kind of cure the word implies—a solution, if you will, to a thorny problem such as unemployment, race relations, etc. The word is built on the Greek **pan** (all) **akeisthai** (healing).

panchromatic: pan + **chrōma**, *"color"*   *adjective*
The word **panchromatic** means "sensitive to the light of all colors." In this sense, many kinds of film are panchromatic. Panchromatic film for an ordinary still camera can be purchased. The secondary word element **chrōma**, unlike those found in **panegyric** and **panacea**, is used in many English words and is well worth learning: **chromosome; monochromatic; achromatic; polychromatic** are but a few. Do not confuse the etymon **chrōma** with **chronos**, meaning "time," as in **chronology**. The latter word element will be studied in a subsequent lesson.

pandemic: pan + **dēmos**, *"people"*   *adjective*
The word **pandemic** means "relating to all people." Its scope is universal, worldwide. In this connection, there are two other words that belong to this family but which are much more confining than the word **pandemic**. These words are **endemic** and **epidemic**. **Endemic** is the least encompassing of these words: "confined to a localized area." The word **epidemic** has the next degree of coverage: "widely prevalent, not necessarily localized." The word **epidemic** also suggests a rapid spread, as in a flu outbreak. Of course, **pandemic** is the word having the most encompassing coverage: "universal, worldwide." Keep in mind that **demos** is a word element well worth remembering. It is the backbone of many other English words: **democracy, demography, demagogue, demophobia,** and **demotic** to name a few.

panorama: pan + **horama**, *"that which is seen"*   *noun*
A **panorama** is "all that lies in a person's field of vision." It usually encompasses an expansive view as, for example, one is afforded while standing atop a promontory, a high point of land. Or it might be on the observation tower of the Empire State Building, which offers a panoramic view of New York City's skyline, an impressive sight. In any case, a panoramic view is both encompassing and unobstructed.

pantheism: pan + **theos**, *"god"*   *noun*
Pantheism is the belief that God is the sum of all natural forces, or it is any religious belief that God and the universe are one. It is built on the Greek word elements **pan** + **theos**, "god." The secondary word

element, **theos**, is used extensively in English, and it should be remembered: **theocracy, theology, theism**, and many others.

pantology: pan + **logos**, *"study of"*   *noun*
The two etymons that make up the word **pantology** actually define it: **pan**, "all" + **logos**, "study of," the study of all knowledge. This is not a helter-skelter approach; it is, rather, a systematic view of the entire body of human knowledge. At one time there was so little known by man that brilliant thinkers could indeed study and master all that was available to humankind. Today it would be a lot more difficult, but not impossible. With the advent of computers, it is quite realistic that all recorded knowledge could be assembled on microchips. In effect it would be the computer that is the pantologist.

panophobia: pan + **phobos**, *"dread, fear of"*   *noun*
Panophobia is "the dread, irrational fear of all things—human or otherwise." A phobia is a fear that is deep-seated, irrational, and persistent. Panophobics have morbid fears. Howard Hughes was said to have been panophobic. His last years were spent as a recluse because he had a dread of the outside world. Phobias are a form of illness, mental illness, and phobics are in need of professional help.

panoply: pan + **hopla**, *"armor"*   *noun*
The word **panoply** as used now has little if anything to do with armor. It is "a complete array of something." For example, "The book of gastronomic recipes presented a **panoply** of exotic dishes that would titillate the palates of the most discerning epicures." The other meaning that attaches itself to the word is "the complete arms and armor of a warrior." For obvious reasons this meaning has become archaic and is no longer in use.

pantheon: pan + **theos**, *"god"*   *noun*
Pantheon has two meanings, one spiritual, the other secular. In the spiritual sense, a pantheon is a temple dedicated to all the gods. The first of these temples was built by the Romans and completed in 27 B.C. All the gods were housed in this temple and worshipped by Romans. The second meaning, and more widely used, is the realm of heroes or persons venerated by any group. For example, Ernest Hemingway earned his place in the **pantheon** of American literature. Babe Ruth did the same and now resides in the **pantheon** of baseball players.

While such men are certainly not gods, they are venerated for their accomplishments in their respective fields.

EXERCISES

A. Write the meaning of each of the etymons below. Then join it with the word element **pan** to form a lesson word.

1. pan + chroma (   ) = _____

2. pan + demos (   ) = _____

3. pan + theos (   ) = _____

4. pan + theos (   ) = _____

5. pan + logos (   ) = _____

6. pan + phobos (   ) = _____

7. pan + hopla (   ) = _____

8. pan + akeisthai (   ) = _____

9. pan + agyris (   ) = _____

10. pan + horama (   ) = _____

B. Complete each word below by providing the missing etymon.

1. pan _____ = laudatory speech

2. pan _____ = a cure-all

3. pan _____ = realm of heroes

4. pan _____ = sensitive to the light of all colors

5. pan _____ = a wide, expansive view

6. pan _____ = doctrine that God is the sum of all

7. pan _____ = pertaining to all the people

8. pan _____ = relating to all forms or shapes

9. pan _____ = study of all knowledge

10. pan _____ = dread, irrational fear of all things

C. Write T if the statement is true or write F if it is false.

1. A **panegyric** might serve well the occasion of a college president's retirement.

2. One might say that AIDS is a **pandemic** disease since its impact has been felt worldwide.

3. Many earlier cultures were **pantheistic**, worshipping the sky, the stars, the mountains, rivers, along with all other natural forces.

4. A **panoramic** view lay before them as they stood at a busy intersection in New York.

5. **Panchromatic** film is an anomaly since it is sensitive to the light of all colors yet gives prints in black and white.

6. Beethoven belongs in the **pantheon** of great composers.

7. The museum displayed three paintings as a **panoply** of abstract art.

8. **Panophobia** relates to the study of all known knowledge.

9. The study of all forms or shapes is referred to as **pantology**.

10. **Panaceas** are cures for some deadly diseases that afflict humankind.

D. Choose two of the following words: panacea, panorama, panoply, pantheon. Use your words in two sentences of your own.

Lesson

9

PHILOS: *"love"*

The Greek word element **philos** means "love." In many instances this reference to love is not to be taken literally. For instance, in the words hemophiliac, philodendron, and thermophile, **philos** means "tendency toward or attraction to something." Incidentally, how do you suppose the city of Philadelphia came up with its name? Check a collegiate dictionary. A hint might be helpful—Philadelphia is known as the "city of brotherly love."

audiophile: audere, *"hear"* + **philos**   *noun*

An **audiophile** is "a person with a keen interest in high-fidelity sound reproduction." This interest includes radios, phonographs, tape recorders, and the like. Audiophile is one of those words in which the etymon **philos** does not mean "love." Rather it suggests a strong attraction for something. In this case, it's high-fidelity sound reproduction. There are many other words grounded in this etymon: **audiometer, audible, audience, audit, auditorium**, and others.

philogynist: philos + **gynē,** *"woman"*   *noun*

A **philogynist** likes women or, put another way, is attracted to the opposite sex. Not all men are philogynists. A German philosopher named Schopenhauer did not like women. He is quoted as having said that women are the sex with long hair and short brains. He was a **misogynist: miseo,** "hatred" + **gynē,** "woman." Philogynists are ordinary, everyday males who are attracted to ordinary, everyday females.

hemophiliac: haima, *"blood"* **+ philos**   *noun*

A **hemophiliac** "suffers from a disease that causes uncontrolled bleeding." Such persons have no clotting factor in their blood. They are often in need of blood transfusions, and this puts them at risk of having tainted blood transfused during the procedure. AIDS and hepatitis are but two of the deadlier diseases that come with contaminated blood. This is tragic. Usually males are hemophiliacs and the gene is transmitted by the mother. There is no known cure for the disease.

thermophile: thermē, *"heat"* **+ philos**   *noun*

A **thermophile** is not someone who likes the sun. Rather it is a bacterium that requires an environment that provides high temperatures. It is common knowledge that bacteria, at least most of them, thrive in an environment of warmth and moisture. The human mouth provides both, and bacteria in the mouth multiply rapidly. This is the cause of halatosis or bad breath. It's the bacteria that are at fault.

bibliophile: biblion, *"book"* **+ philos**   *noun*

A **bibliophile** is "a collector of books—rare editions, or those having fine or unusual printing." **Philos** in this context does not mean "love." What it does mean is "a strong interest or attraction for," in this case, books. Having many books does not make one a bibliophile. The number of books is not as important as the kind of books one owns. There are other words that make use of the etymon **biblion** meaning "book": **bibliography; bibliomania; bibliolatry**; and others.

philately: philos + ateleia, *"exemption from payment"*   *noun*

A **philatelist** has a keen interest in stamps and other related items, such as postmarks. It should be made clear that, as was the case with bibliophiles, philatelists must be serious collectors of stamps and other relevant materials. The Greek etymon meaning "exemption from payment" is possibly a reference to the fact that the sender pays for the stamp; the recipient is "exempt from payment."

philodendron: philos + dendron, *"tree"*   *noun*

A **philodendron** is a climbing plant cultivated as a houseplant. A philodendron has delicate tendrils and cannot support the weight of the plant. It needs help and must find something to which it can cling while climbing up. A piece of bark from a tree will do very nicely. The Greek word elements are right on the mark.

philander: philos + andros, *"male" verb*
See Lesson 5, Dimension Two, Part Two

philanthropist: philos + anthropos, *"humankind" noun*
See Lesson 5, Dimension Two, Part Two

EXERCISES

A. Fill in the missing word to complete the meaning of the sentence.

1. _____ must be careful not to cut themselves because they have no clotting factor in their blood.

2. Most men are attracted to women and are, therefore, _____.

3. _____ collect books, generally those that are very special in some way—unusual printing, first editions, etc.

4. Many _____ have amassed stamp collections that are worth a small fortune.

5. A _____ is not the kind of man a woman wants as a husband.

6. The _____ while clinging to the wooden stake was able to climb upward to a height of 8′.

7. A bacterium that thrives on high temperatures is known as a
_____.

8. _____ have a keen interest in stereo units that offer listeners a high-fidelity sound reproduction.

B. Match the following etymons and their definitions.

1. philos		a. heat
2. haima		b. tree
3. andros		c. book
4. audio		d. blood
5. gynē		e. man
6. biblion		f. woman
7. thermē		g. hear
8. dendron		h. love

C. Write C if the boldface word is consistent with sentence meaning, or write I if it is not.

1. **Philogynists** are book lovers, especially of rare editions.

2. **Hemophiliacs** collect stamps.

3. **Philatelists** pay no income tax on their collections.

4. **Bibliophiles** have a strong attraction to books of rare vintage or having other exceptional features.

5. **Thermophiles** cannot withstand high temperatures and die after such an exposure.

6. A **philodendron** has the capacity to climb up a tree trunk.

7. An **audiophile** is someone who likes to listen to tapes of favorite music.

8. A **misogynist** and a **philogynist** have little in common when it comes to their feelings concerning women.

D. Choose two of the following words: hemophiliac, bibliophile, philately, philodendron. Use your two words in two of your sentences.

Lesson

10

LOQUI: *"to speak"*

Loqui is a Latin etymon that has made a significant contribution to English. In some words **loq** is altered to **loc**, as in circum**loc**ution. **Lucūt is the past participle of loqui,** and more than this cursory explanation is not necessary for our purposes. Bear in mind that **loq** and **loc** mean the same thing—"to speak."

loquacious: loqui + acious, *"abounding in"* *adjective*

Loquacious is built on **loqui + acious,** "abounding in." The suffix **acious** is an adjective ending and is used rather extensively in English words: **mendacious; voracious; veracious; vivacious**; among others. Have you a friend or acquaintance who talks, talks, talks? If so, this person can be characterized as loquacious: "overly talkative, verbose, garrulous." For the most part, loquacious persons have a hard time finding an audience to listen to their endless prattle.

circumlocution: circum, *"around"* **+ loqui** *noun*

Circumlocution is not a speech pattern that fosters clear communication. It's just the opposite. Ask a brief question that requires a yes or no response, and you will get a twenty-minute diatribe that meanders this way and that, never getting to the crux of the matter. In the end, you are not quite sure whether the circumlocution was intended as a yes or a no. It is, in a word, "evasive speech." Keep in mind that circumlocutory speech is no accident. For the most part it is designed to be unclear. Politicians can be masters of circumlocution.

somniloquent: somnus, *"sleep"* + **loqui** *adjective*

One who is **somniloquent** talks in his or her sleep. The word comes from the Roman god of sleep, Somnus. Incidentally, there is an over-the-counter product called Sominex. Can you guess what it is supposed to help you do? It might also be mentioned, parenthetically, that some **somniloquies** have been the cause of more than a handful of divorces. Can you guess why?

ventriloquist: venter, *"belly"* + **loqui** + **ist,** *"one who"*   *noun*

A **ventriloquist** is able to project his or her voice so that it appears to be coming from someone other than the ventriloquist. The trick to ventriloquism is to bring the sound from deep in the diaphragm and not the mouth. In a sense, the sound must come from the **belly.** This is how a ventriloquist is able to give the impression that a wooden dummy is speaking and not the ventriloquist. Charlie McCarthy and Edgar Bergen made up one of the more successful teams. Yes, the late Edgar Bergen is the father of Candice Bergen of television fame. Finally, the suffix **ist** means "one who": **violinist, pianist, dentist, cellist, perfectionist.**

soliloquy: solus, *"alone"* + **loqui**   *noun*

A **soliloquy** is "a speech made by one person, or as though one were alone." It is a dramatic device that allows the writer to share the thoughts of one of the characters in the drama with the audience. How else would the audience know what Macbeth was thinking when he delivers the soliloquy, "Is this a dagger which I see before me . . ." or Hamlet's thoughts when he utters perhaps the most famous soliloquy ever, "To be, or not to be . . ." These are soliloquies, a technique used by writers to allow the audience to be privy to the innermost thoughts of a character.

colloquy: col, *"together"* + **loqui**   *noun*

A **colloquy** is "conversation, especially a formal one." A panel discussion by experts on the economic ramifications of lower interest rates is a colloquy. The key word is **formal.** On the other hand, the word **colloquial,** which is built on the very same word elements, means something quite different. It is an informal conversation. The difference between the words is a matter of formality or the lack of it.

elocution: e, *"out"* + **loqui**   *noun*
eloquence: e, *"out"* + **loqui**   *noun*
The words **elocution** and **eloquence** have a common origin, but they do not mean the same thing. Elocution is "the study and practice of public speaking." Eloquence, on the other hand, means "having the power of fluency, characterized by forceful and appropriate expression." In other words, taking a course in elocution should improve one's eloquence. An important point needs to be made: lessons in elocution are not essential to one's eloquence. Abraham Lincoln never took a course in elocution, but he was an eloquent speaker.

grandiloquent: grandis, *"great"* + **loqui**   *adjective*
A **grandiloquent** speaker is "one who uses grandiloquent language, both pompous and ostentatious." There is another word in English that means the same thing—magniloquent: **magnus,** "great" + **loqui.** Either of these can characterize speakers who project a lofty tone. Of course one should avoid grandiloquence or magniloquence, since both are displays of pompous and affected speech.

EXERCISES

A. Match the words below from Column A with their definitions from Column B.

Column A

1. circumlocution
2. somniloquent
3. soliloquy
4. colloquy
5. ventriloquist
6. grandiloquent
7. eloquent
8. loquacious
9. elocution
10. magniloquent

Column B

a. talking in one's sleep
b. using pompous language
c. forceful, appropriate language expression
d. evasive speech
e. act of speaking alone on stage
f. talkative
g. using formal conversation
h. study of public speaking
i. synonym for grandiloquent
j. one able to project his or her voice

B. Give the meaning of each of the etymons below.

1. solus   6. circum
2. col   7. e(loc)
3. venter   8. grandis
4. acious   9. magnus
5. somnus   10. e(loq)

C. Complete each word below by writing the missing word part.

1. _____ locution   (study of public speaking)

2. _____ loquent   (using pompous language)

3. loqu_____   (talkative)

4. _____ locution   (roundabout expression)

5. _____ loquent   (talking in one's sleep)

6. _____ loquy   (a speech while alone on stage)

7. _____ loquent   (ostentatious language use)

8. _____ loquy   (formal public conversation)

9. _____ loquence   (spoken fluency)

10. _____ loquist   (one able to project his or her voice)

D. Choose two of the following words: loquacious, ventriloquist, soliloquy, eloquence. Use the words in two of your own sentences.

Lesson

11

EU: *"good; well"*

Eu is a Greek etymon and it means "good or well." The Latin equivalent, which will be studied in a subsequent lesson, is **bene**. Also, two words in which **eu** appears are presented in other lessons as well: **eugenics** (Lesson Four, Dimension Two, Part One) and **euthanasia** (Lesson Ten, Dimension One, Part Two). These words are listed in this lesson, but for fuller treatment turn to the lessons noted.

euthenics: eu + **thenein**, *"swelling"* *noun*

Euthenics is built on the Greek **eu** + **thenein** (from the Sanskrit meaning "swelling"). The dictionary defines euthenics as the science which deals with the development of human well-being by improvement of living conditions. Local, state, and federal governments are engaged in euthenic undertakings in an effort to improve the quality of life for those living in depressed areas, especially those areas found in large cities.

euphemism: eu + **pheme**, *"speaking"* *noun*

A **euphemism** is a substitute expression for one that is thought to be overly harsh, blunt, or offensive. There are many such expressions in our language—**pass away** for **die**; in the case of animals **put to sleep** is a substitute for **destroy** or **kill**; the Nazi reference to genocide is perhaps the most tragic—**the final solution**. There are many euphemisms. Should they be avoided? The answer is "no" in many instances. Rather than offend someone, euphemisms are preferred. Be mindful that there are those euphemisms that distort the true meaning intended and should be avoided. For example, to use the euphe-

243

mism **forgetful** for a **thoughtless** person is not justified. If the thoughtless person is offended, then so be it. Good judgment is called for.

eulogy: eu + logos, *"word"*   *noun*

You may recall that in a previous lesson it was pointed out that **logos** has two meanings: "study or science of" and "word." **Eulogy** is a word that uses **logos** to mean "word." It is a praiseworthy speech, a speech of commendation. Such formal addresses are generally reserved for very special occasions. One of the most common of these occasions is a funeral. The speaker will recall to the mourners and friends just how great a person the deceased was. It is a sad fact that oftentimes people wait too long to let people know just how talented and likeable they are in life. It takes their dying to bring this out.

eurythmic: eu + rhythmos, *"rhythm"*   *adjective*

Eurythmic is exactly what one might think it is: "harmonious bodily movements to music." In this sense, aerobic exercise classes that move to music might well be characterized as eurhythmic. The key to determining this for yourself is to know what the word element **eu** means. **Rhythmos** is self explanatory and quite logical in its association with the English **rhythm**. Put them together and **eurythmic** appears.

eutrophic: eu + trephein, *"nourish"*   *noun*

That which is **eutrophic** designates a body of water in which the increase of mineral and organic nutrients has dissolved oxygen, producing an environment that is conducive to plant but not animal life. Granted, you may not have occasion to use this word in your entire life, unless of course you became a botanist. But this is unimportant. It's not the word that we're after. **Learning word elements is our primary goal in this dimension**. For instance, the word **eutrophic** can lead to **dystrophic**, which in turn steers us in the direction of **dyspepsia**, which channels us to **eupeptic** and so on. The words are of secondary importance. Learning etymons will allow you to enlarge your vocabulary almost exponentially rather than one word at a time.

eupepsia: eu + pepsis, *"digestion"*   *noun*

Eupepsia means "good digestion." That is the extent of the meaning provided by collegiate dictionaries. Unlike its counterpart **dyspepsia**, it has nothing whatever to do with one's disposition. Dyspepsia means "bad digestion," but along with this literal meaning there is a figurative definition as well—"morose, gloomy in disposition." Of course, bad digestion could very well put one out of sorts, so the moroseness and gloominess might well be an extension of a "bellyache."

euphoria: eu + pherein, *"to bear"*   *noun*
Euphoria is "a feeling of well-being," especially an exaggerated one having no basis in fact. For example, upon awakening in the morning one is overcome by a feeling of well-being. Only good things can happen on this day. Just why one is influenced by this good feeling cannot be explained. It's just the way one feels. The opposite word for **euphoria** is **dysphoria**—"dissatisfaction, restlessness, fidgeting." Keep in mind that words prefixed with **eu** have something to do with "good;" prefixed with **dys**, the word has something to do with "bad."

euphony: eu + phonē, *"sound"*   *noun*
Euphony is "a pleasant, harmonious sound," pleasing to the ear. As a matter of fact, the sound of the word euphony has a pleasant ring to it. The word having the opposite meaning of **euphony** is **cacophony**—"a harsh, discordant, unpleasant sound." Again, listen to the word's gutteral sound—(ka KOFF o nee.) The repetition of the **k** sound is **cacophonous**. So, here are two words having to do with sound—one good, the other bad.

eugenics: eu + genos, *"birth"*   *noun*
See Lesson 4, Dimension Two, Part One

euthanasia: eu + thanatos, *"death"*   *noun*
See Lesson 10, Dimension One, Part Two

EXERCISES

A. Below are etymons used in conjunction with **eu** to form a word. Write the item that correctly defines the etymon.

1. **thenein:** (a) swelling (b) death (c) thinning (d) to mix

2. **gen:** (a) sound (b) birth (c) swollen (d) jump

3. **pepsis:** (a) dissatisfaction (b) digestion (c) restless (d) harmonious

4. **phōnē**: (a) self (b) digestion (c) heat (d) sound

5. **logos**: (a) word (b) nourish (c) commend (d) faulty

B. Match each word with its definition.

1. euphemism
2. eugenics
3. euthanasia
4. euthenics
5. eupepsia
6. euphoria
7. euphony
8. eulogy
9. eurythmic
10. eutrophic

a. science dealing with the improvement of living conditions
b. substitute expression for one thought to be too harsh
c. literally a good birth (planned breeding)
d. a good death (mercy killing)
e. feeling of well-being for no valid reason
f. pleasant sound
g. good digestion
h. harmonious bodily movements, as in aerobics
i. referring to a body of water conducive to growth of plant life
j. praiseworthy speech

C. Choose a word for each of the blanks below to complete the sentence. Use the words from Exercise B.

1. The minister delivered a _____ over the casket containing the body of the late mayor.

2. _____ is quite common in the breeding of purebred animals.

3. To cut another's life short to end pain and suffering is called _____.

4. Using a _____ is one way to avoid offending someone, substituting a more gentle way of expressing an idea.

5. While the federal government is involved in projects of a _____ nature, precious little progress is in evidence, especially in public housing units found in large metropolitan cities.

6. _____ quite simply means good digestion, unlike its opposite, dyspepsia.

7. A medley of _____ sounds emanated from the cafe beckoning passers-by to stop in and enjoy the music.

8. _____, a feeling of well-being, is generally a state of being that cannot be explained.

9. _____ exercise is both enjoyable and beneficial to those who engage in it.

10. That which is _____ is beneficial, especially to plant life.

D. Choose two of the following words: euphemism, eulogy, eurythmic, euphoria. Use your two words in two sentences.

REVIEW OF LESSONS 6 - 11

A. Match the following items.

Column A   Column B

1. hieros   a. god
2. phone   b. sleep
3. psychē   c. self
4. pater   d. sacred
5. solus   e. sound
6. sōma   f. around
7. philos   g. power
8. theos   h. good; well
9. auto   i. woman
10. somnus   j. alone
11. gynē   k. mind
12. kratos   l. father
13. circum   m. hear
14. eu   n. love
15. audio   o. body

B. Write the meaning of each of the two etymons, and then write the English word derived from them.

1. pan _____ + theos _____ = _____

2. psychē _____ + dēlos _____ = _____

3. audere _____ + philos _____ = _____

4. biblion _____ + philos _____ = _____

5. eu _____ + pheme _____ = _____

6. thermē _____ + philos _____ = _____

7. pan _____ + demos _____ = _____

8. aristos _____ + kratos _____ = _____

9. mono _____ + archon _____ = _____

10. somnus _____ + loqui _____ = _____

11. eu _____ + logos _____ = _____

12. solus _____ + loqui _____ = _____

13. theos _____ + kratos _____ = _____

14. psychē _____ + iatria _____ = _____

15. eu _____ + phonē _____ = _____

   C. Write C if the boldface word is used in a way that is consistent with sentence meaning, or write I if it is not.

1. **Philatelists** collect stamps as a hobby.

2. **Circumlocution** is a much desired characteristic of effective speaking or of eloquent speakers.

3. The armed services of the United States are representative examples of **hierarchical** organizations.

4. **Loquacious** speakers hold their audience's rapt attention.

5. Sometimes **euphemisms** are appropriate and should be used.

6. The federal government seems not to do an effective job when it engages in **euthenic** enterprises.

7. There are few **psychics** who can live up to their reputations in the area of extrasensory perception.

8. **Patriarchies** are limited to governments only.

9. One who has a **psychosis** is psychotic.

10. A **psychogenic** ailment is induced by the mind.

D. Choose any 10 words from Lessons 6-11 and use each of them in a sentence. Don't simply define a word in a sentence: "Somniloquent means to talk in one's sleep." Try to be more creative: **"Somniloquence can be embarrassing to the sleeper if there is someone to listen to what is said."** Try a few for yourself.

Lesson

12

PHŌNĒ: *"sound"*

The Greek etymon **phōnē** is one that is used extensively in English. Any word that is made up in part by the **phōnē** word element has something to do with sound. There are no exceptions. You will find that words are repeated from previous lessons, and this is as it should be. Most etymons enjoy a symbiotic relationship with words—they feed off each other. For example, **tele** was a word element studied in a previous lesson. In it the word **telephone** appears. In other words, **phōnē** is a root word that combines with **tele**, and **tele** combines with **phōnē**. It appears in two places in your work.

aphonic: a, *"without; no"* + **phōnē** *adjective*

The word **aphonic** means "voiceless." Its most common cause is pathological. Throat cancer, for instance, is one such pathology that can cause this condition. It is also used in the study of phonetics; in this context it refers to a letter or letters of the alphabet that are not voiced. The letter **p** is unvoiced, while **b** is voiced.

hydrophone: hydor, *"water"* + **phōnē** *noun*

A **hydrophone** is an instrument that detects sound underwater. It can detect, for example, a running engine, and in this sense is an invaluable tool that submarines use. Fishermen also use this type device to locate schools of fish. One other use of hydrophones is to detect the flow of water through a pipe. Hydraulic companies, those that provide you with drinking water, find that this instrument is very useful in detecting broken water mains.

megaphone: megalas, *"large"* + **phone** *noun*
   A device, usually funnel shaped, used for projecting and directing the voice. Megaphones are still quite popular at football and basketball games, especially at the high school level. Who can resist pounding one's feet at a pep rally with cheerleaders shouting through their megaphones, "Louder!"

cacophony: kakos, *"bad"* + **phone** *noun*
   The word **cacophony** was built into the lesson dealing with **eu,** "good; well." It was used in conjunction with the word **euphony**—a good sound which could be translated into a "pleasant sound." **Cacophony** is its opposite. What might be heard at a bustling international harbor—tugs bellowing their presence, seamen going about their jobs, not too quietly, and cranes lifting heavy containers onto freighters—might well be characterized as cacophonous. If one thinks about it, the word **euphony** has a smooth, melodious ring to it; cacophonous has a harsh gutteral sound attached to it.

xylophone: xylon, *"wood"* + **phōnē** *noun*
   A **xylophone** is a percussion instrument (the striking together of two objects such as cymbals and drums) that is made up of wooden slats of graduated length which when struck by two small mallets produce musical sound. There is a similar instrument which is made up of metal slats, and it is called a **vibraphone.** Keep in mind that the slats of a xylophone are made of wood.

phonics: phōnē, *"sound"* *noun*
   Phonics is a method of teaching reading based on sound. Do you recall a former teacher who, when you were stumped with a word's spelling, would encourage you to **sound it out.** Your teacher was asking you to apply phonetic analysis skills to help you with the word's spelling or its pronunciation. The other method of teaching reading is referred to as the sight method. Hopefully after seeing a word a number of times, you will recall the word's spelling from sight—you have a picture of the word in your mind and simply reproduce it.

polyphony: poly, *"many"* + **phōnē** *noun*
   The word **polyphony** can refer to vocal harmony such as in a choral group. It can also mean music with two or more independent melodies sounded together. The word is used exclusively with reference to music.

EXERCISES

A. Complete each word below by writing the missing word element, one that has been used in this lesson.

1. _____ phony = pleasant sound

2. _____ phone = a percussion instrument

3. _____ phone = instrument for detecting underwater sound

4. _____ phony = harsh, discordant sound

5. _____ phony = vocal harmony

6. _____ phone = device for amplifying sound

7. _____ phone = device that transmits and receives sound from afar

8. _____ phonic = voiceless

9. phon_____ = study of sound system of a language

B. Match the word element with its definition.

1. xylon	a. bad
2. poly	b. well
3. hydor	c. large
4. logos	d. word
5. megalas	e. not; without
6. phone	f. water
7. a; an	g. many
8. tele	h. sound
9. kakos	i. wood
10. eu	j. distance

C. Write T if the statement is true or F if it is not.

1. **Aphonia** is a disease which affects the throat.

2. A **hydrophone** would be invaluable to a scuba diver.

3. The barbershop quartet is one kind of **polyphony**.

4. **Phonics** is one way to teach youngsters to read by teaching them the sounds that make up language.

5. One might expect to hear **cacophonous** sounds at a busy international airport.

6. A **xylophone** is played by striking metal bars of varying length.

7. The words **euphony** and **cacophony** are opposites.

8. **Phonologists** would, of course, study the phonetic composition of a language.

9. A **vibraphone** and a **xylophone** are essentially the same instrument.

10. A **megaphone** works on the same principle as a microphone.

D. Choose two of the following words: megaphone, cacophony, xylophone, phonics. Use the two words in two sentences of your own.

Lesson

13

GRAPHEIN: *"to write; to draw"*
The Greek word **graphein** is one of the ten most commonly used etymons in the English language. It contributes to a great number of words whose meanings are common knowledge: **telegraph; monograph; phonograph; stenography**; and **graphite**. There are many others. The words presented below are not so well known. Bear in mind that the acquisition of new words themselves is not as valuable to you as the learning of etymons which go to make up these words. These word elements extend to countless other words, which will allow you to acquire whole families of words as opposed to one word at a time. One etymon, such as **graphein**, can unlock the meanings of as many as ten, twenty words, which is a much more efficient method of vocabulary development than to learn words one at a time.

bibliography: biblion, *"book"* + **graphein** *noun*
A **bibliography** is a list of titles written by an author, or it may be a list of titles printed by a publisher. A third "might be" is a list of writings on a given subject. As you can easily see, bibliographies are quite adaptable. One of the primary functions of a bibliography in terms of student use is to access references, which will provide additional material on a given subject. In this context, they are invaluable tools of learning too often ignored by students.

orthography: orthos, *"correct"* + **graphein** *noun*
cacography: kakos, *"bad"* + **graphein** *noun*
We have already met the etymon **kakos**, meaning "bad." Do you recall the word **cacophony—kako,** "bad" + **phonē**, "sound"? As you

254

learned, it means harsh, discordant sound, bad sound. **Cacography**, on the other hand, has to do with bad writing—poor penmanship or poor spelling. The word for correct spelling according to established usage is **orthography: orthos**, "correct" + **graphein**. There are other words that make use of the etymon **orthos—orthodox; orthopedics; orthodontic**; and others. All have to do with correctness in one sense or another. The two words are presented as a pair for what should be obvious reasons.

calligraphy: kallos, *"beautiful"* + **graphein**   *noun*
   Calligraphy is "the art of fine handwriting." Actually the Greek etymons together mean "beautiful writing." Calligraphy has nothing to do with spelling and is unrelated to the word orthography except that they share the same etymon **graphein**. The word **calligraphy** is, however, an antonym for the word cacography—poor penmanship. Do you recall the word **calliope**? It too is built on the Greek etymon **kallos**, meaning "beauty."

graffiti: graphium, *"stylus"*   *noun*
   Graffiti is the plural form of **graffito**, which derives from the Latin **graphium**. The Latin alters in Italian to **graffio**, meaning "stylus" or "the scratching of a stylus" (a tracing pen). Graffiti means "rude inscriptions found on sidewalks, building walls (interior or exterior), and large rocks." One must not confuse the word epigraphy and graffiti. Epigraphy is the formal study of inscriptions, rude or otherwise.

topography: topos, *"place"* + **graphein**   *noun*
   Topography is the technique of graphically representing the exact physical features—mountains, rivers, valley, etc.—of a place or region. Such representations are shown on maps. Here is an instance where **graphein** means "draw" rather than "write."

cartography: carte, *"map"* + **graphein**
   Cartography is the art of making (drawing?) maps and charts. The mapmaker is a cartographer. Incidentally, the word topography has to do with mapmaking, too. As a matter of fact, it is the cartographer who draws the physical features of an area on maps—topography.

seismograph: seismos, *"earthquake"* **+ graphein**   *noun*
   Seismographs are "scientific instruments that are used to detect and record relevant data pertaining to earthquakes." They can be found in all parts of the world, but most especially in areas that are earthquake prone such as California. The word for the study of earthquakes is **seismology**, and one who studies it is a **seismologist**.

lexicographer: lexikos, *"of words"* **+ graphein**   *noun*
   A **lexicographer** is a dictionary writer. A lexicon is a dictionary. Enough said!

pornography: pornē, *"harlot"* **+ graphein**   *noun*
   The word **pornography** has an interesting origin. It comes from the Greek **pornographos**, which means "writing about prostitutes." Incidentally, harlot and prostitute are synonyms. When asked for an interpretation of just what constituted pornography, a Supreme Court Justice replied that he couldn't define it, but he knew it when he saw it. Today the word means "sexually explicit behavior portrayed in writing or in pictures to arouse sexual excitement." An historian observed that the pervasiveness of pornography speaks reams about the culture in which it is found.

demography: demos, *"people"* **+ graphein**   *noun*
   Demographers are concerned with the study of human population relative to such features as size, growth, ethnic structure, and individual preferences. The latter is used by advertising executives to determine how an advertisement should be slanted. Another important use of demographics is census taking. Not to be overlooked, pollsters play a pivotal role in politics. Candidates use polls to determine strategy.

epigraphy: epi, *"upon"* **+ graphein**   *noun*
   Epigraphy is "the study of inscriptions, especially inscriptions of an historical nature such as ancient hieroglyphs." It may also take the form of an inscription on a statue such as the Statue of Liberty: "Give me your tired, your poor, . . ." a classic example of epigraphy.

EXERCISES

A. Match the words under Column A with their definitions under Column B.

Column A

1. cacography
2. bibliography
3. pornography
4. seismograph
5. epigraphy
6. demography
7. lexicography
8. calligraphy
9. graffiti
10. topography
11. cartography
12. orthography

Column B

a. list of titles used to access information
b. poor writing
c. correct spelling
d. study of human population for various reasons
e. a scientific instrument used to detect and record earthquake activity
f. study of inscriptions on statues or buildings
g. rude inscription found on walls, for example
h. literally "beautiful writing"
i. the art of map making
j. technique of graphically depicting physical features of land on a map
k. relates to dictionary writing
l. sexually explicit material, graphic or written

B. Write C if the boldface word is consistent with the meaning of the sentence or I if it is not.

1. **Demographers** are pollsters of one kind or another.

2. The earthquake registered 7.2 on the **seismograph**.

3. **Epigraphies** are quite common on many New York City skyscrapers.

4. **Orthography** and **cacography** can be opposites.

5. **Cacography** deals with poor spelling and penmanship.

6. **Graffiti** is commonplace in many areas of large metropolitan cities.

7. **Topography** has nothing to do with mapmaking.

8. **Cartographers** should be well versed with topographical features of areas that they are working on.

9. A **bibliography** might be helpful to a student who is writing a term paper.

10. **Lexicographers** draw maps in fine handwriting called **calligraphy**.

C. Write the meaning of each of the following etymons. Then write the word from this lesson that makes use of this etymon.

	Meaning	Word
1. biblion	_____	_____
2. orthos	_____	_____
3. kakos	_____	_____
4. kallos	_____	_____
5. topos	_____	_____
6. carte	_____	_____
7. seismos	_____	_____
8. epi	_____	_____
9. porne	_____	_____
10. demos	_____	_____

D. Choose two of the following words: bibliography, calligraphy, graffiti, seismograph. Use your two words in two original sentences.

Lesson

14

LOGOS: *study or science of; word or speech*

Countless words in English employ the Greek etymon **logos**. The English version of **logos** is **ology**. This Greek word element has two different meanings: "study or science of" and "word or speech." Usually the meaning of **logos** will be the former. If not otherwise designated, the meaning of **ology** in the following words will be "study or science of."

chronology: chronos, *"time"* + **logos**   *noun*

A **chronology** is a time line of sorts which orders events from the most distant past to the most recent present. History books, for example, are arranged chronologically for obvious reasons. In a different vein, we all have a chronological age—the number of years that have passed since the day of our birth. In brief, chronologies are sequenced in order of time.

paleontology: palaios, *"ancient"* + **logos**   *noun*

Paleontology is a branch of archeology, the scientific study of historic or prehistoric peoples and their cultures, that analyzes artifacts, inscriptions, and fossils that have left tell-tale clues to vanished civilizations. One who studies paleontology is a paleontologist. There is a spelling variant of the word—**palaeontology**.

petrology: petra, *"rock"* + **logos**   *noun*

The study of rocks, their origins, structure, composition changes, and classification is the work of **petrologists**. Be mindful that this endeavor is not a hobby kind of activity. It is a recognized scientific study. Petrology, paleontology, and archeology are interrelated sciences, which overlap on occasion.

tautology: tauto, *"same"* + **logos**, *"word"*   *noun*
A **tautology** is a needless repetition—a redundancy as in the "old woman spinster." A spinster by definition is a woman; hence, woman in the phrase is a tautology—a needless repetition.

ornithology: ornis, *"bird"* + **logos**   *noun*
Ornithologists are people who study a branch of zoology, the science that deals with animals. This branch is the study of birds. Bear in mind that all bird-watchers are not ornithologists. Ornithology is a scientific study as opposed to a casual interest, even an avid interest in birds.

cosmology: kosmos, *"world"* + **logos**   *noun*
Cosmology is the branch of philosophy that investigates the origin and structures of the universe (the cosmos). It is a far more complex study than this, but for our purposes a more detailed explanation of this esoteric science is not needed. Suffice it to say that the cosmos—the entire universe—is the proper study of cosmologists.

necrology: nekros, *"dead body"* + **logos**, *"word"*   *noun*
A **necrology** is a listing of people who have recently died. Sounds a lot like an obituary, doesn't it? Well, it does because it is—an obituary, that is. There are other words that make use of the etymon **nekros** meaning "dead body": **necropolis; necrobiosis; necromancy; necrophobia; necrophilia; necrosis**; and **necropsy**. Check them out. They all have something to do with "death or dying."

ichthyology: ichthys, *"fish"* + **logos**   *noun*
Ichthyology is a branch of zoology that deals with fishes. Again, please don't confuse an ichthyologist with one of your piscatorial friends, an avid fisherman. Ichthyologists are scientists who study a specialized branch of zoology that deals with fish.

ethnology: ethnos, *"race; nation"* + **logos**   *noun*
Ethnology is a branch of anthropology that analyzes cultures with reference to their historical development. It also engages itself in the study that distinguishes characteristics that relate to races that make up humankind. Perhaps now the euphemism **ethnic cleansing** takes on a more significant meaning.

etymology: etymos, *"true"* + **logos**, *"word"*   *noun*

    Etymologies are what we are now engaged in studying—the true meanings of words. In brief, the etymological study of words requires one to trace a word's origin from its earliest known use and its transmission from one language to another. In our case, from any foreign language to English. Not to be confused with **entomology**, the study of insects.

EXERCISES

    A. Match the etymon found under Column A with its meaning found under Column B.

Column A   Column B

  1. palaios   a. same
  2. kosmos   b. time
  3. chronos   c. world
  4. nekros   d. true
  5. ornis   e. fish
  6. petra   f. dead body
  7. etymos   g. rock
  8. ethnos   h. ancient
  9. ichthys   i. bird
10. tauto   j. race; nation

    B. Write C if the boldface word is consistent with the meaning of the sentence or write I if it is not.

1. **Paleontologists** study ancient fossils, among many other things.

2. **Ornithologists** study both flora and fauna.

3. **Ichthyologists** study creatures that live in the sea.

4. A **chronology** arranges items in numerical sequence.

5. A **tautology** is a word that is vital to the sentence meaning.

6. **Ethnicity** has to do with one's race or culture.

7. A **necrology** can be found in one's daily newspaper.

8. Our work in this book, especially this section, deals with **etymologies**.

9. **Cosmologists** study the earth's rotation on its axis.

10. A hobbyist who collects coins is a **petrologist**.

C. Match each word in Column A with its definition in Column B.

Column A   Column B

1. necrology   a. scientific study of humankind
2. cosmology   b. an obituary notice
3. paleontology   c. a branch of zoology that studies fish
4. ornithologist   d. true meanings of words
5. ichthyology   e. a time line, for example
6. etymology   f. the study of rocks, their origin and structure
7. ethnicity   g. study of the universe
8. chronology   h. one who studies birds in a scientific context
9. petrology   i. a needless repetition
10. tautology   j. having to do with one's race or culture

D. Choose two of the following words: chronology, paleontology, ornithology, etymology. Use the two words in two sentences of your own.

Lesson

15

SPECERE: *"to look or to see"*

The Latin **specere** meaning "to look or to see" is an etymon of many English words. It should be noted that **spic, spec**, and **spect** are generally derived from **specere**. Keep in mind that in Dimension Two, learning individual words is **not** one of its goals. Rather, it is to provide you with an opportunity to introduce yourself to etymons that contribute to families of words. The etymon **specere** is one such etymon that extends itself to dozens of English words which together comprise a family of words. Make every effort to learn the word elements; the words will take care of themselves.

perspicacious: per, *"through"* + **specere** *adjective*

The word **perspicacious** comes from the Latin prefix **per**, "through" + **specere**. It is an adjective which characterizes a person of keen mental discernment. A perspicacious mind can't be fooled, for it is like a powerful beacon that would see through the deception in a twinkling of the eye. Perspicacious minds are not that common. Use the word judiciously.

perspicuous: per, *"through"* + **specere** *adjective*

Perspicuous is built on the same two Latin words as **perspicacious**. There is, however, a major difference between the two. Perspicacious applies to mental perception while perspicuous refers to the thing perceived. An argument, for example, is perspicuous if it is clear, unobscure, and unambiguous. It is therefore seen through, or understood, because of its clarity. Perspicacious refers to mind; perspicuous, to things.

specious: speciosus, *"good-looking"* *adjective*

The word **specious** comes from the Latin **speciosus**, meaning "good-looking." Through usage it evolved and eventually came to mean deceptively good-looking, and it is this sense which passed into the English **specious**. Reasoning which is specious sounds plausible and correct, but upon close examination it proves to be faulty. **The reasoning only looks good.** Also bear in mind that the **good-looking** does not apply in a physical sense. It is used to characterize abstract things—an argument, a comment, reasoning, etc.

auspicious: auspex, *"one who predicts by observing birds"* *adjective*

While this may upon first blush appear to be rather absurd, there is in fact a plausible explanation. **Au** derives from **avis**, the Latin word for **bird**. In ancient times prophecies were made by seers or diviners who used their proclaimed powers to advise noblemen and even kings. They could predict things that had not yet happened—at least this was their claim. Obviously they imparted to the nobility only those prophecies that would result in good, never evil. The secret to their power could be found in birds, more specifically the entrails of birds. They would eviscerate a bird and read the entrails for signs which made it possible to look or to see into the future. Hence from **auspex** is derived the word **auspicious**, meaning "of good omen," or **constituting a favorable sign** such as those provided by the seers to the nobility. It is a plausible explanation.

aspect: ad, *"at"* + **specere** *noun*

Aspect has several meanings, nine as a matter of fact. For our purposes two of them take precedence because they are used most frequently. The first of these meanings is "a way in which a thing is perceived or regarded." For example, "Both aspects of the proposition were challenged." The second meaning is the appearance of something to the eye or mind as "the diverse cultural aspect of democracies." The context will help you to determine which of the meanings applies.

introspection: intro, *"within"* + **specere** *noun*

Introspection is the act of self-examination. It is a looking into one's inner self in order to understand better those feelings or states of mind. Introspection is a solitary activity, a kind of soul-searching. Be mindful that there are other **spect** words: **inspect; respect; suspect; spectroscope; spectator**; and others.

prospectus: pro, *"forward"* + **specere**   *noun*

In the world of finance and commerce, a **prospectus** is a report with information relating to a forthcoming project. Many large firms issue a prospectus to shareholders detailing what new projects are on line for the company. Essentially, a prospectus "looks forward or looks to the future."

retrospect: retro, *"back"* + **specere**   *noun*

To examine something in **retrospect** is to look back on it. For instance, you may have bought a car, a Ford Taurus. Some months later in retrospect you thought you made the wrong choice. You should have bought an Oldsmobile. In broadest possible terms, retrospection is a contemplation of the past. It is pretty much the opposite of prospectus, which looks to the future.

specter: specere, *"to see"*   *noun*

A **specter** is a ghost, especially one of a frightening nature. It also has another meaning, equally sinister. A specter is a source of dread or terror. For example, for many college students final exam time is a specter to which they do not look forward. Or, one may think of an IRS audit as a specter. In either case, a specter is something seen as terrifying, frightening.

spectrum: specere, *"to see"*   *noun*

Spectrum has two meanings. One deals with the science of light and color, the other is a broad range of varied but related ideas that go to make up a sequence of ideas, as the political spectrum—conservative, moderate, and liberal. Some fine-tuning can be done in this regard, but for all intents and purposes they embrace the political spectrum as we know it. The meaning attached to light waves is complex, too esoteric for our purposes to be of any value.

EXERCISES

A. Match the word under Column A with its definition under Column B.

Column A

Column B

1. prospectus
2. aspect

a. broad range of varied but related ideas or things

3. perspicacious   b. appearance; view
4. retrospect   c. clear; lucid; unambiguous
5. specter   d. a look back
6. specious   e. marked by keen mental discernment
7. introspection   f. apparition; visible spirit
8. perspicuous   g. favorable; propitious
9. auspicious   h. looking within one's own mind
10. spectrum   i. advance information about an investment
                         j. appearing to be true without being so

B. Write T if the sentence is true or F if it is not.

1. An **aspect** of this debate on social issues could be teenage unemployment among minority youth.

2. An **introspection** is the first part of an introduction.

3. **Perspicuous** presentations are particularly dull and uninspiring.

4. **Specious** reasoning is a ploy oftentimes used by scam artists.

5. One should examine in **retrospect** those things that are to be done in the very near future.

6. A rainbow, for example, displays many colors of the **spectrum**.

7. A **perspicacious** mind will present **perspicuous** arguments.

8. The team's win last night was an **auspicious** beginning to their season.

9. One should read a **prospectus** carefully before making any decisions.

10. The **specter** of final exams overjoyed the student body.

C. Complete each sentence by writing the appropriate word from this lesson.

1. At the seance, a woman insisted that she saw a _____ of her husband who has long been dead.

2. _____, or self-examination, is food for the soul; many of our shortcomings come into sharper focus.

3. The company forwarded to all its stockholders a (an) _____ anticipating the year's profits.

4. Scientists must investigate the entire _____ of possibilities before making any claim to have discovered a cure for a disease, for example.

5. The salesman's _____ reasoning for my purchasing a new car sounded plausible until it was examined carefully.

6. The committee thanked the chairperson for the _____ presentation that he made concerning their work.

7. It was a (an)_____ sign that occurred that day which made him decide to ask his girlfriend to marry him.

8. Her _____ mind countered my every move, and it wasn't long before I lost my queen and bishop and ultimately the match.

9. The murder investigation took on a new _____ when a second body was discovered in an upstairs bedroom.

10. The football coach realized his mistake after thinking about the game in _____.

    D. Choose two of the following words: specious, aspect, retrospect, specter. Use your two words in two original sentences.

REVIEW OF LESSONS 11 - 15

    A. Directions: Listed below find two sets of word elements. Under **Part A** there is a list of secondary etymons which when combined with a primary etymon from **Part B** will form a word. You are to write the word in a lettered list in **Part C**.

Example:

Part A
    a. a, an

Part B
    2. phōnē

Part C
    a. aphonic

Part A

a. a, an	k. kakos
b. ortho	l. carte
c. demos	m. per
d. biblion	n. thanatos
e. retro	o. pro
f. hydor	p. nekros
g. psyché	q. lexikos
h. chronos	r. epi
i. ichthys	s. gen
j. etymos	t. intro

Part B

1. graphein

2. phōnē

3. logos

4. eu

5. specere

Part C

a. _____	k. _____
b. _____	l. _____
c. _____	m. _____
d. _____	n. _____
e. _____	o. _____
f. _____	p. _____
g. _____	q. _____
h. _____	r. _____
i. _____	s. _____
j. _____	t. _____

   B. Write C if the boldface word is consistent with the meaning of
   the sentence, or write I if it is not. If the word usage is incorrect, then explain why this is so. Those boldface words that are
   used correctly require nothing more than the designation C.

   1. It would take a great deal of practice and some considerable tal-
   ent to become expert in the artistic realm known as **calligraphy**.

2. Writing a term paper, in most instances, requires the writer to provide a **bibliography** of the works used in its preparation.

3. A **necrology** can be found on headstones in a cemetery.

4. The United States is a prime example of a **gynocracy.**

5. That which has become **petrified** takes on the appearance and feel of rock.

6. The **Pantheon** in ancient Rome was a temple to all the gods.

7. Loud, harshly grating noises when combined produce a **cacophony** of sound.

8. **Demographers** are very much interested in census information.

9. That which **atrophies** shrinks in size, as muscles in the leg might.

10. **Introspection** and **retrospection** mean pretty much the same thing.

Dimension Two
Part Two

precocious

Prefixes

Prefixes make an important contribution to our language. They add precision to it that would otherwise be difficult to achieve, especially if economy of expression is a goal of language use. For example, take the word **structure**. Add to it the prefix **super** and one meaning is derived. Substitute **sub** for **super** and quite another meaning takes form. A **superstructure** is the part of a building **above** the foundation. A **substructure**, on the other hand, is that part of a building **below** the foundation. It should be obvious that prefixes are versatile enough to change the meanings of words with relative ease. They appear in a never-ending parade of words, one that brings with it a structural design that makes language much clearer than it would be without them. Your work will cover 15 prefixes, ones that are most commonly used. Learn them. They will serve you well.

Finally, as you were told in an earlier section of your book, don't attempt to learn individual words. It is not an efficient method to expand your vocabulary. Try to learn prefixes in this part of your book, prefixes that will allow you to extend them to other words having this same prefix. The key is method. You have been introduced to an efficiently systematic method to build your vocabulary. Follow it. To ignore this advice would be counterproductive in terms of your writers' objectives.

Lesson

1

Anti and ante are two commonly used prefixes. There are virtually hundreds of words to which they are added. A word of caution is in order. There will be occasions when **anti** is actually a spelling variation of **ante**. Since **anti** means "against" and **ante** means "before," the difference in word meaning will be significant. For example, the word **antique** comes from the Latin **antiquus**, meaning "ancient." It has nothing whatever to do with **anti**, meaning "against." In this same vein, the word **anticipate** does not make use of the **anti** meaning "against." It is, rather, the **ante** that comes into play in the word **anticipate**. Other such examples are **antiquity, antiquated**, and **antipasto**. In most cases, the context will make perfectly clear which meaning is to be used—**before** or **against**.

ANTI: *"against; opposed to"*

Word List	Etymology	Word Meaning
antibiotic	bios (life)	a substance checking growth organisms
antipathy	pathos (feeling)	strong aversion; dislike
antidote	didonai (to give)	remedy to counteract effects of a poison or other noxious substance
antiphony	phonē (sound)	alternating responses between 2 groups, especially singers
antiseptic	septikos (putrefying)	capable of destroying organisms that cause disease
antithesis	tithenai (to set)	opposition; contrast of ideas

anti-Semite	none needed	one hostile to Jews
anticlimax	none needed	transition from a significant idea to a trivial one
antichrist	none needed	one who denies or opposes Christ

ANTE: *"before"*

Word List	**Etymology**	**Word Meaning**
antebellum	bellum (war)	before a war, specifically the American Civil War
antechamber	camera (a vault)	entryway into a larger room
antecedent	cedere (to go)	to precede, as a noun preceding a pronoun
antediluvian	diluvium (flood)	specifically before the biblical flood—Genesis 6:8
antemeridian	medius (middle) + dies (day)	before noon (middle of the day)
antemortem	mors (death)	before death
antependium	pendere (to hang)	cloth hanging before an altar or a lectern
anterior	none needed	located at the front
antedate	none needed	coming before in time

EXERCISES

A. Directions: Complete the word whose meaning is listed along side it. You may refer to your word list in this exercise.

1. ante_____ = before the biblical flood; antiquated

2. anti_____ = remedy to counteract the effects of poison

3. ante_____ = cloth hanging in front of an altar or pulpit

4. ante_____ = a waiting room

5. ante_____ = before in time or place

6. ante_____ = before the war (specifically the Civil War)

7. anti_____ = substance checking growth of organisms

8. anti_____ = movement from something important to something trivial

9. ante_____ = before noon

10. anti_____ = opposition; contrast of ideas

11. anti_____ = strong aversion or dislike

   B. Directions: Write the letter I if the boldface word is not consistent with the meaning of the sentence. Write the letter C if it is consistent.

1. **Antemeridian** has to do with the biblical flood.

2. An **antecedent** comes before (as a pronoun referring to the noun that preceded it).

3. His view of the situation was the **antithesis** of mine, and we could not agree on a compromise.

4. The **antebellum** nations that fought World War II joined together to form what is now called NATO.

5. **Antipathies** are much to be desired in civil discourse.

6. The instructor's **antediluvian** views of how the universe was created did not take into account the "big bang theory," which is held by most scientists.

7. A.M. comes from **antemortem** (before death).

8. An **antidote** was administered to the boy who had swallowed poison.

9. An **antiseptic** was applied to the boy's twisted ankle.

10. When flu-like symptoms were reported to the doctor, he prescribed an **antibiotic**.

11. His abrupt reply made clear his **antipathy** in the matter.

   C. Directions: Give the meaning of each of the following etymons. Then write the **ante** or **anti** word to which it contributes. The first one has been done for you.

1. ante + bellum (war) = antebellum

2. ante + cedere _____ = _____

3. anti + septikos _____ = _____

4. ante + diluvium _____ = _____

5. ante + camera _____ = _____

6. ante + pendere _____ = _____

7. anti + didonai _____ = _____

8. ante + mors _____ = _____

9. anti + tithenai _____ = _____

10. anti + phōnē _____ = _____

11. anti + bios _____ = _____

12. anti + pathos _____ = _____

D. Choose two of the following words: antibiotic, antiseptic, antebellum, antecedent. Write the words in two sentences of your
own.

Lesson

2

CIRCUM: *"around; on all sides"*

Word List	Etymology	Word Meaning
circumambulate	ambulare (to walk)	to walk around
circumlocution	loqui (to speak)	talk in circles
circumvent	venire (to come)	to bypass; to go around
circumspect	specere (to look)	watchful; cautious
circumscribe	scribere (to write)	to limit
circumlunar	lūnār (of the moon)	around the moon
circumference	ferre (to carry)	perimeter; boundary line of a circle
circumfluous	fluere (to flow)	surrounded by water
circumsolar	sōl (sun)	around the sun
circa	none needed	approximately

EXERCISES

A. Complete the word whose meaning is listed beside it.

1. circum_____ perimeter; boundary line of a circle

2. circum_____ cautious

3. circ_____ approximately

4. circum_____ surrounded by water

5. circum_____ to limit

6. circum_____ bypass

7. circum_____ around the sun

8. circum_____ roundabout way of speaking

9. circum_____ walk around

10. circum_____ around the moon

B. Write the meaning of each of the following etymons.

1. loqui

2. fluere

3. sōl

4. lūnār

5. ferre

6. venire

7. specere

8. scribere

9. circum

10. ambulare

C. Write the letter C if the boldface word is used in a context consistent with its meaning. Write the letter I if it is inconsistent.

1. The rambling lecture never got to the point, with one lengthy **circumlocution** after another.

2. To have one's movements **circumscribed** is to have them limited in some way.

3. An island is actually a **circumfluous** entity.

4. A burglar would no doubt be **circumspect** while burgling a private home.

5. To **circumambulate** is to talk in circles.

6. A discovery made **circa** 1500 A.D. was made about that time.

7. U.S. spacecraft have made **circumlunar** space flights.

8. The **circumference** of the earth is equal to the boundary line around the equator.

9. To **circumvent** the law is an unethical goal of many criminals.

10. The earth is part of a **circumsolar** universe.

    D. Choose two of the following words: circumference, circa, circumspect, circumvent. Use your words in two original sentences.

Lesson

3

PRE: *"before; prior to"*

Word List	Etymology	Word Meaning
preeminent	eminēre (to stand out)	notable above all others
precocious	praecox (ripened early)	premature development, especially mental development
precursor	currere (runner)	a forerunner
predilection	diligere (love)	a strong preference
prenatal	natus (born)	before birth
preempt	emere (to buy)	to gain possession by purchase or prior right
preclude	claudere (to close)	to prevent
prescient	scire (to know)	knowing of events before they occur
prelude	ludere (to play)	preliminary to main action
premonition	monere (to warn)	a forewarning

EXERCISES

A. Define each of the following etymons.

1. currere

2. emere

3. praecox

4. natus

5. eminere

6. claudere

7. ludere

8. diligere

9. monere

10. scire

B. Write the word which completes the meaning of the sentence.

1. In order to _____ the criminal's escape, the police cordoned off the area in which he was last seen.

2. His _____ awareness astonished even those who did not believe in prophecy.

3. The _____ child was able to play piano pieces from Mozart and Chopin.

4. Dr. Jonas Salk, a _____ medical researcher, discovered the vaccine that prevented the dread disease polio.

5. A _____ for playing golf too often eventually led to marital discord.

6. All pregnant women should seek out _____ care for their unborn child.

7. The psychic's _____ that the man would meet with a fatal accident before his next birthday did not materialize.

8. In many parts of the country, the robin is spring's _____.

9. Hitler's coming to power was the _____ to World War II.

10. The White House requested that all major television networks _____ regularly scheduled programming so that the president could deliver an important message to all Americans.

C. Complete the following items by writing the missing word parts.

1. pre_____ (a strong preference)

2. pre_____ (before the major action)

3. pre_____ (a forerunner)

4. pre_____ (before birth)

5. pre_____ (to prevent)

6. pre_____ (a forewarning)

7. pre_____ (knowing beforehand)

8. pre_____ (standing out)

9. pre_____ (mentally advanced)

10. pre_____ (to be presented in place of)

D. Choose two of the following words: precocious, premonition, prelude, preclude. Use your two words in two sentences of your own.

Lesson

4

POST: *"after"*

Word List	Etymology	Word Meaning
postbellum	bellum (war)	after a war, especially the American Civil War
postmeridian	medius (middle) + dies (day)	after the middle of the day or P.M.
posthumous	postumus (after death)	occurring after death
postnuptial	nuptial (wedding)	after marriage
postscript	scribere (to write)	something added to, as a letter
postmortem	mors (death)	medical exam after death
postdiluvian	diluvium (flood)	after the biblical flood
postlude	ludere (to play)	a concluding piece of music
posthaste	from the phrase "post haste" found on letters	done quickly
posterior	posterus (following after)	located at the rear (adjective); buttocks (noun)

EXERCISES

A. Match each word in Column A with its definition in Column B.

Column A   Column B

1. postscript   a. after one's death
2. postlude   b. after the middle of the day
3. posthumous   c. after the biblical flood
4. postnuptial   d. a concluding piece of music
5. postbellum   e. done quickly
6. postmeridian   f. located at the rear or back
7. postdiluvian   g. exam after death
8. postmortem   h. after marriage
9. posterior   i. something appended to, as a letter
10. posthaste   j. after a war, especially the American Civil War

B. Decide whether the statements below are true or false. Write F if false and T if true.

1. The soldier's medal was awarded **posthumously** at a ceremony held in his honor.

2. The symphony orchestra began its performance with a short **postlude**.

3. The chunky man's **posterior** was amply padded.

4. The **postscript** began with the salutation, "Dear Mr. Smith."

5. The giving of the Ten Commandments was a **postdiluvian** event.

6. A medical examiner would do a **postmortem** examination.

7. A **postnuptial** occasion may occur 10 minutes or 10 years after the wedding.

8. After World War II, the United States entered a **postbellum** period.

9. He was told to deliver the message **posthaste**.

10. The word **postmeridian** has been abbreviated to P.M. which means after the middle of the day.

C. Complete the following words by writing the correct word parts.

1. post_____ after a war, especially the American Civil War

2. post_____ done quickly

3. post_____ after the middle of the day

4. post_____ after marriage

5. post_____ located at the rear or back

6. post_____ added to a letter, for example

7. post_____ after death

8. post_____ exam after death

9. post_____ a concluding piece of music

10. post_____ after the biblical flood

    D. Choose two of the following words: postbellum, postscript, posthumous, posterior. Use your two words in two original sentences.

Lesson

5

COUNTER: *"contrary or opposite"*

Word List	Etymology	Word Meaning
counterpart	none needed	opposite number
counterproductive	none needed	tending to hinder
countervail	valēre (to be strong)	to oppose with equal vigor
counterclaim	none needed	a claim filed in opposition to another claim
counterculture	none needed	a culture whose values run counter to those of the establishment
counterclockwise	none needed	in a direction opposite to the movement of the hands on a clock's dial
counterweight	none needed	weight used to balance other weights
countermeasure	none needed	a measure taken to prevent another measure
countersign	none needed	a second confirming signature, as on a check, or a sign or signal in response to a sign of recognition (used mainly in military)

CONTRA: *"contrary; opposite to"*

Word List	Etymology	Word Meaning
contraception	concipere (to conceive)	prevention of conception
contradict	dicere (to say)	express the opposite of
contradistinguish	none needed	to distinguish by contrasting qualities
contraindicate	none needed	to suggest the inadvisability of
contrariwise	none needed	form a contrary opinion (opposite)
contravene	venire (to come)	to oppose; to act or be counter to
contraclockwise	none needed	same as counterclockwise
contraband	bannus (to decree)	illegal goods; smuggled goods
contralateral	none needed	on the opposite side

EXERCISES

A. Use either a **contra** or **counter** word. The word you are to write is defined beside each item.

1. _____ oppose with actions

2. _____ hindering

3. _____ opposite number

4. _____ oppose with words

5. _____ to distinguish by contrast

6. _____ to reverse a command

7. _____ measure taken to counter another measure

8. _____ to be inadvisable

9. _____ culture opposite of established culture

10. _____ write a confirming signature or sign

11. _____ claim filed in opposition to another claim

12. _____ moving in a direction opposite of hands on a clock's dial

13. _____ weight used to counter other weights

14. _____ prevention of conception

15. _____ on the opposite side

    B. Complete each sentence below by writing the appropriate word from the list provided.

countermand   countermeasure   counterclockwise
contraindicated   contraception   countersign
contraband   counterproductive
counterplot   contradistinction

1. A _____ by the duly established government foiled the goals of the rebel leaders.

2. In _____ to the conservative Democrat, there is the liberal Democrat.

3. The captain could not _____ the general's orders even though he believed them to be in error.

4. _____, a topic that was once not discussed, is now open for debate on television, in schools (as low as 5th and 6th grades), and in print media of all kinds.

5. The bank teller informed the customer that he forgot to _____ the check.

6. Coast Guard cutters intercepted the smugglers' ship and seized one ton of _____.

7. The suggestion would have been _____ and caused havoc among the ranks of hourly wage earners.

8. Absence of fever _____ the doctor's use of an antibiotic.

9. As a _____, the police and city officials responded to the violence by imposing an 11 P.M. curfew.

10. The western dance group was instructed to move in a _____ direction.

C. Choose two of the following words: counterclockwise, counter-sign, contradict, contraband. Use the two words in two sentences of your own.

REVIEW OF LESSONS 1 - 5

A. Directions: Provide the missing prefix that will complete the word whose meaning is listed beside the item. Note that several items can be completed with more than one prefix. You are to use only one.

1. _____ **spect**   cautious; watchful

2. _____ **part**   opposite number

3. _____ **eminent**   notable over all others

4. _____ **meridian**   after the middle of the day

5. _____ **dilection**   a strong preference

6. _____ **thesis**   opposition; contrariwise

7. _____ **cedent**   to go before in time or place

8. _____ **locution**   talk in circles

9. _____ **clude**   to prevent; to block

10. _____ **mand**   to reverse a command

B. Match the word in Column A to its meaning found in Column B.

Column A   Column B

1. precursor   a. a forerunner
2. antemortem   b. before birth
3. posterior   c. having advanced mental development
4. prenatal   d. before death
5. circumscribe   e. to go around; bypass
6. premonition   f. a warning
7. antemeridian   g. knowledge of things before they happen
8. circumvent   h. before the middle of the day
9. precocious   i. to limit
10. prescient   j. located at the rear or back

Lesson

6

TRANS: *"beyond; through; across"*

Word List	Etymology	Word Meaning
transcend	scendere (to climb over)	to go beyond others of its kind; surpass others of the same kind
transgress	gradi (to step)	to sin; to go beyond the limits of
transfuse	fundere (to pour)	to pour liquid from one vessel to another; to administer a transfusion
transient	ire (to go)	transitory; passing away with time
transmute	mutare (to change)	to transform
translucent	lucere (to shine)	permitting light to pass through
transpose	ponere (to place)	reverse; transfer order
transplant	none needed	to transfer (tissue or organ) from one body to another; to uproot and replant
transfix	none needed	to render motionless, as with fright or awe
transcribe	scribere (to write)	to write or type a copy of

EXERCISES

A. Write T if the statement is true and F if it is false.

1. The young girl's eyes were **transfixed** on the gruesome Halloween costume worn by the reveler.

2. **Transients** are generally seen time after time.

3. One of the most macabre **transmutations** in literature must be that of Dr. Jekyll and Mr. Hyde.

4. A secretary was asked to **transcribe** the conversation taking place in the next room.

5. Many women choose a **translucent** material for their attire because they believe it is feminine.

6. Many spelling errors are caused by **transposing** letters, e.g., reciept for receipt.

7. Many **transplanted** immigrants have found peace and freedom in the United States.

8. **Transgressions** are positive if they are done with the right attitude.

9. To hemophiliacs a serious cut may have devastating consequences, if a **transfusion** is not available.

10. The football player **transcended** the goal line for a touchdown.

B. Match the word from Column A with its meaning in Column B.

Column A

1. transcend
2. transient
3. transfix
4. transplant
5. translucent
6. transpose
7. transmute
8. transfuse
9. transgress
10. transcribe

Column B

a. to transfer a liquid
b. transitory; passing with time
c. admitting light
d. to uproot; to replant
e. to reverse
f. to render motionless
g. to write out fully or type a copy of
h. to sin
i. surpass others of the same kind
j. to change form

C. Complete the word whose meaning is listed beside it.

1. trans_____ to sin

2. trans_____ to reverse

3. trans_____ diffusing light

4. trans_____ to surpass; to go beyond

5. trans_____ transitory

6. trans_____ to uproot and replant

7. trans_____ exchange liquids

8. trans_____ to render motionless

9. trans_____ to change form

10. trans_____ to write out fully, as from dictation

D. Choose two of the following words: transfuse, translucent, transplant, transcribe. Use the two words in two sentences.

Lesson

7

Retro is a prefix that means "back or backward." It will be studied together with the prefix **pro**, which is opposite in meaning. Its definition is "before, prior to, or in front of." The pairing of these prefixes should facilitate their learning. To tie related ideas together is an effective tool of learning—**pro** means **"forward"** and **retro** means **"back."** Below are two word lists that will acquaint you with these prefixes.

RETRO: *"back or backward"*

Word List	Etymology	Word Meaning
retrogress	gradus (step)	backward step
retroflex	flectere (to bend)	bent backward
retrospect	specere (to look)	to look back
retroversion	vertere (to turn)	turning backward
retrocede	cedere (to go)	to return; give back
retrospective	specere (to look)	a show exhibiting the work of an artist over a period of years
retrograde	gradi (to step)	moving backward
retroactive	none needed	to have influence on past occurrences
retro-rocket	none needed	rocket engine used to reverse motion of a space craft, missile, or aircraft
retrofire	none needed	to ignite a retro-rocket

PRO: *"before; prior to; in front of"*

Word List	Etymology	Word Meaning
procrastinate	cras (tomorrow)	to delay; put off
procreate	creare (create)	to reproduce, as offspring
prophet	phanai (to speak)	a predictor
profusion	fundere (to pour)	plenty; abundance
progenitor	gen (birth)	a direct ancestor
prognosticate	gnos (to know)	to predict, as weather forecasters
prospectus	specere (to look)	summary of a proposal
proscribe	scribere	to prohibit
proponent	ponere (to set)	an advocate
propensity	pendēre (to hang)	an inclination; predilection

EXERCISES

A. Complete the sentences using one of the words from either the **retro** or **pro** list.

1. Most athletes have a _____ to keep their bodies in good condition.

2. Weathermen _____ phenomena such as blizzards by studying conditions that give rise to such storms.

3. A _____ had a vision and predicted from it a calamitous earthquake.

4. The artist's work was presented as a _____, covering the last ten years of his life.

5. Not only did the student not show progress, he actually _____.

6. To contemplate one's life in _____ can be a learning experience for us all.

7. The doctor _____ drinking alcoholic beverages from his patient's diet.

8. All living things have the power of _____, and that is how the species endures.

9. A _____ of flowers made a spectacular show of colors that daz-
zled the eye.

10. The speaker's unpopular topic made it difficult to find any
_____ in his audience.

B. Match the word from Column A with its meaning found in
Column B.

Column A   Column B

1. retrogress   a. bent backward
2. retrospect   b. direct ancestor
3. retroflex   c. to move backward
4. retrocede   d. to look back upon
5. propensity   e. to delay
6. progenitor   f. to forbid
7. procrastinate   g. to return; give back
8. proscribe   h. inclination; predilection
9. retroactive   i. summary of a proposed venture
10. prospectus   j. applying to an earlier time

C. Complete the words using either prefix—**retro** or **pro**. In several instances either **retro** or **pro** will fit. In such cases, use
only one.

1. _____ flex

2. _____ spect

3. _____ crastinate

4. _____ spectus

5. _____ cede

6. _____ gnosticate

7. _____ genitor

8. _____ version

9. _____ scribe

10. _____ create

11. _____ ponent

12. _____ active

13. _____ pensity

14. _____ fusion

15. _____ gress

    D. Choose two words from the following: retrospect, retro-rocket, procrastinate, profusion. Use your two words in original sentences.

Lesson

8

INTRA: *"within"*

Word List	Etymology	Word Meaning
intradermal	dermis (skin)	within the skin
intrastate	none needed	within a state
intravenous	ven (vein)	within the vein, as in intravenous feeding
intrauterine	uterus (part of female reproductive tract)	within the uterus
intrascholastic	none needed	within a school
intrapersonal	none needed	occurring within one's own mind
intravascular	none needed	within the blood vessel
intracranial	kranion (skull)	within the head
intramuscular	none needed	within the muscle
intramural	mur (wall)	(sports) between teams from the same school

EXERCISES

A. Match the word from Column B with its meaning in Column A.

Column A

1. within the head
2. within the skin

Column B

a. intradermal
b. intramural

3. within the confines of a school

4. within a vein

5. within the walls, as of a school

6. occurring within one's own mind

7. within the uterus

8. within the borders of a state

9. within the blood vessels

10. within the muscle

c. intravenous

d. intrapersonal

e. intramuscular

f. intravascular

g. intrauterine

h. intrascholastic

i. intracranial

j. intrastate

B. Write the missing word part that completes the item whose meaning is given alongside it.

1. intra_____ within the walls, as of a school

2. intra_____ within the head

3. intra_____ within the vein

4. intra_____ within a muscle

5. intra_____ occurring within one's own mind

6. intra_____ within a school setting

7. intra_____ within a state

8. intra_____ within the skin

9. intra_____ within the uterus

10. intra_____ within the blood vessels

C. Write C if the boldface word is used in a way that is consistent with its meaning or I if it inconsistent.

1. **Intramural** sports are played between schools.

2. Removing a brain tumor would involve **intracranial** surgery.

3. An **intrapersonal** experience is a shared experience.

4. Many patients who cannot take food orally are fed **intravenously**.

5. **Intrascholastic** activities are carried on within a school.

6. An **intrastate** bus can take you from one state to another.

7. A dermatologist is concerned with **intradermal** treatments of skin disorders.

8. An **intrauterine** examination for cancer might be done by a gynecologist, a physician who treats ailments exclusive to women, especially regarding reproduction.

9. Heart specialists, or cardiologists, are concerned with **intravascular** treatments.

10. A chiropractor is qualified to give **intradermal** injections.

D. Choose two of the following words: intrastate, intravenous, intrascholastic, intradermal. Use the two words in sentences of your own.

Lesson

9

Lesson Nine will introduce you to a pair of prefixes that mean about the same thing. They are **extra** and **hyper**. Both mean "over, excessive, or beyond." There are other prefixes that also mean "excessive or above": **ultra** and **super**. Most of the words in which these two prefixes appear define themselves, and there is no need to study them in detail: **ultracritical; ultraliberal; ultramodern; superabundant; superstructure; supernatural;** and **superhuman**. All are self-defining. Lesson Nine will concern itself with the prefixes **extra** and **hyper** only.

EXTRA: *"over; excessive; above"*

Word List	Etymology	Word Meaning
extravert or extrovert	vertere (turned)	one who is outgoing; turned outwardly
extramarital	none needed	outside the marital vows
extracurricular	none needed	outside one's normal duties
extramural	muris (walls)	outside the walls of a college
extrasensory	none needed	6th sense; outside the normal range of senses
extralegal	none needed	outside the law
extragalactic	none needed	beyond our galaxy
extraterrestrial	none needed	beyond the earth or its atmosphere
extrapolate	polire (to embellish)	to infer from another source; to go beyond what is known
extraneous	extraneus (outside)	beyond what is vital

HYPER: *"over; excessive; above"*

Word List	Etymology	Word Meaning
hyperactive	none needed	overly active
hyperglycemia	glyco (sweet)	an abnormally high level of glucose in the blood (symptomatic of diabetes)
hyperbaric	bar (atmosphere)	describing pressure higher than the normal atmospheric pressure
hyperextend	none needed	to extend body part beyond normal limits
hyperbole	bolē (throwing)	obvious exaggeration to create desired effect
hypertrophy	trephein (nourish)	increase in the size of an organ
hyperkinetic	kīnēs (movement)	uncontrolled bodily movement; spasm
hyperventilate	none needed	excessively rapid and deep breathing
hypersensitive	none needed	overly sensitive
hyperthermia	thērme (heat)	excessively high fever

EXERCISES

A. If the statement below is true, write T. If it is false, write F.

1. That which is **extrapolated** is inferred from other known facts.

2. A football player is more likely to **hyperextend** his knee than is a housewife.

3. All normal people possess **extrasensory** perception.

4. **Extramural** activities cannot take place outside the walls, as of a university.

5. Information that is critical is **extraneous**.

6. A **hypersensitive** person is apt to be forward in social undertakings.

7. "He was as strong as a lion" is an example of **hyperbole**.

8. A doctor might diagnose a person's fainting as a consequence of **hyperventilation**.

9. A **hyperbaric** chamber restores a person to normal atmospheric pressure very slowly.

10. Going to work each day is an **extracurricular** activity.

B. Complete the word whose meaning is listed beside it. You may use the words from Exercise A.

1. hyper_____ showing uncontrolled body movement

2. extra_____ infer something from known facts

3. extra_____ turned outwardly; concerned with others

4. hyper_____ excessive glucose in one's blood

5. hyper_____ enlargement; swelling out of proportion

6. hyper_____ moving excessively

7. extra_____ beyond our galaxy

8. hyper_____ describing pressures higher than normal atmospheric pressures

9. hyper_____ unusually high fever

10. hyper_____ extravagant exaggeration for effect

C. Write either **extra** or **hyper** to complete each word.

1. _____ **sensitive**   excessively sensitive

2. _____ **legal**   outside or beyond the law

3. _____ **vert**   one who is interested in things outside the self

4. _____ **glycemia**   excessive glucose in the blood

5. _____ **curricular**   outside one's normal duties

6. _____ **thermia**   excessively high fever

7. _____ **marital**   outside the bounds of matrimony

8. _____ **terrestrial**   beyond the earth's atmosphere

9. _____ **trophy**   swelling; enlargement

10. _____ **sensory**   beyond the normal range of senses

D. Choose two of the following words: extracurricular, extraterrestrial, hyperactive, hyperbole. Use your two words in your own sentences.

Lesson

10

The following are word elements and not truly prefixes. They do, however, behave in all respects as prefixes, and in view of this, they will be treated as prefixes. The two elements are **bene** and **male**. They are opposite in meaning, and that is why they are presented in the same lesson. These elements act as prefixes in that they appear only at the beginnings of words and nowhere else. **Bene** means "good or well," and **male** means "bad or ill."

BENE: *"good; well"*

Word List	Etymology	Word Meaning
benefactor	facere (to do)	a kindly helper
benediction	dicere (to say)	a blessing
benignant	gignere (to produce)	favorable; beneficial
benign	gignere (to produce)	of a kind disposition; not malignant, as a tumor
beneficial	facere (to do)	promoting a favorable result
benevolent	volens (wishing)	kindly
beneficent	facere (to do)	performing acts of kindness or charity
beneficiary	facere (to do)	one who receives a benefit

MALE: *"bad; ill"*

Word List	Etymology	Word Meaning
malefactor	facere (to do)	a wrong-doer
malevolent	volens (to wish)	wishing harm or evil

malaise	aise (ease)	unfocused feeling of discomfort
malapropism	apropo (appropriate)	a mistaken use of a word having a humorous effect
malice	malitio (bad)	ill-will
malediction	dicere (to say)	a curse
maladroit	droit (right side)	clumsy in a social sense
malfeasance	facere (to do)	official misconduct
malignant	gignere (to produce)	showing evil; highly injurious, as a tumor
malign	gignere (to produce)	to speak ill of
malinger	gignere (to produce)	to pretend to be ill in order to shirk one's duty

EXERCISES

A. The following exercise is a "potpourri" made up of words studied in this lesson. The items include both **male** and **bene** words.

1. If you slandered a person's reputation, you have _____ his character.
   (a) malingered   (b) maligned   (c) maliced

2. Which of the following would be most likely to utter a benediction?
   (a) a witch   (b) a teacher   (c) a clergyman

3. A kindly person would probably be of a _____ nature.
   (a) benevolent   (b) malevolent   (c) maladroit

4. A criminal or one who disobeys a law is a (a) malingerer
   (b) malefactor   (c) malaise.

5. An awkward, clumsy person is maladroit.
   (a) true   (b) false

6. A person who aided you in your hour of need would be your
   (a) benefactor   (b) malefactor   (c) benediction.

7. The comment "burning her britches behind her" for "burning her bridges" is an example of a malapropism.
(a) true   (b) false

8. The patient's anxiety was relieved when he learned that the tumor was   (a) benign   (b) benevolent   (c) beneficent.

9. Cancer is a   (a) malignant growth   (b) maladroit growth
(c) malevolent growth.

10. One who pretends to be ill in order to avoid work is a
(a) malaise   (b) malevolent   (c) malingerer.

B. Supply a word from this lesson to fit each of the following.

1. lawbreaker: _____

2. curse: _____

3. blessing: _____

4. humanitarian: _____

5. inept; clumsy: _____

6. official misconduct: _____

7. wishing evil; of an evil nature: _____

8. word incorrectly used: _____

9. to slander; to defame: _____

10. feign illness: _____

C. Give a brief definition for each of the following words.

1. malefactor: _____

2. malfeasance: _____

3. benign: _____

4. malediction: _____

5. malinger: _____

6. malicious: _____

7. malaise: _____

8. benediction: _____

9. malapropism: _____

10. benefactor: _____

D. Choose two of the following words: beneficial, beneficiary, malice, malignant. Use your words in two original sentences.

REVIEW OF LESSONS 1 - 10

A. Below are the prefixes studied. Choose the appropriate prefix that will complete each of the word parts below.

hyper	bene	counter
post	contra	pre
circum	trans	anti
ante	retro	pro
intra	mal	extra

1. _____ **meridian**   before the middle of the day

2. _____ **meridian**   after the middle of the day

3. _____ **trophy**   to enlarge excessively

4. _____ **legal**   outside the law; beyond the law

5. _____ **scribe**   limit

6. _____ **ference**   perimeter

7. _____ **mand**   to reverse a command

8. _____ **fix**   to render motionless

9. _____ **gress**   to move in a backward direction

10. _____ **crastinate**   to delay

11. _____ **personal**   occurring within one's own mind

12. _____ **mortem**   after death

13. _____ **spect**   watchful; cautious

14. _____ **cursor**   a forerunner

B. Define the following prefixes.

1. pre _____

2. pro _____

3. ante _____

4. anti _____

5. circum _____

6. extra _____

7. counter _____

8. trans _____

9. contra _____

10. retro _____

11. mal _____

12. intra _____

13. hyper _____

14. post _____

15. bene _____

Dimension Two
Part Three

tripod

*Number and
Amount Prefixes*

Lesson

1

In a previous part you studied prefixes in general. This is not the case with prefixes found in this part. Number and amount prefixes do precisely what they suggest; they indicate "how many" or "how much." You will have already met a few of these affixes, e.g., **tri** meaning "three." Nonetheless, such word parts will be presented again. This is so their meanings will be that much more likely to be remembered.

There may be one small problem that concerns itself with, of all things, the calendar. The prefix **sept**, for example, means "seven," but September is not the seventh month; it is the 9th. Neither is December the 10th month as **deci** meaning "ten" would suggest. The same is true of October and November. The reason for this confusion is that mankind has observed two different calendars. In the year 46 B.C. Julius Caesar fixed the calendar to his liking. Julius Caesar added the month of July for obvious reasons, and the month of August honors Augustus Caesar. In this version December was indeed the 10th month of the year as was November the 9th. This was known as the Julian calendar. In 1582 Pope Gregory XIII took it upon himself to revise the Julian calendar. It, incidentally, is the one we use today. It became known as the Gregorian calendar for obvious reasons. December, which was the 10th month in the Julian calendar, became the 12th month in the Gregorian calendar and so on. Enough said about calendars. Just don't let the discrepancy between the numbers of the months and the numbers of the prefixes confuse you. It's no big deal.

EXERCISES

A. **Directions**: You will be given five number prefixes below. Under each prefix you will find words that employ them. You are to provide a definition for each of these words, making certain that the number the prefix designates appears in it. For example, if you are dealing with the prefix **uni** and the word you are to define is **universal**, your definition should include the word **one** in it. Also, in a couple of instances you will have to find the use of number in the word's etymology, not in its definition. **Quintessence**, for example, will not give the word **five** in its dictionary definition. It will, however, be given in the etymology of **quintessence**. Of course, you are to consult a dictionary for this part of your work.

1. **uni**: one
   a. uniparous:
   b. unipod:
   c. unilateral:
   d. unique:
   e. unison:

2. **mono**: one
   a. monogram:
   b. monopoly:
   c. monophonic:
   d. monoplegia:
   e. monotheism:

3. **du**: two
   a. duologue:
   b. dual:
   c. duo:
   d. duplicate:
   e. duplex:

4. **bi**: two
   a. bilinguist:
   b. bicentennial:
   c. binocular:
   d. bigamy:

e. binary:

f. biped:

5. **tri**: three

a. triplicate:

b. triplets:

c. tricycle:

d. tripod:

e. tricolored:

B. Match the word from Column A with its meaning from Column B.

Column A

1. unilateral
2. monopoly
3. bicentennial
4. monotheism
5. uniparous
6. monoplegia
7. bilingual
8. duologue
9. unipod
10. binary

Column B

a. one-footed stool
b. conversation between two persons
c. belief in one god
d. paralysis involving one limb
e. a 200th anniversary or celebration
f. giving birth to only one offspring
g. controlled by one seller
h. taken by one side only
i. able to speak and write in two languages
j. of or based on the number 2, as the binary numeration system

C. Choose two of the following words: monogram, duplicate, binocular, tricycle. Use your words in two original sentences.

Lesson

2

A. In this lesson you are to do what you did in the previous lesson: write a definition for each of the following words, using in your definition the number that the prefix designates. You may, of course, use a dictionary.

1. **quar, quad**: four
    a. quadriplegia:
    b. quadruped:
    c. quadrant:
    d. quadruplets:
    e. quartile:

2. **quint**: five
    a. quintuple:
    b. quintessential:
    c. quinquagenarian:
    d. quindecennial:

3. **sex**: six
    a. sextet:
    b. sexagenarian:
    c. sextuple:
    d. sexcentenary:

4. **septem**: seven
   a. September:
   b. septuagenarian:
   c. septennial:

5. **octa**: eight
   a. octagon:
   b. October:
   c. octahedron:
   d. octave:
   e. octangular:

B. Match the items below.

Column A

1. septennial
2. quadruped
3. octopus
4. quartile
5. quadriplegic
6. sextet
7. quadrant
8. octagon
9. sexagenarian
10. septuagenarian

Column B

a. animal having 4 feet or legs
b. one who cannot use limbs on either side of the body
c. eight-sided figure
d. a circular arc having an angle of 90°
e. one who is between the ages of 70 and 79
f. a group of persons or things made up of six parts
g. a frequency distribution divided into 4 parts
h. a sea creature having eight tentacles
i. one who is between the ages of 60 and 69
j. occurring every 7 years

C. Choose two of the following words: quartile, quintessential, September, octave. Use your words in two sentences of your own.

Lesson

3

A. In this lesson you are to do what you did in the previous lesson: write a definition for each of the following words, using in your definition the number that the prefix designates. You may, of course, use a dictionary.

1. **novum**: nine
   a. nonagenarian:
   b. November:
   c. nonagon:
   d. novena:

2. **deca, deci**: ten
   a. decade:
   b. December:
   c. Decalogue:
   d. decimate:
   e. decathlon:

3. **cent**: one hundred
   a. century:
   b. centenarian:

316

c. centimeter:
d. centipede:
e. centigrade:

4. **mille**: one thousand
   a. millipede:
   b. millennium:
   c. millisecond:
   d. million:
   e. milliliter:
   f. millimeter:

5. **kilo**: thousand
   a. kilogram:
   b. kilometer:
   c. kiloton:
   d. kilocycle:
   e. kilowatt:

B. Match the following items.

Column A

1. millisecond
2. millennium
3. centigrade
4. decimate
5. nonagon
6. centenarian
7. decathlon
8. centipede
9. millimeter
10. kilogram

Column B

a. nine-sided figure
b. 1,000th of a second
c. insect having what appear to be 100 feet
d. 1,000th of a meter or 0.0394 inches
e. period of 1,000 years
f. one who is 100 years of age or older
g. divided into 100 degrees, as a temperature scale (Celsius)
h. Olympic event encompassing 10 different track and field events
i. 1,000 grams
j. kill a great number (literally to kill every tenth person)

C. Choose two of the following words: November, century, millimeter, kilogram. Use your words in two original sentences.

Lesson

4

The prefixes in this lesson designate **amount**. The first two of these prefixes are **multi** and **poly**, both true prefixes in all respects. Two others—**omni** and **pan**—are really etymons, but each behaves in a manner consistent with prefixes. This being the case, it seems appropriate to treat them as prefixes, and this is why they appear in the lesson.

EXERCISES

A. Follow the format of the lessons dealing with prefixes that came before this lesson—define each word, and in your definition designate the amount intended to be conveyed—**many** or **much**.

1. **multi**: many, much
   a. multiparous:
   b. multifaceted:
   c. multifarious:
   d. multilinguist:
   e. multitudinous:

2. **poly**: many
   a. polygamy:
   b. polytheism:
   c. polyglot:
   d. polygon:
   e. polysyllabic:

3. **omni**: all
   a. omnivorous:
   b. omniscient:
   c. omnifarious:
   d. omnibus:
   e. omnipotent:

4. **pan**: all
   a. pandemic:
   b. panoramic:
   c. panacea:
   d. pantheism:
   e. pandemonium:

5. **semi**: half; partially
   a. semiconscious:
   b. semiliterate:
   c. semicircle:
   d. semitropical:
   e. semitransparent:

B. Match the following items.

Column A

1. multifaceted
2. polygon
3. panacea
4. omnibus
5. polygamy
6. polysyllabic
7. multitudinous
8. omniscient
9. multilinguist
10. multiparous

Column B

a. a cure-all
b. all-knowing
c. one who speaks and writes in many languages
d. very numerous
e. giving birth to more than one offspring at one time
f. closed plane figure
g. having many syllables (as in a word)
h. having several spouses at the same time
i. having many aspects or phases
j. covering many things or classes

C. Choose two of the following words: polysyllabic, omnipotent, panoramic, semicircle. Use your words in two sentences of your own.

REVIEW OF LESSONS 1 - 4

A. Match the word from Column A with its meaning in Column B.

Column A

1. monogram
2. octagon
3. millipede
4. kilogram
5. pantheism
6. tripod
7. polyglot
8. nonagenarian
9. monotheism
10. panorama
11. kilometer
12. multiparous
13. unipod
14. omniscient
15. omnipotent
16. Decalogue
17. omnivorous
18. pandemic
19. unique
20. millennium

Column B

a. initials of a person's name
b. belief in one god
c. one-legged object
d. 1,000 meters or .62137 miles
e. eight-sided figure
f. about 2.2046 pounds
g. all-knowing
h. 3-legged object, as a stool
i. insect having many feet (1 thousand)
j. wide, expansive view
k. one who is between 90 and 99 years of age
l. belief that god is the sum of all things
m. one who speaks several languages
n. giving birth to more than one offspring at a time; multiple births
o. the Ten Commandments
p. period of 1,000 years
q. one of a kind
r. eats both animal and vegetable foods
s. affecting all people
t. all-powerful

B. Add the prefix to the word part to complete the word whose meaning is listed beside it.

1. _____ cracy   rule by one person (generally a despot)

2. _____ lith   a single block of stone very large in size or an undifferentiated mass

3. _____ plicity   double-dealing

4. _____ cuspid   having 3 points, as a tooth

5. _____ hedron   any solid object having 8 faces

6. _____ tet   any group of 5 things or persons

7. _____ lion   1,000 × 1,000

8. _____ ped   animal having 4 feet or legs

9. _____ ton   1,000 tons of an explosive force

10. _____ gram   1,000th of a gram

11. _____ plegia   paralysis limited to one side of the body

12. _____ demonium chaos; confusion; din

13. _____ genarian one who is between the ages of 70 and 79

14. _____ parous   giving birth to more than one offspring at a time

15. _____ theism   the belief in multiple gods (many gods)

C. Write the word that completes the meaning of the sentence.

1. _____ is the belief that many gods exist.

2. _____, having more than one spouse at a time, is illegal in the United States.

3. A _____ speaks several languages.

4. _____ births result in more than one birth at a time.

5. _____ reigned after the home team won the championship.

6. Only God is _____, all-powerful.

7. A _____ view is all-encompassing, usually from a high vantage point.

8. A _____ disease affects all people.

9. God is not only **omnipotent**, He is also _____, all-knowing.

10. Man is _____ in that he eats both animal and vegetable foods.

D. Give the meaning of each of the number/amount prefixes below.

1. mono	11. pan
2. bi	12. omni
3. uni	13. poly
4. tri	14. multi
5. quar	15. cent
6. quint	16. deca
7. sex	17. mille
8. sept	18. kilo
9. octa	19. novum
10. semi	20. du

Dimension Three
Part One

hors d'oeuvres

Foreign Words and Phrases

Lesson

1

Many foreign words and phrases have managed to find their way into the English language based on currency and usage. They are used by a significant block of people, sufficient in number so that foreign languages play a small but important role in language use. Such words and phrases lend color, flavor, and texture to language, thereby making its fabric richer than it would otherwise be. Too often, however, their contribution is subverted, and they become tools of pedants who use them to show off their learning. This is to be avoided. On the other hand, there will be occasions when words from a foreign language more readily express ideas, at least more clearly than equivalent English expressions: For instance, the French **bon mot** means "a clever saying; witticism; or clever turn of phrase." **Bon mot** says it all. To use the French **bon mot** is legitimate in that its meaning is so encompassing. This usage is to be encouraged; it enriches the language.

dos a dos: *(dōé zä dōé)*

> *French:*   a movement in square dancing in which two dancers approach each other and circle back to back, then return to their original positions

de trop: *(də trōé)*

> *French:*   superfluous; too much (overflowing)

mal de mer: *(măl' də mâr)*

> *French:*   seasickness

accouchement: *(ä kōōshé män)*

> *French:*   childbirth; a period of confinement in childbirth
> Literally: a going to bed

table d'hôte: *(tä' bəl dōt)*

> *French:*   1. a communal table for all guests at a hotel or restaurant 2. a full-course meal served at a fixed price in a hotel or restaurant

Zeitgeist: *(tsīt' gīst)*

> *German:*   the taste and outlook characteristic of a period or a generation [from: Zeit (time) and Geist (spirit)]

décolletage: *(dā kōl' təzh)*

> *French:*   a low neckline on a garment

vichyssoise: *(vĭshé ē swäzé)*

> *French:*   a thick, creamy potato soup flavored with leeks and chicken stock, usually served cold

in loco parentis: *(ĭn lōé ko pa rĕné tĭs)*

> *French:*   in place of a parent, as a school may function relative to its students

vis à vis: *(vē zə vē')*

> *French:*   1. opposite to 2. one or two persons or things opposite or corresponding to each other

EXERCISES

> **A.** The following sentences are incomplete because there is in each a missing word or phrase. You are to write this missing word or phrase to complete the meaning of the sentence.

decolletage	vis à vis
vichyssoise	in loco parentis
dos a dos	table d'hôte
accouchement	mal de mer
Zeitgeist	de trop

1. Callers for square dancers make their instructions for a _____ sound as though it were a song.

2. "Any further remarks from the defendant are _____ ," the judge warned the loquacious witness.

3. Many vacationers on the cruise ship retired to their cabins after the rough seas brought on severe cases of _____.

4. Oftentimes _____ is used as a euphemism for childbirth.

5. Because he thought that he got more for his money, Alex usually ordered from the _____ menu.

6. The _____ of the 1980s and the 1990s will be characterized mainly as a culture permeated with drugs and violence.

7. The fashion model wore a sequined gown having a sophisticated but daring _____.

8. Many people don't care for _____ because they do not like cold soup.

9. The dean acted _____ when a decision had to be made regarding the young lady's request for a dorm room change.

10. When confronted _____ with the witness the prosecutor presented, the defendant changed his plea to guilty.

B. Write C if the boldface word is consistent with the meaning of the sentence in which it appears or I if it is not.

1. **Dos a dos** has to do with the deer family.

2. To examine something **vis à vis** is to investigate it with a prejudicial view of the intended outcome.

3. To leave a child with someone **in loco parentis** is for the parents to relinquish all authority and decision-making over their child.

4. **Decolletage** is one of those haute couture designs that change frequently.

5. **Vichyssoise** can be served hot or cold.

6. The **Zeitgeist** of an era can only be judged after that era has passed.

7. Many fine hotels serve **table d'hôte** dinners as well as à la carte menus.

8. **Mal de mer** is a word having to do with malcontents.

9. The judge ordered the defense attorney to cut short his **de trop** summation.

10. The duration of a woman's **accouchement** has shortened considerably over the years.

   C. Match the following items.

Column A

1. de trop
2. mal de mer
3. accouchement
4. Zeitgeist
5. decolletage
6. in loco parentis
7. table d'hôte
8. vichyssoise
9. vis à vis
10. dos a dos

Column B

a. movement in square dancing
b. in place of the parents
c. opposite to
d. superfluous
e. spirit of an age or era
f. full-course meal at a fixed price
g. seasickness
h. low cut garment (at the neck)
i. a thick creamy soup, usually served cold
j. childbirth

   D. Choose two of the following words or phrases: de trop, mal de mer, table d'hôte, vis à vis. Use your choices in two original sentences.

Lesson

2

de rigueur: *(də ri gûr′)*

    French;   strictly required by etiquette, usage, or fashion.

sine qua non: *(sīn′ ă kwä nŏn)*

    Latin: an essential element or condition

la dolce vita: *(lä dəl′ che vē′ tä)*

    Italian: the good life, a way of life devoted to pleasure or expressions of self-indulgence

hors d'oeuvres: *(ôr dûrv′)*

    French: an appetizer; often served on crackers or small pieces of toast

Dominus vobiscum: *(Dō′ mi noŏs vō bis′ koŏm)*

    Latin: The Lord be with you

joie de vivre: *(zhwä′ də vēvr)*

    French: hearty or carefree enjoyment of life

concierge: *(kŏn syärzh′)*

    French: hotel employee who provides information or anything else guests may require—theater tickets, etc.

bourgeoisie: *(boŏr zhwä zē')*

> *French:*   the middle class

noblesse oblige: *(no blĕs' ō blezh')*

> *French:*   benevolent and honorable behavior considered to be the
> obligation of persons of high rank or birth

chargé d'affaires: *(shär' zhā də fär')*

> *French:*   governmental official temporarily placed in charge of
> diplomatic affairs while the ambassador is absent

diva: *(dē' və)*

> *Italian:*   an operatic prima donna; a very high-strung, vain, and
> temperamental person

EXERCISES

joie de vivre	divas	sine qua non
concierge	chargé d'affaires	
la dolce vita	bourgeois	
noblesse oblige	hors d'oeuvres	
Dominus vobiscum	de rigueur	

A. Complete the sentences below. Use a lesson word or phrase.

1. Wearing gloves is strictly _____ when presented to members
of a royal family.

2. _____ is the _____ for people whose only aim in life is to find
pleasure.

3. We all looked forward to dining at Aunt Rose's house because
she prepared such tasty _____.

4. "_____," said the priest to those who had donated food and
clothing to his needy parish.

5. Most Disney animated characters embody a _____, especially

Mickey Mouse, whose ever-present smile has made millions of children deliriously happy.

6. The hotel's _____ managed to get us two tickets to the opera house which was featuring the music of Chopin and Mozart.

7. _____ dictated that the king accept the invitation to his birthday party given by his subjects.

8. The Marxist demonstrator shouted to the speaker that his ideas were middle-class, a product of _____ thinking.

9. The United States Consulate's _____ arranged an appointment to see the ambassador next week.

10. _____, very talented performers, are oftentimes difficult to work with because they can be so demanding.

B. Match the meanings from Column B with the items from Column A.

Column A

1. la dolce vita
2. Dominus vobiscum
3. concierge
4. bourgeoisie
5. sine qua non
6. hors d'oeuvres
7. de rigueur
8. noblesse oblige
9. chargé d'affaires
10. diva

Column B

a. very talented performer
b. behavior that is seen as an obligation
c. an appetizer
d. hotel employee
e. the Lord be with you
f. the good life (pleasure)
g. strictly required by etiquette
h. middle class
i. an essential element
j. government official placed in charge while ambassador is absent

C. Write the letter T if the statement is true, or write F if it is not.

1. **La dolce vita** has to do with obligatory behavior of the rich.

2. The Latin phrase that a priest no doubt utters frequently is **Dominus vobiscum**.

3. There are those persons who hold high rank and who are completely lacking in **noblesse oblige** and treat their subordinates rather shabbily.

4. To wear a tuxedo at one's high school prom is **de rigueur**.

5. A **concierge** is a very talented performer, one who at times can be unreasonably demanding.

6. The **bourgeoisie** make up a society's middle class.

7. That which is **sine qua non** is that which cannot be done without.

8. An **hors d'oeuvre** is served after dinner.

9. A **chargé d'affaires** is temporarily in charge of a government embassy in a foreign country.

10. A **diva** is a mediocre opera performer.

D. Choose two of the following words or phrases: de rigueur, la dolce vita, hors d'oeuvres, joie de vivre. Use your choices in two sentences of your own.

Lesson

3

rapprochement: *(ra prōsh män')*

    French: an establishment of harmonious relations, as between nations

requiescat in pace: *(rĕk wē es' kat in paé chā)*

    Latin: may he or she rest in peace

entre nous: *(än tra nōō')*

    French: between ourselves; confidentially

carte blanche: *(kärt' blanch')*

    French: full discretionary power; free hand; a blank sheet of paper given to someone to write what he or she pleases

anno Domini: *(an ō dom' ə nī [or] nē)*

    Latin: in the year of our Lord; since Christ was born (A.D.)

cause célèbre: *(kôz sə leb')*

    French: any controversy that attracts great public attention

non pareil: *(non pə rĕl')*

    French: having no peer; unparalleled

lettre de cachet: *(lĕ´ trə də kA shā´)*

> *French:*   a letter under the seal of a sovereign, especially order-
> ing imprisonment

a priori: *(ā pri ōr´ ī [or] ē)*

> *Latin:*   from cause to effect; from general to particular

a posteriori: *(ā pō stēr ē ōr ī [or] ē)*

> *Latin:*   from effect to cause

EXERCISES

A. Complete the sentences below. Use a lesson word or phrase.
You may refer to these items when doing this exercise.

1. The peace process begun by the leaders of the warring nations
   eventually led to a _____ and peace.

2. "_____," the chaplain intoned over the fallen soldier who had
   stepped on a land mine.

3. "Don't tell anyone what I just told you about Judy," June admon-
   ished Beverly. "It's strictly _____."

4. Because our friend's father owned the baseball team, we were
   given _____; anything we wanted was ours for the asking.

5. The Magna Carta was signed by King John in June, 1215 _____.

6. _____ generally do not hold the public's attention for long.

7. Winston Churchill was a charismatic leader of the British people; without a doubt he was a statesman _____.

8. Charles Darnay, a character in the novel A TALE OF TWO CIT-
   IES by Dickens, was imprisoned as a result of a _____ written
   in his name.

9. Reasoning _____, the gardener decided the sun shining on the grapes caused them to ripen.

10. The gardener's wife, reasoning _____, replied, "Well, the grapes certainly didn't cause the sun to shine."

B. Match the following items.

Column A

1. requiescat in pace
2. lettre de cachet
3. cause célèbre
4. non pareil
5. entre nous
6. rapprochement
7. anno Domini
8. carte blanche
9. a priori
10. a posteriori

Column B

a. in the year of our Lord
b. between ourselves
c. having no equal
d. letter under seal of a sovereign
e. a notorious incident
f. a free hand
g. from effect to cause
h. from cause to effect
i. harmonious relations, as between states
j. may he or she rest in peace

C. Again, as in the previous lesson, write T if the statement is true or F if it is false.

1. To reason **a priori** is to do so in a way that moves from the particular to the more general.

2. A **lettre de cachet** is a love letter that is sent to a ruler under his seal of authority.

3. To arrive at a solution **a posteriori** is to move in a cause-to-effect fashion.

4. That which is considered **non pareil** is without equal.

5. The words **anno Domini** are generally designated by the letters A.D.

6. If one has **carte blanche**, this person is bound by the restrictions imposed on him or her.

7. When a secret is revealed **entre nous**, it is not to be repeated.

8. **Requiescat in pace** is a blessing bestowed by a priest at the time of one's death and during a requiem, a mass for a deceased person.

9. A period of **rapprochement** between the United States and Russia accompanied the dissolution of the Soviet Union.

10. A **cause célèbre** is a famous person who celebrates his good fortune with accolades and much public attention.

D. Choose two of the following words or phrases: entre nous, carte blanche, cause célèbre, non pareil. Use your choices in two original sentences.

Lesson

4

avant-garde: *(ă vânt' gärd')*

>*French:* a group active in the invention and application of new technology in a given field, especially the arts. The word **vanguard** comes from **avant-garde**, meaning "in the **forefront**."

billet doux: *(bil ē doo')*

>*French:* love letter

carpe diem: *(kär' pe dē' em)*

>*Latin:* enjoy the present as opposed to placing all hope in the future; don't worry about tomorrow; seize the day.

prix fixe: *(prē feks')*

>*French:* price at which a table d'hôte meal is offered; **prix fixe** signs abound in European shop windows informing patrons that prices could not be bargained down.

alfresco: *(al fresé ko)*

>*Italian:* out-of-doors; open air

ad nauseam: *(ad nôé zē əm)*

>*Latin:* to a sickening or disgusting degree (literally, it means to the point of seasickness)

bon mot: *(bôn mō')*

   French: a clever saying; witticism; clever turn of phrase

au jus: *(o zhōos')*

   French: served in its natural juices obtained from cooking

bête noire: *(bet nwär')*

   French: someone or something one particularly dislikes or seeks
   to avoid (literally, meaning "a black beast")

sub rosa: *(sub ro' zə)*

   Latin: in secret; privately (The rose at one time was a symbol
   of secrecy.)

EXERCISES

   A. Write a lesson word to complete each sentence.

sub rosa	bon mot
carpe diem	billet doux
bête noir	prix fixe
alfresco	au jus
ad nauseam	avant-garde

1. The artist was considered _____ because he worked with a medium never before used.

2. Emma found an old yellowed _____ in the hollow of a tree, but she never did learn who the lovers were.

3. "Gather ye rosebuds while ye may,/ Old Time is still a-flying" is taken from a poem whose author was a follower of the _____ theme so prevalent during the 17th century.

4. Patrons at the Cafe Noir knew that a _____ always applied to a table d'hôte menu.

5. One of the most delightful attractions of St. Mark's Square in Venice, Italy, is eating _____ at one of the sidewalk cafes.

6. The woman in the television talk show went on and on _____, relating her husband's shortcomings.

7. After it had been reported that Samuel Clemens had died, he replied with his now famous _____: "The reports of my death have been grossly exaggerated."

8. We order roast beef at our favorite restaurant because the beef always comes drenched _____.

9. Having to prepare my income tax return is a horrid nightmare— a _____, in fact.

10. All meetings between heads of state are conducted _____, especially those of a delicate nature.

    B. Write the letter C if the boldface word or phrase is used correctly or I if it is not.

1. To go on **ad nauseam** on a given topic is commendable.

2. A **billet doux** is not something one would want made public.

3. To have a beef steak **au jus** is not possible.

4. A meeting held **sub rosa** has to do with roses.

5. An **avant-garde** theater group was experimenting with new approaches to presenting Shakespeare.

6. To dine **alfresco** is not possible in many restaurants.

7. A **bête noire** is a big black beast.

8. The Roman shopkeeper hung a sign in his window reading **prix fixe**, which meant his prices were negotiable.

9. "Seize the day" could well be the cornerpiece of the **carpe diem** philosophy.

10. Samuel Johnson (1709–84), English writer/lexicographer, had a sharp wit. One of his better **bon mots** is: "It is better to live rich, than to die rich."

C. Write the letter of the item that most closely defines the bold-face word or phrase.

1. **billet doux**
   (a) the billets that soldiers occupy   (b) a love letter
   (c) out-of-doors

2. **sub rosa**
   (a) a floral arrangement   (b) in secret   (c) a witticism

3. **bête noire**
   (a) an Alaskan black bear   (b) privately   (c) that which one particularly dislikes

4. **prix fixe**
   (a) enjoy the present   (b) open air   (c) a fixed price

5. **au jus**
   (a) natural juices from cooking   (b) sickening   (c) in the forefront

6. **carpe diem**
   (a) live for today   (b) a clever saying   (c) a love letter

7. **avant-garde**
   (a) a dueling term   (b) don't worry about tomorrow   (c) in the
   vanguard

8. **ad nauseam**
   (a) sickening to a disgusting degree   (b) out-of-doors
   (c) privately

9. **bon mot**
   (a) a beast   (b) a clever turn of phrase   (c) good food

10. **alfresco**
    (a) a cold drink   (b) open air   (c) fresh air

D. Choose two of the following words or phrases: avant-garde,
prix fixe, bon mot, bête noir. Use your two choices in two of
your own sentences.

Lesson

5

bon vivant: *(bôn vē vän′)*

    French: a person who lives luxuriously and enjoys good food and drink, among other things

bonsai: *(bōn′ sī)*

    Japanese: a potted tree or shrub that has been dwarfed (made to grow much smaller than normal size)

borscht: *(bôrshté)*

    Russian: soup containing beets and cabbage, served hot or cold, often with sour cream

paparazzi: *(päp ə rät′ sē)*

    Italian: photographers who are aggressive (perhaps too much so) in pursuit of candid photos of celebrities

nota bene: *(nō′ tə bĕ nē′)*

    Latin: used to direct attention to something particularly important (generally used in abbreviated form—N.B.)

inamorato: *(ĭn ăm ə rä′ tō)*

    Latin: a man with whom one is in love (inamora**ta** is a woman with whom one is in love)

maven: *(mā′ vən)*

> *Yiddish:*   an expert; an authority; a person having special knowledge (often used derisively)

objet d'art: *(ŏb zhā′ där)*

> *French:*   ornamental article, usually of some artistic value

déclassé: *(dā klə sā′)*

> *French:*   reduced to or having low status; fallen in social standing

caveat emptor: *(kā′ vē ăt emp′ tôr)*

> *Latin:*   the principle that the seller cannot be held responsible for the quality of his product unless guaranteed in a warranty (literally, "let the buyer beware.")

EXERCISES

A. Write the lesson word or phrase that will complete the meaning of each sentence. Use the words above.

1. The steel magnate's son, a noted _____, spent extravagant sums of money in his travels.

2. An exhibit of _____ trees and shrubs captured the fancy of onlookers because of their uniqueness.

3. "I like a bowl of _____ occasionally," replied Tom, "but I like it hot, not chilled."

4. The constant hounding of the _____ with their flash cameras popping can be for many celebrities their **bête noir**.

5. The letters N.B. designate _____, indicating that the reader should pay close attention to that part so marked.

6. Maria wailed inconsolably, "My dearest _____ has left me for another woman."

7. Should anyone want advice or counsel, the neighborhood _____ was available.

8. The sheik's palatial home was filled with paintings and other
   _____.

9. Many people feel that smoking in public today is definitely
   _____.

10. When dealing with mail order houses, the admonition _____ is
    particularly appropriate.

B. Match the following items.

Column A

1. objet d'art
2. paparazzi
3. borscht
4. bonsai
5. caveat emptor
6. nota bene
7. inamorato
8. maven
9. bon vivant
10. déclassé

Column B

a. person who lives luxuriously
b. a man with whom a woman is in love
c. item of artistic value
d. having low status
e. an expert
f. indication that something is particularly
   important
g. aggressive photographers
h. small potted tree or shrub
i. beet soup served cold or hot
j. "Let the buyer beware"

C. Without referring to previous exercises, define the following.

1. bon vivant:

2. borscht:

3. paparazzi:

4. bonsai:

5. objet d'art:

6. maven:

7. déclassé:

8. caveat emptor:

9. inamorato:

10. nota bene:

D. Choose two of the following words or phrases: bon vivant, paparazzi, maven, dé classé: Use your choices in two original sentences.

REVIEW OF LESSONS 1 - 5

A. Match the following items.

Column A

1. de trop
2. table d'hôte
3. de rigueur
4. non pareil
5. rapprochement
6. billet doux
7. sub rosa
8. alfresco
9. bonsai
10. objet d'art
11. caveat emptor
12. mal de mer
13. decolletage
14. noblesse oblige
15. bourgeosie
16. anno Domini
17. carte blanche
18. maven
19. déclassé
20. entre nous

Column B

a. strictly by etiquette or usage
b. in secret
c. a potted tree or shrub that has been dwarfed
d. a full-course meal at a fixed price
e. out-of-doors; open air
f. without equal
g. buyer beware
h. harmonious relations, as between nations
i. seasickness
j. middle class
k. low neckline on a garment
l. benevolent behavior considered an obligation of those of high rank or birth
m. artistic ornament of some value
n. a love letter
o. an expert
p. having low status
q. free hand
r. between ourselves
s. in the year of our Lord
t. superfluous

B. Write C if the boldface word is consistent with sentence meaning, or write I if it is not.

1. The **decolletage** of wearing apparel is generally dictated by women's fashion designers.

2. One can visit the **concierge** in a hotel to obtain theater tickets.

3. An argument **a priori** moves from specific to general.

4. Any **cause célèbre** is in the public eye.

5. A **carpe diem** philosophy is one that promotes living for the day and not worrying about tomorrow.

6. An **avant-garde** movement is behind the times, and its primary concern is the past, not the present.

7. **Borscht** is a light wine served with seafood dinners.

8. A **bon vivant** is miserly, penny-pinching, and reclusive.

9. **Vichyssoise** and **borscht** have in common the fact that both are soups that must be served piping hot.

10. An era's **Zeitgeist** is a reflection of its spirit.

Lesson

6

dishabille: *(dĭs ə bēl')*

French: a state of being carelessly or partially dressed

bona fide: *(bō' nə fid)*

Latin: real; genuine; in good faith

outré: *(ü' trā)*

French: violating convention or propriety

savoir faire: *(săv wär fâr')*

French: ability to say or do the correct thing in any situation

ersatz: *(ĕr' zäts)*

German: substitute; artificial

raison d'être: *(rĕ zŏn' dĕ é trə)*

French: reason or justification for existing

mélange: *(mā länzh')*

French: a mixture (literature, music, languages, etc.)

mea culpa: *(mē ə kŭl' pə)*

Latin: an acknowledgment of a personal error or fault

fait accompli: *(fāt ë kŏm plē')*

> *French:*   an accomplished and presumably irreversible deed or fact

faux pas: *(fō pä')*

> *French:*   a social blunder

EXERCISES

raison d'être   mea culpa
ersatz   bona fide
savoir faire   dishabille
mélange

> **A.** The following is a mélange of items relating to the words you just studied. What you are to do will be obvious.

1. Which phrase has to do with the reason for one's existence?

2. Generally, a person's _____ is reflected in his or her slovenly housekeeping habits.

3. How would you write in Latin, "It's my fault" ?

4. Almost everyone wants to possess this ability to be able to respond correctly to almost any situation.

5. A mix of music from the 1940s through the 1980s is a _____.

6. A counterfeit $100 bill is not this.

7. Someone possessing **savoir faire** would never be guilty of **outre** behavior. (True or False?)

8. The word **bona fide** and _____ are opposites.

9. Most **faux pas** are really inconsequential social shortcomings. (True or False?)

10. A **fait accompli** is that which has not yet been done. (True or False?)

B. Match the following items.

Column A

1. ersatz
2. fait accompli
3. dishabille
4. mea culpa
5. outré
6. mélange
7. savoir faire
8. raison d'être
9. faux pas
10. bona fide

Column B

a. carelessly or partially dressed
b. genuine
c. violating convention or propriety
d. ability to do or say the correct thing
e. artificial
f. reason for existing
g. a mix
h. acknowledgment of a personal fault
i. a done deed
j. a social blunder

C. Define the following words and phrases. Be brief in your response.

1. bona fide:

2. savoir faire:

3. ersatz:

4. raison d'être:

5. mélange:

6. mea culpa:

7. faux pas:

8. fait accompli:

9. outré:

10. dishabille:

D. Choose two of the following words or phrases: bona fide, ersatz, mea culpa, faux pas. Use your choices in two of your own sentences.

Lesson

7

imprimatur: *(ĭm prə mä' tur)*

Latin: official approval or license to print or publish, especially under conditions of censorship; official sanction

nouvelle cuisine: *(no͞o vĕ l' kwĭ zēné)*

French: school of French cooking that downplays the customary heavy sauces laced with butter and cream; light low-calorie sauces and stocks substituted

quid pro quo: *(kwĭdé prō kwō')*

Latin: an equal exchange or substitution

sotto voce: *(sōt ō vō' chē)*

Latin: softly, so as not to be overheard, a direction on the musical score

sobriquet: *(sō brĭ kā')*

French: an affectionate or humorous nickname; an assumed name

non sequitur: *(non sĕk' wĭ tər)*

Latin: a conclusion that does not follow from the evidence or premises; a statement that does not logically follow from the preceding one

nosh: *(nŏsh)*

> *Yiddish:*   to eat snacks between meals (from the Yiddish **nosherei** meaning "tidbits")

nolo contendere: *(nō lō kun ten' da rē)*

> *Latin:*   means "I don't want to fight"; a plea made by a defendant tantamount to an admission of guilt, but which allows him to change his plea later.

metier: *(mā tyā')*

> *French:*   work or activity for which a person is particularly well suited

klutz: *(klŭtz')*

> *Yiddish:*   a clumsy person

EXERCISES

A. Match the following items.

Column A	Column B
1. non sequitur	a. a conclusion that does not logically follow
2. imprimatur	b. French style of cooking
3. nouvelle cuisine	c. something for something
4. quid pro quo	d. softly
5. sotto voce	e. a humorous nickname
6. sobriquet	f. a "guilty" plea that can be changed
7. nolo contendere	g. a clumsy person
8. nosh	h. work that one is well suited for
9. metier	i. eat snacks
10. klutz	j. official sanction

B. Write the word that is called for in each of the following.

1. A clumsy person is a _____.

2. Statements that are not logical are _____.

3. An equal exchange or something for something is a _____.

4. That which is spoken softly so as not to be overheard is done
_____.

5. To snack between meals is to _____.

6. That work for which a person is best-suited is his/her _____.

7. _____ means "I don't want to fight."

8. One's nickname is his/her _____.

9. French cooking that downplays heavy, rich sauces is _____.

10. The government's _____ was stamped boldly on the cover page
of the magazine.

nosh	sobriquet
metier	imprimatur
klutz	non sequiturs
nolo contendere	quid pro quo
nouvelle cuisine	sotto voce

C. Choose the item that best fits the definition of the word or
words.

1. **nosh**
(a) clumsy person   (b) an affectionate nickname   (c) to eat
snacks between meals

2. **metier**
(a) official approval   (b) work for which one is particularly well-
suited   (c) slowly

3. **nouvelle cuisine**
(a) a publication that is censored   (b) French school of cooking
(c) softly

4. **klutz**
(a) a clumsy person   (b) an equal exchange   (c) it does not logically follow

5. **non sequitur**
(a) makes no sense   (b) softly   (c) a substitution

6. **imprimatur**
(a) a conclusion   (b) one's strength   (c) official approval

7. **sotto voce**
   (a) softly   (b) humorous nickname   (c) to shout loudly

8. **nolo contendere**
   (a) rest in peace   (b) to contest a criminal charge   (c) a plea
   equivalent to an admission of guilt

9. **sobriquet**
   (a) music played softly   (b) a nickname   (c) something which
   one is particularly well-suited to do

10. **quid pro quo**
    (a) an equal exchange   (b) rest in peace   (c) an illogical statement

D. Choose two of the following words or phrases: sotto voce, nosh,
metier, klutz. Use your choices in two original sentences.

Lesson

8

nouveau riche: *(noo̅ vo̅ rēsh')*

> *French:*   one who has recently become rich, especially one who flaunts his good fortune

forte: *(fôrt')*

> *French:*   something at which a person excels

déjà vu: *(dā̅ zhä vü')*

> *French:*   the illusion of already having experienced something that is actually being experienced for the first time

ex cathedra: *(ĕks kə thē̅' drə)*

> *Latin:*   with authority derived from one's position (from **ex** "out," **cathedra**, "chair," which is an oblique reference to the seat of a bishop)

toute de suite: *(to̅ot swē̅t')*

> *French:*   at once; immediately

tour de force: *(to̅or' də fôrs)*

> *French:*   an exceptional achievement

cul-de-sac: *(kŭl' di săk)*

> *French:*   dead-end street; an impasse (literally, "the bottom of the sack with no way out")

tout le monde: *(tōō lə mônd')*

    French: everybody (literally, the "whole world")

tabula rasa: *(tăb é yə lə rä' zə)*

    Latin: clean slate; the mind prior to its receiving impressions coming with experience. The philosopher John Locke believed that man was born with a mind that was lacking any impressions, and from this **tabula rasa** was born—"an erased board."

haute cuisine: *(ōt kwĭ zēn')*

    French: elaborate or skillfully prepared cuisine

EXERCISES

haute cuisine	tout le monde
nouveau riche	ex cathedra
déjà vu	forte
tout de suite	cul-de-sac
tabula rasa	tour de force

A. Write the lesson word or words to complete each sentence.

1. The _____ are looked down upon by the long-established wealthy aristocracy.

2. Hitting home runs was the slugger's _____, and it brought him a 20 million dollar contract for signing with the Yankees.

3. The tourist scanned the familiar surroundings, commenting that she had a distinct feeling of _____, although she had never been there before.

4. The Holy See published _____ the papal stand on divorce and other pressing matters.

5. "I want you home _____," Pierre's mother said in a very serious tone of voice.

6. To watch two young lovers walk hand-in-hand down the avenue in Paris calls to mind that _____ loves lovers.

7. General Patton's achievements during World War II have become a legendary _____.

8. The French term _____ has become a synonym for a dead-end street in America.

9. Whether the mind at birth is a blank, a _____, or has inborn impressions and sensations stamped upon it is a matter of debate.

10. Any dining establishment that has earned the reputation of _____ will offer fare as eminently high-priced.

   B. Match the following items.

Column A

1. forte
2. cul-de-sac
3. tour de force
4. tout de suite
5. déjà vu
6. nouveau riche
7. ex cathedra
8. tout le monde
9. tabula rasa
10. haute cuisine

Column B

a. newly rich
b. immediately
c. skillfully prepared food
d. everybody
e. an exceptional achievement
f. an illusion of having experienced something
g. something at which one excels
h. authority from one's office or position
i. dead end
j. clean slate, referring to the mind

   C. For each definition below, write the foreign word or phrase that fits most closely.

1. newly rich:

2. at once:

3. the "whole world":

4. dead end:

5. authority derived from one's position:

6. illusion of having experienced something:

7. an exceptional achievement:

8. something at which one is very good:

9. John Locke's hypothesis:

10. elaborate, skillfully prepared cuisine:

D. Choose two of the following words or phrases: déjà vu, tout de suite, cul-de-sac, tabula rasa. Use your two choices in two original sentences.

Lesson

9

beau monde: *(bō mond')*

    French: the world of fashionable society

mot juste: *(mō zhyst')*

    French: the exact or appropriate word

double entendre: *(dub' əl än tän' drə)*

    French: a double meaning, one of which is off color—risqué

au gratin: *(ō grät' an)*

    French: baked or cooked with a topping of bread crumbs and/or cheese. The French **au gratin** means **the burnt part**, an obvious reference to the toasted bread crumbs and cheese.

habitue: *(ha bich' oo āé)*

    French: a frequenter of a place or particular kind of place, especially one offering entertainment

angst: *(ängkst)*

    German: a feeling of anxiety; anguish or dread

demitasse: *(də mē täs')*

    French: a small cup of strong black after-dinner coffee or the cup itself in which the coffee is served

cloture: *(klō' chər)*

> *French:*   a method of closing debate and causing an immediate vote to be taken

café au lait: *(kaf' ā ō lā')*

> *French:*   hot coffee poured in equal portions with scalded milk

croupier: *(krōō' pē ər)*

> *French:*   an attendant at a gaming table who collects and pays bets

EXERCISES

A. Write T if the statement is true or F if it is false.

1. **Demitasse** or **café au lait** is served as an after-dinner beverage.

2. **Angst** is a celebratory feeling one would experience on a joyful occasion.

3. **Cloture** refers to a letter under the seal of a sovereign.

4. A **habitue** of a nightclub would be well known to those who work there.

5. **Double entendres** are intended to be humorous, but at times they are offensive, especially in mixed company.

6. One can reasonably expect a dish prepared **au gratin** to be piping hot.

7. A **mot juste** is the precise use of a word.

8. The **croupier** in an establishment will gladly serve patrons food and drink.

9. Edith Wharton's characters in THE AGE OF INNOCENCE epitomized the **beau monde** of New York in the late 19th century, a time of high fashion.

10. **Café au lait** is made by combining equal amounts of coffee and hot milk.

B. Write the lesson word or phrase that completes the meaning of each sentence.

1. Oftentimes the **nouveau riche** are not prepared socially to be a part of the _____, the world of fashionable society.

2. The linguistics professor managed to end his lecture with a _____ that clearly demonstrated the importance of choosing words carefully.

3. A dish prepared _____ may be served with either bread crumbs or cheese, unless one prefers both.

4. _____ that are contrived should be used with utmost care lest someone is offended by the suggested indelicacy.

5. The police were able to track down the drug dealer because he was a known _____ of a disco in Manhattan.

6. _____ was a very real part of the American scene during the Vietnam conflict, especially for those who opposed the war.

7. For many Americans _____ is much too strong a beverage, although it is quite popular in Europe.

8. Invoking _____ and closing debate is a common ploy in the United States Senate.

9. The hostess who served _____ to her guests recommended that they try it at home by combining equal amounts of coffee and scalding milk.

10. The _____ informed the roulette table that no more bets would be taken.

C. Match the item from Column A with its meaning from Column B.

Column A

1. café au lait
2. croupier
3. mot juste
4. double entendre
5. habitue
6. cloture

Column B

a. the world of fashionable society
b. hot coffee (half coffee + half scalded milk)
c. a small cup for serving after-dinner drinks (hot black coffee)
d. attendant at a gaming table who collects and pays off bets

7. demitasse
8. angst
9. au gratin
10. beau monde

e. a dish prepared with a covering of cheese and/or bread crumbs
f. the exact or appropriate word
g. feeling of anxiety
h. frequenter of a place
i. word having a double meaning
j. method of closing debate causing immediate vote to be taken (often used in U.S. Senate)

D. Choose two of the following words or phrases: double entendre, habitue, angst, demitasse. Use your two choices in two of your own sentences.

Lesson

10

cogito ergo sum: *(kṓé gi tō er' gō soŏm)*

   Latin: I think, therefore I am (philosopher René Descartes' first universal truth)

bodega: *(bō dā́' gə)*

   Spanish: a grocery store, especially among Spanish-speaking Americans

à la carte: *(ä lə kärt')*

   French: with a stated price for each dish offered on a menu

nom de plume: *(nom də plōom')*

   French: pen name

detente: *(dā tänt')*

   French: a relaxing or easing, as of tensions between nations

du jour: *də zhoŏr')*

   French: of the kind being served today, as soup du jour

pro bono publico: *(prō bō' nō poo' bli kō')*

   Latin: for the public good

femme fatale: *(fĕm fə tä l´)* *(plural form: femmes fatales)*

French: a woman whose seductive charms may lead a man into a compromising or dangerous situation

enfant terrible: *(än fän´ te rē´ blə)*

French: one whose unconventional behavior causes embarrassment or dismay; a prodigy whose behavior is somewhat less than agreeable

esprit de corps: *(ĕ sprē´ də kôr)*

French: common spirit of comradeship, enthusiasm, and devotion among a group's members

EXERCISES

A. Write the lesson word or phrase to complete the meaning of each sentence.

cogito ergo sum   detente
esprit de corps   bodega
enfant terrible   à la carte
nom de plume   du jour
pro bono publico   femmes fatales

1. René Descartes concluded that if he could think, and he proved that he could, then he must exist, and thus was born the famous dictum _____, "I think, therefore, I am."

2. Luis offered to stop in at the _____ and pick up a quart of milk.

3. Generally _____ dinners are more costly than are those taken from a table d'hôte menu.

4. Samuel Clemens used the _____ Mark Twain.

5. At present a _____ exists between the United States and Russia.

6. The luncheonette featured a sandwich and a cup of soup _____ at a special low price.

7. The phrase _____ has been shortened in the legal profession to pro bono—a lawyer's taking on a case with no recompense.

8. Perhaps Delilah was the most famous or infamous of all the biblical _____, and she was known primarily for her betrayal of Samson to the Philistines.

9. His reputation as an _____ preceded him, and the precocious young pianist noticed that people made a habit of avoiding his company.

10. It is said that the varsity team's _____ is what helps them win so many games.

B. Write T if the statement is true or F if it is false.

1. An **enfant terrible** would be greeted with enthusiasm by friends and acquaintances.

2. An **esprit de corps** is what sets the United States Marines apart from other branches of service.

3. **Cogito ergo sum** suggests that thinking and existence are intimately intertwined.

4. **Bodegas** are dairies where milk can be purchased.

5. An **à la carte** meal has a fixed price.

6. A **nom de plume** is a humorous nickname, much like a sobriquet.

7. **Detente** between governments is not a good sign for the future relations of those countries.

8. A **du jour** special on food, for example, carries over from one day to the next.

9. **Pro bono publico** is that which is done for the public good.

10. A **femme fatale** is a seductress.

C. Match the item from Column A with its meaning from Column B.

Column A

1. du jour
2. pro bono publico
3. detente
4. bodega
5. esprit de corps
6. enfant terrible
7. cogito ergo sum
8. nom de plume
9. femme fatale
10. à la carte

Column B

a. prodigy whose behavior is less than agreeable
b. relaxing or easing of tension
c. stated price for each dish on a menu
d. of the kind being served today
e. seductive woman whose charm could lead men into dangerous situations
f. pen name
g. grocery store, especially among Spanish speaking people
h. René Decartes' first universal truth, "I think, therefore I am."
i. common spirit or comradeship among a group's members
j. for the public good

D. Choose two of the following words or phrases: à la carte, nom de plume, detente, esprit de corps. Use your two choices in two original sentences.

REVIEW OF LESSONS 6 - 10

A. Write the letter of the item whose meaning most closely matches the numbered word or phrase.

1. a mixture
   (a) fait accompli   (b) mélange   (c) outré

2. violation of convention or propriety
   (a) outré   (b) tout le monde   (c) haute cuisine

3. substitute; artificial
   (a) sobriquet   (b) imprimatur   (c) ersatz

4. something for something
   (a) metier   (b) quid pro quo   (c) non sequitur

5. softly, as a whisper
   (a) forte   (b) tour de force   (c) sotto voce

6. at once; immediately
   (a) tout de suite   (b) tout le monde   (c) déjà vu

7. something at which a person excels
   (a) tout de suite   (b) tout le monde   (c) metier

8. a feeling of anxiety
   (a) mot juste   (b) detente   (c) angst

9. a pen name
   (a) du jour   (b) a bodega   (c) nom de plume

10. spirit of comradeship
    (a) carpe diem   (b) esprit de corps   (c) sub rosa

B. Choose the response that best answers the question posed.

1. In whose company would you least likely enjoy yourself?
   (a) an enfant terrible   (b) an avant-garde person   (c) an habitue

2. Which would you be most likely to be served with your dinner, especially in Europe?
   (a) sobriquet   (b) demitasse   (c) metier

3. Which of the following would most likely use a **sobriquet**?
   (a) a clergyman in prayer   (b) a lawyer to a judge   (c) friends to each other

4. Which of the following phrases would a priest be most likely to use?
   (a) quid pro quo   (b) non sequitur   (c) requiescat in pace

5. Where might a **faux pas** most likely occur?
   (a) in one's home in privacy   (b) at a formal dinner table   (c) at a picnic

6. **Dishabille** would most closely describe which of the following?
   (a) a well-dressed business executive   (b) a person who is carelessly attired   (c) a person who made a faux pas

7. That which is already accomplished is a
   (a) fait accompli   (b) faux pas   (c) mea culpa

8. To snack on "nibblies" is to do what?
   (a) klutz   (b) nosh   (c) maven

9. The head of the Catholic church speaks with the authority of his position, which is
   (a) the pontifical bridge   (b) ex cathedra   (c) a tabula rasa

10. Where would a **croupier** be most likely found?
    (a) at a swank hotel   (b) at a gambling casino   (c) at a restaurant

C. Write the missing word or words.

1. **Dishabille** has to do with one's being _____ dressed.

2. A **fait accompli** is a deed that has already been _____.

3. That which is _____ is done **sotto voce**.

4. An **imprimatur** is that which is done with _____ sanction.

5. One's **forte** is that which is done _____.

6. A **tour de force** is an _____ achievement.

7. **Haute cuisine** is _____ prepared cuisine.

8. **Angst** is a feeling of _____.

9. **Double entendre** is a statement having two meanings, one of which is _____.

10. A **demitasse** is a strong _____ coffee served as a(n) _____ drink.

D. Write the letter of the appropriate response.

1. a social blunder
   (a) ersatz   (b) outré   (c) faux pas

2. acknowledgment of personal fault
   (a) mea culpa   (b) savoir faire   (c) imprimatur

3. softly, as a whisper
   (a) sobriquet   (b) sotto voce   (c) metier

4. to eat snacks between meals
   (a) haute cuisine   (b) nosh   (c) nouvelle cuisine

5. at once
   (a) tout de suite   (b) tout le monde   (c) detente

6. of a kind being served today, as a soup
   (a) mélange   (b) vichyssoise   (c) du jour

7. violation of convention
   (a) faux pas   (b) outré   (c) dishabille

8. reason for existing
   (a) non sequitur   (b) sobriquet   (c) raison d'être

9. a clumsy person
   (a) a nosh   (b) a klutz   (c) an inamorata

10. an equal exchange
    (a) quid pro quo   (b) raison d'être   (c) cloture

Dimension Three
Part Two

optometrist

Medical Specialities

It is common knowledge that in recent years there has been a virtual explosion of innovative medical advancements. Laproscopic surgery, angioplasty, microsurgery, and cryosurgery are but a few.

While this explosion was taking place, the area of specialized medicine did the opposite. It imploded. Physicians became more and more specialized. This is clearly evident. Check the yellow pages in your phone book. There are specialists who treat the eyes, the kidneys, the digestive system, cancers, the heart, the blood, and so on. The general practioner, a family doctor, is fast becoming an anachronism, belonging to a time long gone. It is a combination of these factors, the exploding innovations taking place in the field of medicine and the shrinking numbers of general practioners, that can bring about the public's interest and awareness of the seemingly never-ending changes that are taking place. With each new advancement there is an attendant increase in the number of specialists. One should keep abreast of these changes. After all, one of them might save your life.

What follows is a list of specialists, specialties, and procedures. The list is by no means complete, but it will do nicely for our purpose, which is in the nature of a broad introduction to medical specialties.

Lesson

1

oncologist

The doctor who specializes in the treatment of tumors, especially malignant tumors—cancers. The word is built on the Greek **onkos**, which means "mass." Oftentimes, a tumor is referred to as mass, a body of matter with no specific shape. Oncologists are specialists in the treatment of cancers.

nephrologist

The doctor who deals with kidneys, especially their function. The general field is referred to as nephrology. Aptly enough, the Greek word for kidney is **nephro**. Other words using this same word element are: **nephrectomy**—the excision of a kidney; **nephritis**—the chronic inflammations of the kidney; **nephrosis**—the disease of kidneys marked by degenerative lesions; and **nephrotomy**—surgical incision into the kidney, but not its removal.

hematologist

The Greek **haima** means "blood." Hematology is the science dealing with the pathology and therapies relating to blood disorders, e.g., **hemophilia** (a word you have already studied) and **leukemia**, from **leuco**, "white" + **haima**, "blood," a cancer caused by white blood cells proliferating at an unsustainable growth rate, thereby retarding the increase in number of healthy red blood cells.

urologist

The Latin **urina** means "urine" and is the origin of the word urologist. This doctor specializes in the study of the urogenital tract, which involves both urinary and genital functions. Urologists treat both genders—men and women.

podiatrist

Podiatry is a practice that does not require the practioner to hold a medical certificate that doctors of medicine are required to have. Podiatrists are physicians who specialize in treating the feet, e.g., corn and callous removal, treatment of bunions, etc. The Greek **pod** means "foot," and **iatreia** means "healing."

chiropractor

As in the case of podiatrists, chiropractors do not need an American Medical Association-endorsed license to practice. While chiropractors do not need AMA endorsement, they must submit themselves to rigorous testing before they are allowed to practice their speciality. Chiropractic is a system of therapy in which disease is considered the result of neural dysfunction, and manipulation of the spinal column and other structures is the preferred method of treatment. It is built on the Greek **kheir**, "hand" + **practkos**, "effective." Chiropractors cannot prescribe medications. Most treatments involve the use of the **hands** in some manipulative way.

endodontist

Endodontists are dentists who deal with the cause, diagnosis, prevention, and treatment of disease of the dental pulp. The procedure most often performed by the endodontist is referred to as pulpotomy or root canal therapy. The Greek etymon **endo**, "within" + **dens**, "tooth," combine to form the words endodontia and endodontist.

orthodontist

The similarity between endodontia and orthodontia should be obvious. Both end with the Greek etymon **dens**, which has changed in English to **don**(tia). The other Greek element is **ortho**, which means **correct**. Hence, an orthodontist's job is to correct misaligned, or maloccluded, teeth. In a word, he or she straightens teeth by applying pressure against those teeth that are to be moved by plastic braces or braces of another kind, such as rubber bands.

dermatologist

The Greek **dermato** means "skin." The dermatologist treats diseases of the skin such as acne, eczema, skin cancer, warts, and dermatitis, among a host of other skin pathologies. Dermatologists are board-certified doctors of medicine.

otorhinolaryngologist

This is certainly a formidable-looking word, but it's not as bad as it looks. The Greek **otikos** means "ear"; **rhino** means "nose"; and **larrungo** means "throat." Essentially these doctors treat ailments relating to the ear, nose, and throat. More often than not, doctors who specialize in these areas are referred to as ear, nose, and throat specialists since otorhinolaryngologist is a mouthful, to say the least.

EXERCISES

A. Write C if the boldface word is used in a way that is consistent with its meaning, or write I if it is not.

1. A **podiatrist** can prescribe drugs to a patient in much the same manner as a medical doctor.

2. A **urologist's** practice is limited to conditions relating to the urogenital tract in women.

3. If you had a kidney disease, your best bet would be to visit a **hematologist**.

4. A **nephrologist** is a specialist who treats disease of the lymph glands.

5. **Chiropractors** can't prescribe medications requiring a prescription authorized by a medical doctor.

6. An **orthodontist** would prefer his patients to be young, when the teeth can be moved more easily.

7. A skin rash may prompt you to visit a **dermatologist**.

8. **Endodontists** do root canal therapy among other things.

9. If you have a problem with your eyes, ears, or kidneys, you should see an **otorhinolaryngologist**.

10. **Oncologists** specialize in the treatment of malignant tumors.

B. Match the item from under Column A with its meaning under Column B.

Column A

1. podiatrist
2. hematologist
3. dermatologist
4. endodontist
5. chiropractor
6. otorhinolaryngologist
7. orthodontist
8. nephrologist
9. urologist
10. oncologist

Column B

a. specializes in treatment of tumors
b. treats the feet
c. treats urogenital tract diseases
d. specializes in pathologies of the blood
e. corrects teeth misalignments
f. treats diseases of the skin
g. treats nose, ears, and throat
h. performs root canal therapy
i. treats kidney diseases
j. manipulates spinal column

C. Write the medical specialist one might visit for a disease or symptoms listed in the following.

Disease or Symptoms

1. cancer

2. urinary tract problems

3. skin rash

4. need of root canal therapy

5. a sore back or neck

6. an ear infection

7. need for teeth to be straightened

8. a blood disorder

9. a foot problem

10. a kidney infection

D. Choose two of the following words: hematologist, chiropractor, dermatologist, orthodontist. Use your words in two original sentences.

Lesson

2

periodontist

Periodontia is that branch of dentistry that treats gum disease. The Greek **perio**, "around" + **dens**, "teeth," combine to form the word. A periodontist works around the teeth, namely the gums, which may have contracted such pathologies as gingivitis, inflammation of the gums.

cardiologist

The Greek **kardia** means "heart," and a cardiologist treats heart disease and disease of the vascular system in general. Other words related to this branch of the medical profession are: cardiovascular, cardiogram, cardiopulmonary, carditis, and cardiogenic.

endocrinologist

An endocrinologist is a medical doctor who treats the endocrine glands: thyroid, parathyroid, adrenals, pituitary, and the pancreas. Endocrine glands secrete internally the body's hormones directly into the blood. The pancreas, for example, secretes insulin directly into the blood to break down sugar intake. Two Greek elements form the word: **endo**, "within" + **krinein**, "separate." The only logical explanation for this derivation is that the endocrine glands are indeed separate, and do in fact work as separate systems.

cryosurgeon

Cryosurgeons practice a branch of cryogenics, the science of low-temperature phenomena. It is specifically a surgical procedure that uses extreme cold to destroy tissue for therapeutic purposes. It is built on the Greek **kruos,** meaning "icy cold." The use of extreme cold is a technique that is quite young, but it does appear to have a promising future in medicine.

orthopedist

An orthopedist corrects bone malformations, misalignments, common bone fractures, etc. The word comes from the Greek **ortho,** "straight" + **paid,** "child." The orthopedist would much prefer to correct bone malformations in a child, when the bones are still malleable.

gynecologist

Medical specialists dealing with the care of women, especially with regard to the reproduction organs. The Greek **gyne,** "woman" + **logos,** "science," are the sources of the word.

anesthesiologist

A physician who specializes in anesthesiology, the science of administering anesthetics—drugs that produce physical insensibility to pain. The word is built on the Greek etymons **an,** "without" + **aisthesis,** "feeling."

ophthalmologist

An ophthalmologist is a licensed physician who treats diseases of the eye—cataracts, glaucoma, retinopathy, etc. Ophthalmologists also examine the eyes and prescribe prescriptive lenses when needed. They also perform surgical procedures on the eye, such as cataract removal. Again, Greek contributes to English: **ophthalmos,** "eye" + **logos,** "study" + **ist,** "one who."

osteopath

Osteopaths emphasize the manipulation technique for correcting specific bodily abnormalities. In short, osteopathy is a therapeutic system that restores health by manipulation of skeleton and muscles, not too much unlike the chiropractor. It is built on the Greek **osteon,** "bone" + **path,** "disease."

geriatrician

Geriatricians treat the pathologies of the elderly. This has become a fast-growing branch of the medical practice since so many of us are living to ripe old ages. This was not the case fifty or so years ago. It is built on the Greek **gēra**, meaning "old age."

A. Write C if the statement below is consistent with the meaning of the boldface word or I, if it is not.

1. A **cardiologist** is concerned with the use of extreme cold temperatures.

2. An **endocrinologist** is a physician who treats glandular disease or dysfunction.

3. A woman who has an illness common to women only would visit a **gynecologist**.

4. **Geriatricians** treat disease of the bone by manipulation.

5. An **osteopath** and an orthopedist practice the same kind of medicine.

6. One might visit a **periodontist** for treatment of gum disease.

7. **Ophthalmologists** perform surgeries to the eye.

8. **Anesthesiologists** are required for major surgeries.

9. **Orthopedists** treat bone disease in children only.

10. A **cryosurgeon** destroys unhealthy tissue by subjecting it to extreme cold temperatures.

B. Match the following words from Column A with its meaning from Column B.

Column A

1. orthopedist
2. osteopath
3. cardiologist
4. anesthesiologist
5. ophthalmologist

Column B

a. one who renders a patient insensible to pain
b. practice that treats the elderly
c. a doctor who treats ailments common to women

6. endocrinologist
7. geriatrics
8. periodontist
9. gynecologist
10. cryosurgeon

d. a physician who treats bone
   malformations, among other things
e. restores health by manipulating skeleton
   and muscles
f. a physician who treats eye disease
g. treats glandular problems
h. a doctor who treats cardiovascular disease
i. a dentist who treats gum disease
j. a doctor who uses extreme cold
   temperatures to destroy unhealthy tissue

C. Write a lesson word to complete the meaning of each sentence.

1. An **orthopedist** treats conditions that have to do with _____.

2. A **cardiologist** treats diseases of the _____ along with the vascular system.

3. **Ophthalmologists** care for their patients' _____.

4. A **cryosurgeon** performs surgeries that involve the use of extreme _____ temperatures.

5. An **osteopath** manipulates _____ and _____ to restore patients' health.

6. An **endocrinologist** specializes in the treatment of _____ conditions, such as diabetes.

7. **Gynecologists** treat ailments common to _____, generally involving the reproductive system.

8. **Geriatricians** care for the _____.

9. A **periodontist** treats diseases that affect the _____.

10. An **anesthesiologist** renders patients insensible to _____.

D. Choose two of the following words: orthopedist, anesthesiologist, ophthalmologist, geriatrician. Use your words in two sentences of your own.

Lesson

3

maxillofacial surgeon

Maxillofacial surgeons are dentists who treat disorders of the mouth, teeth, or jaw. They also treat children having congenital facial malformations. There are a number of conditions that such surgeons are best qualified to deal with—maloccluded wisdom teeth, dental implants, jaw surgery, and the list goes on. The word maxillofacial comes from the New Latin **maxla**, meaning "upper jaw, cheekbone."

prosthodontist

From the Greek **prostithenai**, meaning "to add," and **odont**, meaning "tooth," the word prosthodontist is derived. The prosthodontist's special area of expertise is in the replacement of missing teeth by the use of bridges, dentures, or implants. These doctors also specialize in crowning teeth when conventional fillings are inappropriate. One can see in part of the word **prosthodontics** the similarity to the word **prosthetics**, the replacement of missing parts with artificial structures—a leg or an arm, for example.

obstetrician

Obstetrician comes from the Latin **obstetrix**, meaning "midwife," one who delivers babies but who is not part of the traditional medical establishment. An obstetrician is a physician who specializes in the care of women during and after pregnancy. The obstetrician's patient is the mother. A pediatrician cares for the newborn baby.

pediatrician

From the Greek **pedo**, meaning "child," the word pediatrician is born. The Greek **pedo** is not to be confused with the Latin **pedi**, meaning **foot**, as in **pedestrian**. A pediatrician is a physician who specializes in the care of children.

gastroenterologist

Gastro comes from the Greek and it means "stomach." A gastroenterologist treats digestive disorders, not exclusively but primarily. Such ailments are known collectively as gastrointestinal conditions. Gastroenterologists are best trained to treat such illnesses.

epidemiologist

An epidemiologist is a doctor whose primary concern is diseases, especially those that affect many people. One can virtually see in the word **epidemi**ologist the word **epidemic**. These doctors try to eliminate diseases that vary in severity from AIDS to flu-type illnesses. Do you recall the word element **demos** meaning "people"? Together **epi** and **demos** mean literally "among the people," and that's precisely what an epidemic does—it finds its way **among the people**, infecting them in wholesale numbers.

neurosurgeon

A neurosurgeon performs surgeries to any part of the nervous system—the brain, spinal cord, nerves, or ganglia. The word comes from the Greek **neuron**, and it means "tendon" or "nerve." The neurosurgeon's work, especially on the brain, is probably the most delicate of all surgeries.

radiologist

The Latin **radius** means a "beam" or "ray," and from it is derived the word **radio**, which has to do with radiation. Radiologists are physicians who use x-rays for diagnostic purposes. Such services as mammograms, chest x-rays, or CAT scans (cross sectional x-rays of the body) produced by CAT scanners (**c**omputerized **a**xial **t**omography). Radiologists can x-ray just about any part of the body. Without the services of radiologists, modern medicine could not function as it now does.

psychoanalyst

A physician who follows the teachings of Sigmund Freud and who uses Freudian techniques such as dream interpretation and free association is a psychoanalyst. Psychoanalysis is far more complex than can be explained here. One would have to read some of Freud's writings to have a fuller understanding of it. The word **psyche** is the Greek for "mind."

optometrist
   Optometrists belong to a profession called optometry. Those belonging to this professional group can examine, measure, and treat visual defects that do not require a physician, that is, a doctor who is approved by the American Medical Association. This limits what optometrists can do. They may examine eyes, and when necessary prescribe corrective lenses. Optometrists may also check patients for such eye diseases as glaucoma and cataracts. Bear in mind that treatment of these visual defects is the province of ophthalmologists, not optometrists. In short, what optometrists can do to patients is quite limited. They carry the designation "doctor of optometry," not doctor of medicine. There is another troublesome word—optician. Opticians take the prescription for corrective lenses and actually grind them to specification. There is not much else opticians can do other than sell frames and other nonprescription items. Optometrist comes from the Greek **optikos**, "of sight" + **metr**, "measure." Optician is built on this same root—**optikos**, "of sight."

EXERCISES

   A. Write the word that completes each sentence. Use the following word list.

prosthodontist	pediatrician
gastroenterologist	obstetrician
epidemiologist	maxillofacial surgeon
radiologist	neurosurgeon
psychoanalyst	optometrist

   1. A pregnant woman would visit an _____ before using the services of a pediatrician.

   2. My teacher's ulcer required him to see a _____.

   3. After John's jaw was diagnosed as broken in two places, he was referred to a _____.

4. The disease raged through two New England states before being identified by an investigating _____.

5. Having lost her teeth to gum disease, the woman consulted a _____ for a set of dentures.

6. Since her young child was running a temperature of 103°, a call was put in to the child's _____.

7. A _____ probes deeply into a patient's psyche employing Freudian techniques as therapies.

8. The primary work of an _____ is to examine eyes and prescribe corrective lenses.

9. The _____ took x-rays of the boy's leg to determine whether it was broken or not.

10. Brain surgery was required to remove a blood clot that posed a life-threatening danger to the patient, and a _____ was called in to perform the procedure.

B. Match the following items.

Column A

1. prosthodontist
2. pediatrician
3. obstetrician
4. maxillofacial surgeon
5. gastroenterologist
6. radiologist
7. psychoanalyst
8. neurosurgeon
9. epidemiologist
10. optometrist

Column B

a. treats disorders of the mouth, jaw, or teeth
b. treats mental, emotional, and nervous disorders
c. replaces missing teeth
d. uses x-rays for diagnostic purposes
e. studies diseases of epidemic proportion
f. specializes in the care of women during pregnancy
g. performs surgeries to any part of the nervous system
h. treats children
i. treats digestive disorders
j. one who examines, measures, and treats visual defects not requiring the services of a physician

C. Respond to the following sentences with the missing word.

1. To whom would you go if you had a problem digesting food?

   _____

2. A doctor who specializes in the care of pregnant women is called a(n) _____.

3. If you needed to have teeth replaced with dentures, you might visit a _____.

4. Those having a problem with the jaw, such as a badly broken jaw, should consider having a _____ surgeon treat the condition.

5. After the birth of her child, a mother might place the infant in the care of a _____.

6. If widespread disease appeared in a community, an _____ might be called in to study the problem.

7. Doctors who use x-rays for diagnostic purposes are called

   _____.

8. Those who need operations to remove tumors from the brain might consult a _____.

9. A _____ treats mental, emotional, and nervous disorders.

10. _____ are eye doctors who themselves are not physicians.

   D. Choose two of the following words: pediatrician, radiologist, psychoanalyst, optometrist. Use your words in two original sentences.

Lesson

4

What follows is a list of words that are common to the field of medicine. These words are not esoteric jargon known to doctors alone. Quite to the contrary, they are known by many average Americans with an average education. Adding such specialized words to your vocabulary will make it infinitely richer and more interesting.

apnea

The word **apnea** comes from the Greek **a**, "not" + **pnèein**, "to breathe." Literally they mean together "not breathing" and that is precisely what the word apnea means, a temporary suspension of respiration or breathing. Apnea occurs during sleep. The sleeper for some unexplained reason stops breathing. Almost always, the sleeper awakens before anything serious happens. It is, however, a condition that should be brought to the attention of a physician.

carcinogen

A carcinogen is a cancer-causing agent—pesticides, cigarettes, and many other agents such as asbestos. The word comes from the Greek **karkinos**, meaning "crab" + **genos**, meaning "origin." Coincidentally, the crab is also the fourth sign of the zodiac, coming between Gemini and Leo. The zodiacal name for this sign is, as you may have already guessed, Cancer, and its pictorial representation is the **crab**. The word **cancer**, is derived from the Latin **cancer**, meaning "crab" or "gangrene." Perhaps in days of yore before the medical profession became more scientific in its pursuits, it was thought that cancers were gangrenous, from the Greek **gangraina**, an "eating sore."

cirrhosis

Once again the Greek language makes a contribution to English. The Greek **kirros** means "tawny," a dark yellowish or dull yellowish-brown color. This is precisely the color of a liver with cirrhosis. The healthy liver is reddish-brown in color. Cirrhosis is a chronic disease of the liver which can and often does lead to death. Liver transplants are being done today with success, but finding a donor match is the difficult part of such a procedure.

embolism

An embolism is an air bubble, a mass of bacteria, or a clot of some kind that obstructs or occludes a blood vessel. Depending on which of the blood vessels is occluded, a heart attack or a stroke is a very likely eventuality. One of the more common causes of an embolism is thought to be a high level of cholesterol in the blood. It clings to the walls of a blood vessel, and eventually builds up sufficiently to occlude the vein or artery.

metastasis

The Greek prefix **meta** means "change," and this is exactly what the word **metastasis** suggests. Technically it is the transference of disease-producing organisms from the original site to other parts of the body. This is what happens to cancer cells when they metastisize— they **change** their location from one site to another. In a word, when a disease such as cancer or tuberculosis metastisizes, it **spreads** from the original site to a secondary site.

tachycardia

The Greek etymons **tachy**, "swift" + **kardis**, "heart," combine to make the word **tachycardia**, which is an excessively rapid heart beat. To extend the element **tachy** further, most automobiles of recent vintage have as part of their instrument panels a tachometer which measures the engine's rpm. Specifically, it measures how fast the engine is turning over. Another word using this word element is **tachyon**, a hypothetical particle that travels faster than the speed of light. At this point, tachyons belong to the realm of science fiction. Getting back to the word **tachycardia**, one should consult a physician if such an episode occurs.

hyperglycemia

Hyper is a Greek prefix that means "above" or "excessive." **Glyco**, the other part of hyperglycemia, means "sugar." Literally the word elements when combined mean "excessive sugar." Hyperglycemics, or diabetics, have too much sugar in their blood. On the other hand, **hypoglycemics** have too little sugar in the blood, which can also lead to serious health problems. In either case, both hyperglycemics and hypoglycemics need professional care. The prefix **hypo** as you may have already surmised means "less" or "under."

rhinoplasty

Rhinoplasty involves surgery of the nose. Most such procedures are done for cosmetic reasons. The patient did not like the way his or her nose looked and wanted it reshaped. The word comes from the Greek **rhino** meaning "nose" and **plast** meaning "formed" or "shaped." Plastic surgeons do rhinoplasties.

renal

The Latin **rēn** means "kidneys." Its English equivalent means "pertaining to the kidneys or the surrounding regions." Renal illnesses can best be served by a nephrologist. When the kidneys fail and cease to cleanse the blood, the condition is known as renal failure. Thankfully there are available dialysis machines that do the work of the kidneys, extending the lives of patients with renal failure.

-ectomy/-otomy

Neither of these is a word. They are word endings, but important word endings in medicine. The Greek **tom**, meaning "to cut," is the derivation. An **ectomy** is a complete excision while an **otomy** is a partial excision. For example, a tonsillectomy is a complete removal of the tonsil. A tonsillotomy is a procedure that excises only the diseased part of the tonsil. Keep in mind that an ectomy is a complete removal, an otomy a partial removal.

EXERCISES

A. Match the following items.

Column A

1. carcinogen
2. hyperglycemia
3. apnea

Column B

a. a disease of the liver
b. relating to the kidneys
c. spreading of a disease from site to site

4. metastasis   d. temporary suspension of breathing
5. rhinoplasty   e. too rapid heart beat
6. renal   f. surgery of the nose for cosmetic reasons
7. -ectomy/-otomy   g. excessive sugar in the blood
8. tachycardia   h. cancer causing agent
9. embolism   i. a complete excision; a partial excision
10. cirrhosis   j. a blockage of a blood vessel

B. Write C if the statement is consistent with the boldface word or I if it is not.

1. **Rhinoplasty** is a procedure that is done by a prosthodontist.

2. A **hyperglycemic** who takes insulin to control sugar levels is a diabetic.

3. A **renal** ailment involves the liver.

4. **Apnea** causes the person to lose consciousness when hyperactive.

5. It is a well-documented fact that cigarette smoke can cause cancer and is classified as a **carcinogen**.

6. When a disease spreads from its original site, it is said to have **metastasized**.

7. A too slow heart beat is referred to as **tachycardia**.

8. An **embolism** can result from a too high level of cholesterol.

9. The word endings -**ectomy** and -**otomy** have to do with the tonsils.

10. **Cirrhosis** is a disease of the kidneys.

C. Give a brief definition of each of the following.

1. embolism:

2. cirrhosis:

3. tachycardia:

4. carcinogen:

5. hyperglycemia:

6. metastasis:

7. renal:

8. -ectomy/-otomy (define both):

9. rhinoplasty:

10. apnea:

    D. Choose two of the following words: carcinogen, embolism, hyperglycemia, rhinoplasty. Use your words in two sentences of your own.

Lesson

5

rheumatic fever

Rheumatic fever is a disease affecting the joints which become very painful due to inflammation. It mainly affects children. Aside from the pain that accompanies this illness, there can also be permanent damage to the heart's valves. One other point: it is an infectious disease that can be passed on to others. The word rheumatic comes from the Greek **rheum**, meaning "flow." This is one of those rare occasions when a word's etymology makes no linguistic sense. It happens. Incidentally, there is a word **rheum** in English, which is a cold that causes a running nose and tearing eyes. The **flow** makes sense here, but it does not carry over to rheumatism or rheumatic. So, here is a mystery for you to solve. How did the words rheumatism and rheumatic find their origins in **rheum** meaning "flow"?

melanoma

A **melanoma** is a dark-pigmented malignant tumor much like a mole in appearance. Be sure to understand that not all moles are malignant. A dermatologist would be best suited to make this determination. The word melanoma is built on the Greek **melas**, "black" + **nom**, "a sore." You may be interested to know that there is in the human body a chemical called **melanin** which determines the darkness of one's skin. The more melanin present in the body, the darker the skin. Albinos lack this chemical altogether.

arthritis

Arthritis is an inflammation of the joints. The word comes from the Greek **arthro**, meaning "joint," and **itis**, a word ending meaning "inflammation." Many words end in **itis**: appendicitis, bursitis, sinusitis, and periotonitis are but a few. Keep in mind that **itis** means "inflammation."

pulmonary

The word **pulmonary** has to do with the lungs in the human body. It comes from the Latin **pulmo**, which means "lung." Several pulmonary diseases are tuberculosis, emphysema, and lung cancer. Many medical scientists believe that cigarette smoke is the cause of many pulmonary diseases.

mammogram

A **mammogram** is an x-ray of a woman's breast to determine whether or not tumors are present. A mammogram can pinpoint a tumor that can't be detected during a routine physical examination. It is a simple, noninvasive procedure that literally takes minutes to perform. A mammogram is recommended for women past 40 years of age. Of course, women of any age can have a mammogram done if it sets their minds at ease. The word is built on the Late Latin **mammalis**, "breast" + **gram**, "a record."

glaucoma

Glaucoma is a disease of the eye characterized by increased pressure within the eyeball. A progressive loss of vision can be expected if treatment is not received. An ophthalmologist is the specialist who can best treat patients with glaucoma. The word is built on the Greek **glaūkōma** meaning "opacity of the eye lens." It can be compared to looking through a piece of sheer silk. One's vision is not at all clear.

cataract

Persons having cataracts also have vision problems. The eyes' lenses, as in glaucoma, become opaque, causing impaired vision. The difference between the diseases is the cause. In glaucoma it is pressure on the eyeball that causes the problem; with cataracts, it is a thin film or growth through which the patient sees and which causes impaired vision. If not treated, blindness can occur. Cataracts, unlike glaucoma, can be treated by surgical removal. After such procedures, patients generally have restored the vision that they had prior to the cataract. The word comes from the Greek **kata**, "down" + **rassein**, "to dash, as in a waterfall." This is precisely what cataract patients experience. They seem to be looking through water cascading over the eye, causing vision that is opaque.

cardiovascular

The **cardiovascular** system in humans is made up of the heart and blood vessels, covering a lot of territory in the body. Cardiovascular surgeons, for example, do such procedures as angioplasties (to open clogged arteries), by-pass surgery, and even heart transplants, which are rare today because medical science has yet to find a way to prevent the body's immune system from rejecting foreign tissue. The word is built on the Greek **kardio**, "heart" + Latin **vasculum**, "vessel."

anorexia

There are two kinds of **anorexia**. The first is a pathological loss of appetite due to illness. The patient simply does not want to eat. In such instances, the patient is fed intravenously. The second form of anorexia is **anorexia nervosa**, a pathological loss of appetite occurring mainly in young women. Its origin is thought to be the mind. There are no medical reasons to explain this fasting. In either case, food is shunned. Regarding the latter of the conditions, victims of **anorexia nervosa** can literally starve themselves to death. The word anorexia is built on the Greek **an**, "no" + **orexis**, "appetite" + **nervosa**, "nervous."

bulimia

The Greek **boulima** means "hunger of an ox." Bulimics go on food binges and eat inordinate amounts of food. They do indeed have the "hunger of an ox." The problem is that after having glutted themselves, they induce vomiting, oftentimes returning to their bingeing. It is a paradox that bulimics can also starve to death. The food does not provide them with sustenance since it never stays in the stomach to be digested. The disease strikes young women for the most part.

EXERCISES

A. Match the following items.

Column A

Column B

1. melanoma

2. bulimia

a. disease affecting the joints and possibly the heart's valves

3. mammogram
4. cardiovascular
5. pulmonary
6. anorexia nervosa
7. rheumatic fever
8. cataract
9. glaucoma
10. arthritis

b. having to do with the heart and blood vessels
c. pertaining to the lungs
d. disease of the eyes marked by increased pressure within the eyeball
e. a thin growth or film over the eye causing impaired vision
f. x-ray of a woman's breast to detect tumors
g. an inflammation affecting the joints
h. bingeing on food and then inducing vomit
i. a malignancy having the appearance of a mole
j. pathological loss of appetite that could lead to death; psychogenic in nature

B. Write **C** if the statement is consistent with the boldface word or **I** if it is not.

1. **Anorexia nervosa** strikes young women who oftentimes starve themselves to death.

2. **Bulimia** is not as severe as is **anorexia nervosa** and does not require medical attention.

3. It is recommended that all women take annual **mammograms**.

4. **Rheumatic fever** can have lasting effects on those it strikes.

5. **Cataracts** are caused by too much pressure within the eyeball.

6. **Arthritis** and **rheumatic fever** have the same medical outlook.

7. All **pulmonary** disease is caused by smoking.

8. **Melanomas** should be checked by a gastroenterologist.

9. **Cardiovascular** disease affects the heart and blood vessels.

10. **Glaucoma** can be treated by an ophthalmologist.

C. Write the lesson word that completes the meaning of each sentence.

1. Those who binge on food and then induce vomiting are called ____.

2. A _____ is a dark-pigmented malignant tumor.

3. Inflammation of the joints is known as _____.

4. A _____ causes impaired vision due to a thin growth or film that covers the eye.

5. _____, on the other hand, is caused by increased pressure within the eyeball.

6. The heart and blood vessels in humans make up the _____ system.

7. _____ is a pathological loss of appetite.

8. A _____ is an x-ray of a woman's breast to determine whether or not tumors are present.

9. The word _____ has to do with the lungs in humans.

10. _____ fever is a disease affecting the joints and is acutely painful.

    D. Choose two of the following words: melanoma, cataract, anorexia, bulimia. Use your words in two sentences of your own.

Lesson

6

holistic medicine

Holistic medicine is one of the newer entries found in the age of specialization. It is concerned with the whole patient, not just that body part that is not well. The holistic practitioner believes that the whole transcends the sum of the parts. What this implies is that humans are more than a collection of arms, legs, vital organs, etc. All are interconnected, and to treat any one of them the physician must understand the whole person. This holistic approach is catching on. In education now it is the shibboleth—the whole child. In ecology it is the same thing. Scientists cannot address one part of the ecosystem without understanding its relationship to all other parts. In short, holism sets forth the belief that the whole is made up of organic or unified parts, and it is far greater in meaning than collective parts.

anemia

Anemia is a pathological deficiency of red blood cells. This condition may cause a pale colored skin, weakness—and even breathlessness. Anemia is not an illness to be ignored. The doctor best suited to treat this disease is a hematologist. The word anemia comes from the Greek **an**, "without" + **haima**, "blood."

liposuction

Liposuction is a relatively new surgical procedure. Its primary purpose is to remove excess fat (from the thighs, legs, face, buttocks, and arm). This is done by making incisions in the area to be treated and inserting a tube-like apparatus into the incision and fat is then literally sucked out. The procedure exposes patients to minimal risk due to complications, and it can be done in a doctor's office in as little as an hour's time. For the most part, this procedure is done for cosmetic reasons. The word comes from the Greek **lipos**, meaning "fat." The **suction** part takes care of itself. One final point: the word is so new that it does not appear in most dictionaries.

arthroscopic surgery

This surgery is done with the aid of an ultrascope that is inserted into a small incision made by the surgeon directly over the area to be treated. The ultrascope has a fiber-optic light source and sends images to a screen that is monitored by the surgeon. By viewing the monitor, the surgeon is able to effect repair to the injured part without having to make a large incision that would be required if conventional therapy were used. Arthroscopic patients are able to resume their normal activities in a far shorter time than those who underwent conventional treatment. It is also quicker, safer, and much less painful. This is a widespread treatment for athletes who injure a leg, an arm, or an ankle or foot. The word arthroscope is built on the Greek **arthro**, meaning "joint" + **scopein**, meaning "to see."

migraine

Migraines are recurrent headaches—not your run-of-the-mill headache. The pain is intense. The strange part of this is that the migraine strikes only one side of the head. The word's etymology makes this quite clear; it is built on the Greek **hemi**, "half" + **cranion**, "cranium." The first two letters of **hemi** are dropped in the English version, and what we are left with is migraine—a headache that affects only one side of the head.

muscular dystrophy

Muscular dystrophy, better known as MD, is a disease characterized by progressive muscular deterioration. This breakdown is both gradual and irreversible. MD is not a contagious disease. Scientists have been working at finding a cure for this crippling disease without much success. Its origin is unknown. The words derive from the Latin **musculus**, "muscle" and the Greek **dys**, "bad" + **tre-**

phein, "nourish." Literally it means that the muscles are badly nourished.

phlebotomy

Actually a **phlebotomist** is one who draws blood from a patient's arm for some diagnostic purpose. The word itself has a rather interesting origin. The Greek word that gave rise to our Anglicized version is **phlebotomia**, which is remarkably close to the English **phlebotomy**. Back to the Greek **phlebotomia**. It meant "opening a vein." This in turn came from the Greek word elements **phleps**, "vein" + **tomos**, "cutting." Put the two together and you have it—phlebotomy.

laryngitis

Laryngitis is an inflammation of the larynx. In the more serious episodes, laryngitis can render one speechless. Otherwise, a hoarseness is the most prominent symptom. It can be caused by any of a number of things—the common cold or allergies. The word comes from the Greek **larungo** and it means "larynx." An otorhinolaryngologist is a physician best trained to treat laryngitis.

hepatitis

This disease is characterized by an inflamed liver which has several distinct symptoms: jaundice, fever, and a general lassitude. Other bodily systems can also be affected. It is not a disease to fool with. Also, bear in mind that it is a highly communicable disease which is oftentimes spread by food handlers, especially in restaurants and diners. Immediate treatment is required both for the sake of the patient and for those with whom he comes into contact. The word is built on the Greek **hepat**, meaning "liver," and **itis**, a word ending you have already met meaning "inflammation."

mastectomy

A **mastectomy** is a surgical procedure that involves the removal of a breast. After a mammogram determines there is a tumor in a human breast, the growth is then biopsied to learn whether or not it is malignant. If it is cancerous, an oncologist is the specialist of choice for treatment. The word is built on the Late Latin **mammalis**, meaning "breast," and **ectomy** is an ending you have already met. It means "to cut."

EXERCISES

A. Match the items found below.

Column A

1. anemia
2. hepatitis
3. migraine
4. laryngitis
5. holistic medicine
6. liposuction
7. arthroscopic surgery
8. muscular dystrophy
9. phlebotomy
10. mastectomy

Column B

a. headache affecting half the head
b. an inflamed liver condition
c. the science of drawing blood, generally from the arm
d. surgical removal of a woman's breast
e. an inflamed larynx
f. treats the whole person, not just the patient's specific illness
g. deficiency of red blood cells
h. removal of body fat
i. surgery done on camera, so to speak
j. disease marked by progressive muscular deterioration

B. Would you agree with these following statements or would you disagree? Write A if you agree or D if you disagree.

1. **Liposuction** procedures are done mainly for cosmetic reasons.

2. **Arthroscopic surgery** is an ideal procedure for an athlete.

3. **Muscular dystrophy** is a crippling disease.

4. A **mastectomy** involves the removal of the tumor in a human breast.

5. **Holistic medicine** entails caring for patients as individuals—whole persons.

6. **Laryngitis** can leave one speechless.

7. A **migraine headache** affects only the left side of the head.

8. **Hepatitis** is a disease of the liver.

9. **Anemia** is caused by an insufficiency of red blood cells.

10. Those who work as **phlebotomists** would undoubtedly use syringes in their day-to-day responsibilities.

C. Write the lesson word that completes the meaning of each sentence.

1. _____ concerns itself with the whole patient, not just the body part that is not well. (Two words are needed.)

2. A _____ is a headache that affects only one side of the head.

3. A disease marked by progressive muscular deterioration is known as _____. (Two words are needed.)

4. One who draws blood from a patient for diagnostic purposes is called a _____.

5. A radical _____ is the surgical removal of the entire breast.

6. One who has an inflamed liver suffers from a disease known as _____.

7. An inflammation of the larynx is known as _____.

8. Surgery done with the aid of an ultrascope inserted into the incision is known as _____ surgery.

9. The removal of excess fat by a surgical procedure known as _____ is relatively new to medicine.

10. A pathological deficiency of red blood cells is known as _____.

D. Choose two of the following words: holistic medicine, anemia, liposuction, laryngitis. Use your words in two original sentences.

REVIEW OF LESSONS 1 - 6

A. Match the word(s) from Column A with its meaning from Column B.

Column A

1. endocrinologist
2. podiatrist
3. orthodontist

Column B

a. treats ailments of the nose, throat, and ears
b. a surgeon who uses extreme cold

4. otorhinolaryngologist
5. orthopedist
6. epidemiologist
7. cryosurgeon
8. pediatrician
9. obstetrician
10. geriatrician
11. nephrologist
12. cardiologist
13. ophthalmologist
14. oncologist
15. maxillofacial surgeon

   temperatures to destroy unhealthy
   tissue
c. treats glands, such as the pituitary
   and adrenal glands
d. cares for children
e. treats the feet for such complaints
   as corns and bunions
f. treats pathologies of the elderly
g. a dentist who corrects misaligned
   teeth
h. a doctor concerned with the
   identification and elimination of
   epidemic diseases
i. corrects bone malformations
j. cares for women before and
   immediately after childbirth
k. treats disorders of the mouth, jaw,
   and teeth
l. treats diseases of the eye
m. treats malignant tumors
n. treats disorders of the kidneys
o. treats ailments of the heart and
   cardiovascular system

B. Choose the item that best answers the questions posed. Write the letter of that choice.

1. To which doctor might you go to treat a condition known as **tachycardia?**
   (a) a cardiologist (b) a gastroenterologist (c) a urologist

2. If you had a **malignant tumor**, to which of the following might you go?
   (a) a cryosurgeon (b) an oncologist (c) an orthopedist

3. A person wishing to have a **rhinoplasty procedure** done would visit which of the following?
   (a) a urologist (b) a nephrologist (c) a plastic surgeon

4. **Renal failure** can best be treated by which of the following?
   (a) a nephrologist (b) an endocrinologist (c) an orthopedist

5. A **partial excision** (cutting out) of the tonsils would require which of the following?
(a) a tonsillotomy (b) a tonsillectomy (c) a tonsillitis

6. A **melanoma** is which of the following?
(a) a disease affecting the joints (b) a dark-pigmented malignant tumor (c) a sleep disorder

7. A person who experiences episodes of **apnea** suffers a pathological disorder relating to which of the following?
(a) digestion (b) breathing (c) glucose levels that are high

8. **Mammograms** are generally done in the offices of which of the following?
(a) osteopaths (b) oncologists (c) radiologists

9. That branch of medicine that holds treatment of the **whole patient** is paramount is which of the following?
(a) hologramology (b) holographic medicine (c) holistic medicine

10. A disease characterized by **liver inflammation** is called which of the following?
(a) phlebotomy (b) anemia (c) hepatitis

C. Which branch of specialized medicine is best suited to deal with the following? Choose one of the words from the list provided below.

radiology	otorhinolaryngology	geriatrics
ophthalmology	endocrinology	gastroenterology
periodontia	hematology	pediatrics
nephrology	oncology	neurology
cardiology	urology	gynecology

1. disease of the blood

2. an elderly person

3. the nervous system

4. mammography

5. an intestinal disorder

6. cataracts

7. hypothyroidism

8. an embolism, or a blood clot

9. renal failure

10. laryngitis

11. a malignant tumor

12. urogenital tract disorder

13. care of a child

14. gum disease

15. ailments common to women only

Dimension Three
Part Three

previously owned car

Special Terms and Word Forms

Lesson

1

Euphemisms

Euphemisms are verbal niceties that are meant to soften a more direct, a more blunt, use of language. For example, **senior citizen** is a widely accepted euphemism. A senior citizen is actually an elderly person. However, some senior citizens resent the term **elderly**. Or take the phrase **capital punishment**, which serves to tone down the dramatic effect that would accompany the phrase **put to death**. The language is replete with such niceties which in truth are gentler than the more direct approach to language use. For instance, to refer to an overweight woman as **full-figured** is a considerate use of language. On the other hand, there are those euphemisms that should be avoided. For example, to say that a felon convicted of a brutal murder is **incarcerated** is softening the fact that the felon is **imprisoned**. If you mean imprisoned, then say imprisoned.

The word euphemism is built on the Greek **eu**, "good; well" + **phēmē**, "speech." When these etymons are combined in Greek, the word **euphemos** is formed and it means using an **auspicious word**. Actually, euphemisms are intended to be auspicious. They are meant to be less harsh, more favorable (auspicious?).

EXERCISES

A. **Directions**: Here are sentences containing a few commonly used euphemisms. You are to recast the sentence and substitute your own words for the euphemism. You may of course use a dictionary if needed. After rewriting the sentence, decide which version you like better—the one containing the euphemism or your rewrite. Then give the reason for the choice you made. The first two are done for you.

1. John's mother, after a long battle with a **wasting disease**, finally succumbed to it and **passed away**.

   Rewrite: John's mother, after a long battle with cancer, finally succumbed to it and died.

   Which sentence do you like more? Why? The rewrite is better because "died" and "cancer" are more direct.

2. Billy's teacher informed his mother that he was exhibiting signs of **social aggression**.

   Rewrite: Billy's teacher informed his mother that he was exhibiting behavior that was bullying his classmates.

   Which sentence and why? The use of the euphemism is appropriate. "Bullying" may be too strong a word for Billy's parents to accept.

3. Not only was Billy socially aggressive, he was also **nonconforming**, which presented still another problem.

4. John's wife was concerned about just how **unmindful** her husband had become after he forgot their wedding anniversary.

5. The convicted felon was **incarcerated** at the state prison for a period of five years.

6. The shoe company **downsized** its work force to improve its profit margin.

7. The auto dealership advertised a special on a **previously owned car**.

8. John was told by his teacher that he was an **underachiever**.

9. The caller was told that the firm's executive officer was **indisposed** and could not see him.

10. John admitted that he was **strong-willed**, but he also added that his wife Ellen was even more so.

B. In this exercise you will find a list of euphemisms. For each of them you are to write a more direct way of saying what you think the writer had in mind. You may use a phrase or a clause as your response.

Example: previously owned car: a used car

1. inappropriate language use:

2. fiercely independent:

3. not adaptive:

4. monopolizes class time:

5. cadaver:

6. demise:

7. not altogether unattractive:

8. inebriated:

9. strong-willed:

10. hyperactive (as a youngster at school):

C. Think of a word or phrase that softens the meaning of each of the items listed below.

Example: emaciated: thin

1. janitor:

2. thoughtless:

3. stubborn:

4. foul-mouthed:

5. drunk:

6. hostile:

7. lied:

8. nuisance:

9. a crook:

10. a dead body:

D. Think of a euphemism that you have heard at home or at school. Use it in a sentence that you might hear again.

General Review of Euphemisms

Essentially euphemisms are verbal niceties that take the bite, the harshness, out of language. In many instances, euphemisms serve a useful purpose. For example, to refer to a mother's child as "mentally retarded" is an insensitive use of language. The euphemism "slow learner" or some other substitute expression is much kinder, much more compassionate. On the other hand, to suggest that someone who told a bald-faced lie "fabricated the truth" is not an appropriate use of euphemisms. A bald-faced lie is a bald-faced lie. Nothing less! But you must also bear in mind that there are lies and there are lies. They can be slotted into several levels. For instance, the "white lie" is one that is intended to assuage another's feelings. It is not meant to deceive. In such a case, the euphemism "embroidering the truth" might be more appropriate than a bald-faced lie. Finally, there are a few euphemisms that outrage the imagination—"the final solution" and "ethnic cleansing" to name but two.

In short, there are occasions when a euphemism is called for, but having said that, one must be careful not to soften language that ought not be softened. For the most part words that state an idea directly are much to be preferred over euphemisms.

Lesson

2

Oxymorons

An oxymoron is a contradiction in terms. One of the words appearing in the expression contradicts another of the words. Take, for example, the oxymoron **almost perfect**. A thing is either perfect or it is imperfect. It can't be almost perfect since the word **perfect** is an absolute, that which cannot be qualified or limited by exceptions or restrictions. Another oxymoron one can hear used frequently is **most unique**, as in "It presented me with a most unique situation." Again, a thing is unique or it is not unique. It simply can't be **most unique**. There are many such oxymorons that appear in English that reflect a careless use of language. The word **oxymoron** comes from the Greek **axumoros**, which means "pointedly foolish." Following are some of the more commonly used oxymorons.

EXERCISES

A. Explain in as few words as possible why the following are oxymorons. How do the words contradict each other? One of the items is not an oxymoron. Simply write "correct."

1. holy war:

2. real potential:

3. qualified success:

4. biased opinion:

5. nondairy cream:

6. original copies:

7. open secret:

8. justifiably paranoid:

9. linear curve:

10. vaguely aware:

B. Match each item under Column A with an item from Column B so that together they form an oxymoron. Write your answers in a list numbered 1-10. The first one is done as an example.

Column A   Column B

1. acute   a. unsung   acute dullness
2. games   b. elevated   _____
3. tragic   c. randomly   _____
4. simply   d. superb   _____
5. subway   e. dullness   _____
6. organized   f. deliberately   _____
7. normal   g. deviation   _____
8. thoughtless   h. confused   _____
9. clearly   i. war   _____
10. hero   j. comedy   _____

C. Can you pick out the oxymorons in the following sentences? Write your answers.

1. The contractor was asked by his customer for an exact estimate to build an addition to his home.

2. The audience was told that the show was being shown nation-wide, and that its subject was the life of an unsung hero.

3. He responded that he was vaguely aware of the problem.

4. The teacher told the boy's parents that he had real potential.

5. He was told that he had inherited a small fortune.

6. He used a nondairy cream in his coffee.

7. The small manufacturing plant owner was told that a large conglomerate was interested in a friendly takeover of his plant.

8. Chocolate is my least favorite ice cream.

9. The mother described her daughter's new punk hairstyle as perfectly awful.

10. The beauty pageant contestant whispered to one of her friends that for her to win would take a minor miracle.

D. Think of an oxymoron that you have heard in everyday conversation. Use it in a sentence of your own.

General Review of Oxymorons

Oxymorons are pairs of words that are contradictory. Some are as humorous as they are illogical, and they have taken a firm hold on the English language and are determined not to let go. A day rarely passes when one or more oxymorons have not been heard or not been seen in print by most of us. But you remark, "Nonsense, I haven't heard or seen an oxymoron ever." Well, the truth of the matter is that such illogical word pairings are so widely used that they have literally become acceptable English usage. Put another way, if an oxymoron were used in your presence, you didn't hear it because it has been accepted as standard usage. The same holds true for reading. You didn't see it because there was nothing to see. This being the case, why remember it? Oxymorons can be perceived only when one is alert to their folly.

How to avoid oxymorons is quite simple. Think! Read words with a critical eye. Hear spoken language with an ear that is sensitive to such illogical pairings of words. How often have you heard the phrase "only choice," an obvious oxymoron? **Choice** implies options. The word **only** eliminates these options. **If there is but one course of action, there is no choice**. Having said this, it should be pointed out that it would be quite easy to accept "only choice" as standard usage because its wide usage has made it part of the English language. There are dozens of popularized oxymorons. How often have you heard or used the phrase "the larger half"? When looked at with a critical eye, the phrase sounds and is ridiculous. It's simply not possible to have or to give "a larger half." How about "pretty ugly"? Perhaps one you can identify with is "least favorite," as in ice cream flavors. Such phrases, no matter how popular, are illogical and should be avoided. Think about what words really mean. Listen! Really listen to what the words say.

Oxymorons have made inroads into language that are so indelible that expunging these contradictions requires a conscious effort. Oxymorons, fair or not, say much about a person's capacity to think logically. Avoid them if at all possible.

Lesson

3

Acronyms

An **acronym** is a word that is made up of initial letters of a group of words: **MAD** is an acronym for "mutual assured destruction." The word **scuba** is an acronym formed as follows: (s)elf-(c)ontained (u)nderwater (b)reathing (a)pparatus. **Radar** is an acronym: (ra)dio (d)etecting (a)nd (r)anging. Bear in mind that acronyms are pronounceable as words. The initials FBI are not an acronym since the letters are said separately, not as a pronounceable word. The word **acronym** comes from the Greek **akros**. It is a learned borrowing that means "extremity or height." In the case of the word **acronym**, the former is appropriate. Letters are taken from the first part of words (extremity?). On the other hand, such words as **acrobat** or **acrophobia** do indeed concern themselves with **height**. Add to **akros** the word element **onoma**, which means "name," and the word **acronym** is formed. In the case of acronyms, **name** has come to mean "word." The following is a list of acronyms. It is by no means complete, but it is a good start toward that end.

AIDS:	Acquired Immune Deficiency Syndrome
ASCAP:	American Society of Composers, Authors, and Publishers
COBOL:	Common Business-Oriented Language
MAD:	Mutual Assured Destruction
MADD:	Mothers Against Drunk Driving
RADAR:	Radio Detecting and Ranging
SALT:	Strategic Arms Limitation Talks

413

UNESCO: United Nations Educational, Scientific, and Cultural
          Organization
UNICEF: United Nations International Children's Emergency
          Fund
VISTA: Volunteers in Service to America
WASP: White Anglo-Saxon Protestant
HUD: Housing and Urban Development
CORE: Congress of Racial Equality
NATO: North Atlantic Treaty Organization
ASEAN: Association of Southeast Asian Nations
DEW: Distant Early Warning
WAC: Women's Army Corps
AWOL: Absent Without Leave
NASA: National Aeronautics and Space Administration
PAL: Police Athletic League
PAC: Political Action Committee
CAP: Civil Air Patrol
LED: Light-Emitting Diode (calculator's digital display)
YUPPIE: Young Urban Professional
ZIP: Zone Improvement Plan (Postal Service)

EXERCISES

A. Write the words from which each of the following acronyms was formed. You may, of course, refer to the list.

1. AIDS:

2. HUD:

3. ZIP:

4. WAC:

5. CORE:

6. WASP

7. PAC:

8. UNICEF:

9. MADD:

10. UNESCO:

11. COBOL:

12. AWOL:

13. SALT:

14. NASA:

B. Now work in the opposite direction from that of the previous exercise. Write the acronym for each of the below. A few are not on the lesson list; see if you can figure them out.

1. zone improvement plan

2. young urban professional

3. Congress of Racial Equality

4. Common Business-Oriented Language

5. Mothers Against Drunk Driving

6. Federal Insurance Contribution Act

7. Museum of Modern Art (New York)

8. absent without leave

9. acquired immune deficiency syndrome

10. World Health Organization

11. Organization of Petroleum Exporting Countries

12. Volunteers in Service to America

13. self-contained underwater breathing apparatus

14. individual retirement account

15. Commodity Exchange (New York)

C   In this exercise you will create acronyms of your own. It could be an acronym for something that is real, or it may well be fiction, pure and unadulterated. Either of these will do nicely. For instance, you could use the acronym **SCAR** for **S**tudents

Committed **A**gainst **R**acism. This is fiction. There is no such group, but that's all right! Real or imagined—makes no difference. There is one caveat. The acronym that you create must be pronounceable as a word. The letters **BKRS** cannot qualify as an acronym since the letters cannot be said as a word. Other than this imposition, you have free rein. Have fun with this! Now you will write ten acronyms of your own, and you must designate what each of the letters of your acronym stands for. Copy the chart and fill it in.

Acronym   Meaning

1.

2.

3.

4.

5.

6.

7.

8.

9.

10.

D. Use two of your acronyms in sentences of your own.

General Review of Acronyms

Acronyms simplify language by compressing long titles and using one, or more, of the letters from each word. A clear example of the compression referred to is the acronym SCUBA, which is derived from **S**elf-Contained **U**nderwater **B**reathing **A**pparatus—quite a mouthful. Another such example is the word RADAR. It comes from **Ra**dio **D**etecting **a**nd **R**anging. Clearly the acronyms are much preferred to the long phrases. Acronyms abound in English, and their use is quite legitimate. Having said that, you must be reasonably sure that your audience will know their meanings. For example, it is **not** reasonable to expect that most people know what the acronym COMEX means, unless, of course, they are stockbrokers, for whom the **Com-**

modities **Ex**change is essential. In another arena it is equally unlikely that many people will know what the acronym UNESCO means— United **N**ations **E**ducational, **S**ocial, and **C**ultural **O**rganization. UNESCO compresses the unwieldy name to a six-letter word. This is the major contribution that acronyms make to English.

Be mindful that all acronyms must be pronounceable as words. FBI, for example, is not an acronym since it can't be pronounced as a word. Feel free to use acronyms, especially those that are in the public eye, such as ZIP, MADD, and PAL.

Lesson

4

Neologisms and Portmanteau Words

In this lesson you will be introduced to **neologisms** and **portmanteau words**. Neologisms are words that are new to the language, or they are already established words which have been designated a new meaning. For example, the word **mouse** is a neologism when used to mean "a small device that controls movement of the cursor on a computer screen." A new meaning has been assigned to an already established word—**mouse**. The other meaning of neologism is a word new to language. The word **fax**, for instance, is a neologism in this sense. It is an abbreviated form of the word **facsimile**. Interestingly enough, the word neologism comes from the Greek **neo**, "new" + **logos**, "word."

Next, **portmanteau words** will be presented for study. A portmanteau is a trunk or large suitcase that opens into halves much like a book. The word's derivation is from the French word **portmanteau** and means "a cloak carrier." Well, today portmanteaus carry much more than cloaks. They may, for example, carry the needs of a vacationer or business traveler. The key here is that portmanteaus open into halves. Portmanteau words are made up of two halves, the beginning of one word and the end of another. For instance, insulin used by diabetics to control blood sugar levels is gotten from, of all things, a pig. An alternative was searched for and eventually an artificial **human insulin** was created. Well, a noun was needed to name this innovative product. The two words **human** + **insulin** formed the basis for this new word, this noun, and it took shape pretty much as follows: **HUM**an + ins**ULIN**, and the word **humulin** was born. This is a portmanteau word. Keep in mind that while the word **humulin** is indeed a portmanteau word, it is also a neologism, just as all newly coined portmanteau words were when coined. Perhaps now you can appreciate why neologisms and portmanteau words are presented in the same lesson.

Finally, with regard to neologisms, just how new must a word be to qualify itself as a neologism? The question is open to discussion. How long is long? It's one of those kinds of things. Just keep in mind that the English language dates back as far as A.D. 449, over 1500 years. A few years in this context makes a thing recent. As close as one might come to answering this question is that "new words" must be of recent vintage. While this is admittedly a vague response to the question, it's about as precise as one can be.

As was mentioned in the introduction to this lesson, most neologisms find their way into language via new technologies. This is especially true in the field of computer technology. An entirely new language was forged to provide names for the countless new ideas and innovative products that spilled over into the marketplace. New words and new meanings bombarded the language, and this is, in part, how many neologisms found their way into the English language. Now this in no way is meant to suggest that technology is the only source of neologisms. It is not. Listed below are a few neologisms followed by a handful of portmanteau words.

bells and whistles

This phrase is a neologism in that it gives new meaning to words already a part of our language. The meaning of the phrase has little to do with "bells and whistles" as you know them. Rather, it is a slang term that is part of computer jargon. It means "added features that a computer program offers." An analogy might be the options the automotive dealerships offer. Such options might be considered the "bells and whistles" of the auto industry.

nanosecond

One-billionth of a second is a nanosecond. **Nano** is a prefix meaning "one-billionth." Until hi-tech (a portmanteau word?) computers arrived on the scene, it was virtually impossible to conceive of one-billionth of anything. The technology to measure so small an amount or distance was not available until the high-powered computers came upon the scene. This is a relatively new word, and as such qualifies as a neologism.

cyborg

Cyber is a prefix that means "anything electronic in origin." There are words such as **cyberspace** and **cybernetics**, things that are electronic in nature. The word **cyborg** comes from **CYB**ernetic + **ORG**anism. Cyborgs are fascinating creatures that appear from time to time on science fiction shows, especially fiction that relates to space travel. Any "trekkie" could tell you what cyborgs are, and he or she would no doubt inform you that they are controlled cybernetically, having bodily processes, again, electronically controlled. One might also guess that "trekkies" would also inform you that cyborgs are not nice. They are generally portrayed as unfeeling creatures that behave very badly.

bus

A bus is another neologism in that new meaning is given to an already established word. Suffice to say that we all know what a bus is. How many of us know the meaning of the word bus as it is used in the jargon of computerese? Not too many, one would guess. A bus sends or transports electrons from place to place, forming a pathway, an electronic pathway, over which information travels between the microprocessor and other computer parts. Not much like the bus we all know, is it?

Internet

The word **Internet** is both a neologism and a portmanteau word. It is a neologism inasmuch as it is a relatively new word to the language, and it is a portmanteau since it is built on two words from which parts were taken: International Network (**INTER**national **NET**work). It is a worldwide computer network that makes possible the user's connecting with many other computers worldwide. For example, a man living in Greece can access the library records of the University of Chicago simply by punching a number of keys. Money can be transferred to anywhere in the world in seconds. There is not too much that it can't do, and it has earned the appellation Information Superhighway.

virus

Everyone knows the meaning of the word **virus** in a medical context. Who among us has not been at one time infected by a virus? Well, in a very different context a virus is something about which many people know very little or nothing at all. A virus in this latter context applies to computers. Essentially, a virus when introduced into a computer system can do irreparable damage to it. It can also do harm to other computer systems which are tied to the one that has had the virus introduced into it. It should be said, but rather obvious, that modification of computer programs by a virus is an illegal act for which one can be jailed. **Hackers**, those who introduce the virus, are oftentimes the culprits. Did you pick up on the fact that the word "hackers" in this context is itself a neologism? It is. In order to counter these sorties by hackers, antiviruses have been introduced to computer systems, and they can be used to scan computer systems to detect the presence of viruses and eliminate them before they are able to do damage.

byte

A **byte** is the amount of memory needed to store something in a computer's memory, things such as letters or numbers. The word **byte** is obviously a neologism in that it is a word new to language. To delve into kilobytes, megabytes, and gigabytes would be too technical for us to derive anything worthwhile. You should, however, get a general idea that these bytes provide computers with a rather large capacity to store information.

bit

The word **bit** is another word that is both a neologism and a portmanteau word. It is a neologism since it gives new meaning to the word **bit**, and it is also a portmanteau word in that it is made up of parts of two words: **BI**nary digi**T**. A bit can be either a 0 or a 1, and it measures the potential of a processor to do its work, which is essentially taking raw data and processing it. That's all you need to know about bits. Keep in mind that in this lesson you are being exposed to neologisms and portmanteau words in a very general way.

hung

The word **hung** is a neologism inasmuch as a new meaning has been assigned to it. Again, it is the language of computer users. Hung, to them, is "a computer that doesn't work." A context sentence may help: **John notified his boss that he could not get any work out be-**

cause his computer had been "hung" since early that morning. The meaning of hung in this context is a far cry from what is considered a standard definition of the word hung.

lox

This word belongs to the vocabulary of space travel, too. **Lox** is what makes space flight possible. It is a rocket fuel oxidizer. The word is built on **L**iquid **OX**ygen. It also gives new meaning to the word **lox**, a smoked salmon. In this instance, the portmanteau word **lox** gives new meaning to an already established word, making it a neologism.

chortle

Chortle is a portmanteau word made up of two word parts: **CH**uck**LE** and sn**ORT**. One must presume that the letters **LE** were taken from chuck**LE**. The word means "to chuckle with glee," and it was coined by Lewis Carroll in his work **Through the Looking Glass** (1872).

motel

Motel is a portmanteau word that was coined by combining parts of two words: **MO**tor and ho**TEL**. Enough said about motels.

chunnel

Chunnel is both a portmanteau word and a neologism. The word chunnel comes from two words: **CH**annel and t**UNNEL**. Actually it is a tunnel that connects France and England. The chunnel was built, of course, under the English Channel.

smog

Smog too is a portmanteau word. It is built on two words: **SM**oke and f**OG**. There isn't too much else that can be said about smog other than that we can do very nicely without it.

comex

Comex is built on the words **COM**modity **EX**change. It is one of the exchanges in the New York financial district. More than this you need not know, unless you intend to jump into the market on a "hot tip" from one of your friends.

slithy

Slithy is another portmanteau word, which means "moving along by gliding," much as a snake does. In addition to this, the thing doing the gliding is also **slimy**. From **SLITH**er and slim**Y** the word **slithy** is born.

brunch

Let's not forget one of America's most popular dining-out experiences—**brunch**. It is a portmanteau word built on **BR**eakfast and l**UNCH**. There is not much else that can be said that you don't already know about the word.

hobol

The word **hobol** is a portmanteau word. Its origin is found in two words—**homing** and **bomb**. Let's try that once again: **HO**ming and **BO**mb. These bombs have guidance systems built into them and are extremely accurate. The letter **L** was no doubt added to avoid referring to these bombs as **HOBO** bombs. That just would not do.

EXERCISES

A. The following lists of words are examples of neologisms and portmanteau words. They are all words new to the language. Never before has anyone uttered these words or seen them in print. They belong to whoever created them. Notice how the words that make up neologisms are formed. Etymons are combined in a way that the new word has a logical meaning attached to it. Study the neologisms below. Then, using any etymons in this book, create five neologisms of your own. Also study the portmanteau words below and create five of your own.

Neologisms

1. **lithoglyph: lith**, "rock," + **glyph**, "carving"
   Meaning: a rock carving

2. **monoglyph: mono**, "one" + **glyph**, "carving"
   Meaning: a carving made of one rock or stone (marble, porcelain, or any other kind of stone)

3. **dermechino: derm,** "skin" + **echino,** "spiny"
   Meaning: having a spiny skin, as a porcupine

4. **leptosomata: lepto,** "slender" + **somata,** "body"
   Meaning: having a slender body

5. **malegenic: mal,** "bad" + **gen,** "origin or kind"
   Meaning: having a bad origin or being a bad kind, as a tumor

6. **eupathic: eu,** "good or well" + **path,** "feeling"
   Meaning: feeling good about oneself, much like the word
   euphoria.

7. **micrographic: micro,** "small" + **graph,** "write"
   Meaning: too small to read with the naked eye

8. **malegraphy: mal,** "bad or evil" + **graph,** "write"
   Meaning: pornographic material in written form, as a novel

9. **panalogue: pan,** "all" + **logos,** "word"
   Meaning: a discussion that embraces topics that are wide-
   ranging in both scope and analysis

10. **macrographic: macro,** "large" + **graph,** "write"
    Meaning: very large writing, as in sky writing or books hav-
    ing very large print that enables the partially sighted to read
    them.

Portmanteau Words

1. **spork:** a shaft with tines at one end and a spoon at the other end
   SPoon and f**ORK**

2. **sitcom:** a TV program whose format is a
   SITuation **COM**edy

3. **dramedy:** a movie or TV program that combines
   DRAMa and com**EDY**

4. **autoway:** an auto highway
   AUTOmobile high**WAY**

5. **surgop**: surgical operation
   SURGery **OP**eration

6. **expeed**: excessive speed
   EXcessive s**PEED**

7. **musicom**: a musical comedy
   MUSIcal **COM**edy

8. **resortel**: a resort hotel
   RESORt ho**TEL**

9. **limon**: lemon and lime mix
   LIme le**MON**

10. **agricorp**: agricultural corporation
    AGRIcultural **CORP**oration

B. **Directions**: Match the **neologism** found in Column A with its meaning found in Column B. Remember, these are made-up words.

Column A

1. aphotic
2. gynotheism
3. pantospective
4. macrophonic
5. anthrophobic
6. eugamy
7. cybertology
8. androcide
9. polyphobic
10. bitheism

Column B

a. a good marriage; a happy marriage
b. study of cybernetics
c. killing a man
d. having no light; absence of light
e. having an amplified (large) sound
f. belief that there are two gods
g. belief that god is a woman
h. pathologically afraid of people
i. attentive to all (details, surroundings, etc.)
j. pathologically afraid of many things

C. **Directions**: Match the word pairs from Column B with the **portmanteau word** found in Column A.

Column A

1. swatch
2. telethon
3. heliport

Column B

a. information commercial
b. snarled and tangled
c. capsule and tablet

4. snangled   d. teletypewriter connected to a telephonic
5. infomercial   system or exchange
6. telex   e. helicopter airport
7. sitcom   f. situation comedy
8. caplet   g. camera recorder
9. camcorder   h. television marathon
10. telegenic   i. television and photogenic
                 j. Swiss watch

D. Give a meaning to the following neologisms. They are words that have never been used, completely new to the language. You must use the etymologies to help you in your work.

For example: **bitheism** bi (two) + theos (god). Obviously the word **bitheism** must mean the "belief in two gods." Now you do the same for the remainder of the items below, all of which are neologisms.

1. aphotic:

2. androcide:

3. polyphobic:

4. gynotheism:

5. pantospect:

6. anthrophobic:

7. macrophonic:

8. cybertology:

9. eudemic:

10. eugamous:

E. Read the following instructions carefully before you begin your work. In this exercise you will make or, if you prefer, create five of each—neologisms and portmanteau words. Regarding neologisms, you may not designate new meaning to words already in use. Your words must be new, must never have been seen before, and they must be defined. Use etymons to help you with your work. Look back to previous exercises. Check again Exercises A through D of this lesson.

Neologisms	**Meanings**
1. _____	1. _____
2. _____	2. _____
3. _____	3. _____
4. _____	4. _____
5. _____	5. _____

Portmanteau Words	**Meanings**
1. _____	1. _____
2. _____	2. _____
3. _____	3. _____
4. _____	4. _____
5. _____	5. _____

General Review of Neologisms and Portmanteau Words

A neologism can be derived in two different ways. It can be a word that is new to language, or it can be a word that is already a part of a language, but one that takes on a new meaning. In the case of the former, the words, at least many of them, used in computer technology are neologisms: **bits** and **bytes**, not to mention **cyborgs** and **Internet**. The language is replete with such neologisms, and they are by no means limited to the technology of computers. When new products are introduced into the marketplace, new words are needed to name these innovations. Take for example the neologism **condotel**. It is a combination of parts of two words: **CONDO**minium and ho**TEL**. Actually a condotel is a hotel that offers the amenities of a condominum—multiple rooms, dining room, fireplaces, etc. Or it might be a word related to the technology of space flight. **Liquid oxygen** is used in spaceflight as a propellant to boost a rocket into deep space. Well, **liquid oxygen** eventually became **lox** from **L**iquid **OX**ygen. In this instance, the neologism is the result of giving new meaning to a word already in use: **lox**, "smoked salmon."

All portmanteau words were at one time neologisms. When a portmanteau word is first coined, it is both neologism and portmanteau word at the same time. Both are vital to language. They allow it to grow, to enrich itself by filling a void created by the many words in

English that have fallen by the wayside and are no longer in current use. Some portmanteau words and neologisms are already a part of your daily life, and one cannot conceive of English without them. Finally, keep in mind that **portmanteau** must be followed by **word**, or it will mean "a large suitcase."